JOHN WESLEY'S DOCTRINE OF JUSTIFICATION

Mark K. Olson

John Wesley's Doctrine of Justification

Nashville

JOHN WESLEY'S DOCTRINE OF JUSTIFICATION

Copyright © 2023 by Abingdon Press

All rights reserved.

No part of this work may be reproduced or transmitted in any form or by any means, electronic or mechanical, including photocopying and recording, or by any information storage or retrieval system, except as may be expressly permitted by the 1976 Copyright Act, the 1998 Digital Millennium Copyright Act, or in writing from the publisher. Requests for permission should be addressed to Permissions, Abingdon Press, 810 12th Avenue South, Nashville, TN 37203-4704, or emailed to permissions@abingdonpress.com.

Library of Congress Control Number: 2023950815

ISBN: 9781791031268

Scripture quotations unless noted otherwise are from The Authorized (King James) Version. Rights in the Authorized Version in the United Kingdom are vested in the Crown. Reproduced by permission of the Crown's patentee, Cambridge University Press.

Scripture quotations marked NRSVue are taken from the New Revised Standard Version Updated Edition. Copyright © 2021 National Council of Churches of Christ in the United States of America. Used by permission. All rights reserved worldwide.

MANUFACTURED IN THE UNITED STATES OF AMERICA

CONTENTS

Introduction	vii
Chapter 1: The Doctrine of Justification in Wesley's World	1
Religious Landscape	2
Anglican High Church Tradition	5
Historical Review	10
Chapter 2: Seeking Righteousness as an Anglican High Church Divine: 1703–37	29
Early Years	30
Oxford	37
Georgia	52
Chapter 3: Aldersgate and Early Controversies over Justification: 1738–49	62
Moravian/Lutheran Period	63
Moderate Reformed Period	78
Evangelical Sacramentalism	87
Justification and Assurance, Part One	91
Chapter 4: Explanatory Notes and Debates over Christ's Righteousness: 1750–69	95
Explanatory Notes upon the New Testament	96
Treatise on Baptism	106

Imputed Righteousness Controversy	113
Justification and Assurance, Part Two	125
Chapter 5: The Minutes Controversy and Degrees of Justification: 1770–91	**129**
1770 Conference Minutes	130
Degrees of Acceptance	146
Primacy of Present Justification	159
Conclusion: Enduring Themes	**167**
Economic Trinity	168
Covenant Theology	170
Degrees of Acceptance	171
Trinitarian Roles	172
Repentance, Faith, and Good Works	178
Bibliography	**181**
Scripture Index	193
Author Index	195
Subject Index	197

INTRODUCTION

The doctrine of justification was a fundamental truth of the Christian faith for John Wesley (1703–91). He made this clear on several occasions, as when he stated in 1746 that justification is the "foundation of all our hope" and twenty years later the "pillar and ground of that faith" from which "alone cometh salvation."[1] He likewise listed it as one of the two organizing truths around which he explicated his doctrine of salvation.[2] A third way Wesley stressed its centrality was to include justification in the "analogy of faith," the "grand scheme of doctrine" found throughout Holy Scripture.[3] So essential was this fundamental truth that Wesley claimed in later life that he never wavered nor varied a "hair's breadth" on it.[4]

Even with this claim of fidelity, Wesley's views on justification did develop over the course of his life. Most significant was the metamorphosis of 1738 when he adopted an evangelical understanding of the gospel. In the mid-1740s Wesley shared about his prior ignorance of

---

1. "Justification by Faith" §1 and *The Lord Our Righteousness* §4 in *The Works of John Wesley*, bicentennial edition, 35 vols., gen. eds. Frank Baker, Richard Heitzenrater, and Randy L. Maddox (Oxford: Clarendon Press, 1975–83; Nashville: Abingdon Press, 1984–Present), 1:106, 182, 451 (Hereafter: *Works*).

2. Wesley listed justification and sanctification as the two "general parts" or "grand branches" of Christian salvation (*The Scripture Way of Salvation* I.3; *On Working Out Our Own Salvation* II.1; *Works*, 2:157; 3:204). The same point is suggested in *On God's Vineyard* I.5 and *On the Wedding Garment* §10 (*Works*, 3:505; 4:144).

3. *Explanatory Notes upon the New Testament*, 2 vols. (Grand Rapids: Baker, 1980), Rom. 12:6.

4. Letters, April 24 and May 14, 1765 (John Telford, ed., *The Letters of the Rev. John Wesley, A.M.*, 8 vols. London: Epworth Press, 1931), 4:295, 298; *On the Wedding Garment* §18 (*Works*, 4:147).

gospel justification and admitted that at Oxford he "knew nothing of that righteousness of faith in justification."[5] Two decades later in his *Short History of Methodism* he recalled that in 1738 he became convinced of three essential truths: by nature everyone is dead in sin, justification is by faith alone, and the fruit of justifying faith is inward and outward holiness.[6] At the time he reminded his Calvinist critics that this was what he "constantly believed and taught" since 1738.[7] While these statements show that Wesley's views went through a major transition in 1738, they leave on the table questions about his prior views and what changed in 1738. They also lead scholars to ponder developments after 1738 since his soteriology continued to evolve in significant ways. These subjects will be explored at length in this study.

Given that justification played such a pivotal role in Wesley's religious and theological development, scholars and historians have taken a keen interest in the subject.[8] To list some examples, William Cannon's *Theology of John Wesley* was published in 1946 and up until now has been the only full monograph on the subject.[9] Following George Croft Cell's influential study that repositioned Wesley in the shadow of the Protestant Reformation, Cannon presented a more Reformed viewpoint of his justification doctrine.[10] In so doing, he somewhat misread eighteenth-century Anglican views and erroneously concluded that the early Wesley was semi-Pelagian. Fourteen years later Colin Williams surveyed Wesley's doctrine of justification in relation to current ecumenical discussions and the *ordo*

---

5. *A Further Appeal to Men of Reason and Religion* VI.1, 2; Conference Minutes, 1746 (*Works*, 11:176–77; 10:175).

6. *A Short History of Methodism* §10 (*Works*, 9:369).

7. *The Lord Our Righteousness* II.6 (*Works*, 1:456).

8. Nearly all the standard histories of Wesley address his rediscovery of the evangelical doctrine of justification leading up to his evangelical conversion at Aldersgate. For a survey, see Mark K. Olson, *Wesley and Aldersgate: Interpreting Conversion Narratives* (New York: Routledge, 2019), 10–26.

9. William Ragsdale Cannon, *The Theology of John Wesley: With Special Reference to the Doctrine of Justification* (Lanham, MD: University Press of America, 1974, orig. 1946).

10. George Croft Cell, *The Rediscovery of John Wesley* (New York: Henry Holt & Co., 1935).

salutis (order of salvation).[11] Williams emphasized the inner coherence and contemporary relevance of Wesley's theology. In so doing, his discussion on justification is preceded by several chapters on prevenient grace, original sin, and repentance, followed by atonement, regeneration, assurance, and sanctification. Of interest to our study, Williams distinguished the *faith of a servant* from the *faith of a son* in Wesley's theology by attributing justifying faith only to the latter. The servant/son metaphor would later become one of the more contested issues connected to Wesley's justification doctrine.[12]

Several more recent studies deserve mention. In 1994 Randy Maddox produced an influential work that seeks to organize Wesley's practical theology around the orienting concern "responsible grace."[13] This orienting perspective is further framed within an east-west tension of therapeutic and juridical accounts of salvation, with the former stressed as Wesley's primary concern. Moving away from Williams's *ordo* approach, Maddox presented justification as a stage in the *via salutis* (way of salvation) that accents inward renewal within the salvation process. Whether intentional or not, justification is demoted as a structural doctrine in Wesley's soteriology even though Maddox captured many of the nuances in Wesley's double-justification doctrine. The doctrine's structural importance is re-emphasized in Kenneth Collins's *Theology of John Wesley* (2007) in which an entire chapter is devoted to Wesley's theology of objective righteousness.[14] Framed within a Catholic and Protestant conjunctive of cooperant and free grace, Collins highlighted justification as a sovereign gift of divine grace and the first focus of the Wesleyan *ordo salutis* (the second being Christian perfection). Several years later a four-volume compendium of

---

11. Colin W. Williams, *John Wesley's Theology Today: A Study of the Wesleyan Tradition in Current Theological Dialogue* (Nashville: Abingdon Press, 1960).

12. By the early years of the current millennium, two views developed on the soteriological standing of the servant. One position deemed the servant as justified and the other position considered the servant as not justified. For the first position, see Laura Bartels Felleman, "John Wesley and the 'Servant of God,'" *Wesleyan Theological Journal* 41–42 (Fall 2006): 72–86. For the second position, see Kenneth Collins, *The Theology of John Wesley: Holy Love and the Shape of Grace* (Nashville: Abingdon Press, 2007), 182–84.

13. Randy L. Maddox, *Responsible Grace: John Wesley's Practical Theology* (Nashville: Kingswood Books, 1994).

14. Collins, *Theology of John Wesley*, 155–94.

John Wesley's Teachings (2012) was released in which Thomas Oden proposed that Wesley belongs theologically to the Great Christian tradition reaching back to the primitive church and that no major Christian doctrine is omitted from his teaching homilies.[15] Oden's approach was to survey Wesley's writings to expound his theology, and for the doctrine of justification he examined several sermons and tracts written from 1738 and thereafter.

These scholars and others have contributed much to our understanding of Wesley's doctrine of justification. However, a tendency of past scholarship has been to focus almost exclusively on the post-Aldersgate Wesley to explicate his doctrine of justification. On first thought, this makes sense given Wesley's post-1738 remarks. But this study proposes a different starting point. It will be shown that Wesley already had a doctrine of justification long before his rediscovery of the evangelical gospel in 1738 and that foundational concepts of his early doctrine continued to inform his viewpoint long after he adopted his "new gospel." Even though Wesley claimed his views did not change after 1738, it will be shown there were significant developments over the decades. Thus, Wesley's doctrine of justification is as much a story to be told as it is a doctrine to explain.

Part of the story is that Wesley drank from many theological streams, and this led him to form a conjunctive approach to the subject. His full doctrine of justification includes several dialectic tensions, such as present and final, sacramental and non-sacramental, imputed and imparted, condition and merit, relation and real, servant and son, monergism and synergism, faith and works. Wesley therefore developed a theology of objective righteousness that is eclectic in nature and expression. From his wide range of religious experiences and theological controversies, Wesley became convinced there are degrees of acceptance in the favor of God. How these developments took place is another focal point of our story.

The doctrine's complexity is another reason for this study. By looking at the whole Wesley (early, middle, and late) and his essential writings on justification in each period—not only his sermons, journals, letters, and tracts, but also his hymns and sacramental works—a comprehensive and

---

15. Thomas C. Oden, *John Wesley's Teachings*, 4 vols. (Grand Rapids: Zondervan, 2012).

integrative evaluation can be made of what the doctrine meant to Wesley at different stages of his life and career. There is much to "chew on" in this study. The detailed nature of the subject, the subtle arguments over minute matters, and the sheer amount of material will inevitably lead to different interpretations. But the doctrine is too vital to Wesley's theology and his explication of gospel salvation for us to simply ignore or to miss the mark on its nature and ramifications. Therefore, this study aims to spur renewed interest in the subject and to encourage dialogue and constructive debate as the different strands of Wesley's full doctrine of justification are studied and evaluated. For some, novel concepts will be proposed, but the reader is encouraged to check the references, read the sources, and to critically engage in the arguments and analysis before drawing conclusions. As iron sharpens iron, this author welcomes the exchange.

Our study begins with the background sources that influenced Wesley. The primary traditions were Roman Catholicism, the Protestant Reformation, Anglicanism, Puritanism/Calvinism, and Pietism, with Wesley situated within the High Church tradition of the Church of England. A historical sketch of the doctrine follows from the Protestant Reformation to Wesley's own day in Hanoverian England. In this review attention is given to how the doctrine was nuanced regarding the principal issues of debate that would involve Wesley. These issues include matters of definition and formal cause, but also the nature of Christ's imputed righteousness, whether justification is complete at conversion or final judgment, and its relationship to the new birth and good works.

The next four chapters tell the story of how Wesley's doctrine of justification developed over the course of his lifetime. This approach is the best way to learn the particulars of his justification doctrine and to contextualize and evaluate his writings on the subject. Chapter 2 covers his early life from Epworth up to the eve of his evangelical conversion in 1738. It begins with Wesley's upbringing in the Anglican High Church tradition and its sacramental view of justification. The narrative then moves to his spiritual awakening in 1725 and his immersion into the holy living tradition that linked justification to holy living. Following his crisis of doubt during his voyage to North America in late 1735, the Pietists pointed

Wesley toward a non-sacramental view of justification grounded on faith alone. Chapter 3 addresses Wesley's rediscovery of the Reformation's message of justification by faith alone. At the time he adopted a Moravian/Lutheran perspective of present justification based on the imputation of Christ's active and passive righteousness. However, by the mid-1740s he moved toward a moderate Reformed position that asserted the imputation of Christ's passive righteousness to refute the antinomian errors of the Calvinists and Moravians. He also began to reemphasize the doctrine of double justification and introduced a concept of degrees into his theology of objective righteousness.

The next two chapters cover the last four decades of Wesley's life. Chapter 4 examines his justification doctrine from 1750 to 1769. His New Testament commentary, tracts on baptism, remarks on assurance, and the imputation controversy with the Calvinist James Hervey form the substance of this chapter, leading to his mature statement on imputation in *The Lord Our Righteousness*. The concept of five degrees of acceptance took shape during this period as prevenient grace became more prominent in Wesley's descriptions of the "scripture way of salvation." Chapter 5 covers the last two decades in which Wesley reasserted the necessity and conditionality of good works during the Minutes Controversy. He also employed the dispensationalism of John Fletcher to develop further his concept of degrees in the favor of God. This includes his use of the servant/son metaphor and his mature remarks on the soteriological standing of the responsive unregenerate (those who have never heard of Christ). At the same time his editorial decisions in the *Sunday Service* articulated his settled position on sacramental justification. With such complexity and nuance in his viewpoint, the aim of this study is to capture John Wesley's full perspective on the subject.

The study closes by retracing the themes that this author considers enduring in Wesley's theology of objective righteousness. Wesley is presented as a doctrinal theologian for how he interwove the central themes to form a comprehensive theological understanding of justification. Some of the themes surveyed are the economic Trinity and Wesley's nuanced view of grace; his Arminian reinterpretation of the divine decrees and his use of covenant theology to articulate a concept of degrees; the employment of the Triune roles to internally structure his doctrine; and Wesley's understanding of repentance, faith, and good works as conditions in his doctrine of double justification.

Now that the study's aim and methodology have been spelled out, we are ready to begin our story with the background of John Wesley's doctrine of justification.

CHAPTER ONE

THE DOCTRINE OF JUSTIFICATION IN WESLEY'S WORLD

John Wesley's doctrine of justification involves a story as well as a theology. It is a narrative that begins with his early years in the parsonage at Epworth and reaches its climax during his final years as head of the Wesleyan Methodist movement. It is a story of contrasting moods and scenes—his upbringing in the High Church tradition, his heartfelt pursuit of piety at Oxford, his tutelage under and separation from the Moravians, his evangelical conversion at Aldersgate, his rediscovery of his Anglican Reformation heritage, his reflective reading of the Pietists and Puritans, his ardent praise and vehement criticism of Martin Luther, his single-minded passion to know the "way to heaven,"[1] his unending debates with the Calvinists, and his thoughtful reflection on the soteriological standing of the non-Christian (the responsive unregenerate). With such contrasts and disparities, the narrative becomes complex and calls for nuance. This is a story that has not been fully told before.[2]

Scholars often divide Wesley's career into three periods: early (1725–38), middle (1738–65), and late (1765–91). This division is useful to identify patterns and transitions in his religious life and thought. The

---

1. Preface §5 to "Sermons on Several Occasions" (*Works*, 1:105).

2. As was noted in the introduction, past studies have focused almost entirely on the post-Aldersgate Wesley, ignoring important developments in his early period. The same can be said for the late Wesley, whose views on degrees of justification were influenced by John Fletcher.

early Wesley is remembered for his ardent passion for holy living; the middle Wesley for his commitment to the Protestant message of salvation by faith; and the late Wesley for his integration of both emphases into a theological tradition that is known as "Wesleyan."[3] Our story is similar in that it employs a parallel framework to examine Wesley's doctrine of justification at each phase of his life. It also looks at how developments in the doctrine contributed to these transitions in his career and theology. In the end, this is an account of how the father of the people called Methodists grappled with what it means to be in right relationship with God, given the complexities of life and religious experience.

We begin with Wesley's religious context in the eighteenth century. Hanoverian England reflected the diversity found in western Christianity two centuries after the Protestant Reformation. The doctrine of justification remained a contested issue between Roman Catholics and Protestants, and between the different branches of Protestantism. It was in this religious climate that Wesley formulated his doctrine of justification. The main sections below include a brief sketch of the religious landscape in the English-speaking world, with special attention given to Wesley's Anglican context. This is followed by a historical review of the doctrine of justification from the Protestant Reformation up to Wesley's day in Hanoverian England.

Religious Landscape

The English-speaking religious world of the eighteenth century was spread over nine regions on both sides of the Atlantic Ocean. England, Scotland, Wales, and Ireland were in the British Isles while New England, the Mid-Atlantic, the American South, the West Indies, and Canada were in the new world.[4] Wales was annexed to England during the reign of

---

3. For a similar overview of the three periods and their central themes, see Randy L. Maddox, *Responsible Grace: John Wesley's Practical Theology* (Nashville: Kingswood Books, 1994), 20.

4. Mark A. Noll, *The Rise of Evangelicalism: The Age of Edwards, Whitefield and the Wesleys* (Downers Grove, IL: InterVarsity Press, 2003), 33.

Henry VIII and Scotland and England (and Wales) joined together in 1707 to form Great Britain. At the mid-century mark the population for all nine regions was estimated by Mark Noll at over twelve million.[5]

Throughout much of the English-speaking world the Church of England served as the established church, with the British monarch as its head. Henry Rack lists approximately 90 percent of the population in England as members, though the numbers were much lower in those regions with a different state church or where no established church was formed.[6] Most Anglicans considered their church the best national church in Christendom, in terms of its liturgy and traditions.[7] Wesley shared this sentiment.[8] Past historians criticized the Hanoverian Church for being lethargic and ill-equipped to meet the transformative changes introduced by the Enlightenment and the Industrial Revolution. Recent scholarship has corrected this negative portrayal by showing there was a strong resurgence of piety and philanthropy in the post-Restoration church as it entered the eighteenth century.[9]

Brent Sirota has shown that the late-seventeenth-century Anglican renewal was "staunchly anti-Calvinist" as well as anti-Catholic. It embodied a popular "sacramental piety" that sought to restore the "Eucharist to

---

5. Noll, *The Rise of Evangelicalism*, 31.

6. Henry D. Rack, *Reasonable Enthusiast: John Wesley and the Rise of Methodism*, 3rd ed. (London: Epworth Press, 2002), 10; Noll, *Rise of Evangelicalism*, 34–35.

7. Rack, *Reasonable Enthusiast*, 10.

8. Geordan Hammond, *John Wesley in America: Restoring Primitive Christianity* (Oxford: Oxford University Press, 2014), 197.

9. See J. C. D. Clark, *English Society 1660–1830* (Cambridge: Cambridge University Press, 2000); Jeremy Gregory, "The Long Eighteenth Century," in *The Cambridge Companion to John Wesley*, ed. Randy L. Maddox and Jason E. Vickers (Cambridge: Cambridge University Press, 2010), 15–16; Noll, *The Rise of Evangelicalism*, 39–42. General studies on the eighteenth century include William E. H. Lecky, *A History of England in the Eighteenth Century*, 8 vols. (New York: Appleton & Company, 1888); Roy Porter, *English Society in the 18th Century*, rev. ed. (New York: Penguin Books, 1991); Leslie Stephen, *History of English Thought in the Eighteenth Century*, 2 vols., 3rd ed. (London: Smith, Elder & Co., 1902); Keith Thomas, *The Ends of Life: Roads to Fulfilment in Early Modern England* (Oxford: Oxford University Press, 2009).

the center of Anglican worship."[10] The church included a spectrum of viewpoints ranging from High Church to latitudinarian to Deist. High Churchmanship was on the ascendency in the opening decades of the eighteenth century, as was holy living theology. Even though the majority of Anglican clergy leaned Arminian, a Calvinist minority remained that would later include Anglican evangelicals. A wave of philanthropy led to the formation of several religious and reforming societies by the end of the seventeenth century, such as the Society for Promoting Christian Knowledge, the Society for the Propagation of the Gospel in Foreign Parts, and the Society for the Reformation of Manners.

Nonconformity in the British Isles was made up of several groups. Presbyterians made up more than half of English and Welsh dissenters, with Congregationalists, Baptists, Quakers, Moravians, Catholics, and other groups filling up the ranks. In Ireland most of the population was Catholic, though there was a sizable Presbyterian presence and a small but wealthy Anglican Church. Scotland, by contrast, had a Presbyterian state church with Scottish Episcopalians and splinter Presbyterian groups filling the ranks of dissent.[11]

Moving across the Atlantic, the situation was quite different. New England had a Congregational state church that was established by the Puritan settlers. By the eighteenth century, Baptists, Quakers, and a handful of Anglican churches made their presence felt. Up north in Nova Scotia there were several communions, including Anglicans, Congregationalists, Baptists, Lutherans, and Roman Catholics. Further west at Quebec, the Catholic Church functioned as a state church since this area was ruled by France until the end of the Seven Years' War (1756–63),

---

10. Brent S. Sirota, *The Christian Monitors: The Church of England and the Age of Benevolence, 1680–1730* (New Haven, CT: Yale University Press, 2014), 26, 32–36. For the religious pulse of the early modern period, see Ted A. Campbell, *The Religion of the Heart: A Study of European Religious Life in the Seventeenth and Eighteenth Centuries* (Columbia: University of South Carolina Press, 1991). For surveys of the Church of England in the early eighteenth century, see William Gibson, *The Church of England 1688–1832: Unity and Accord* (London: Routledge, 2012); Richard P. Heitzenrater, *Wesley and the People Called Methodists*, 2nd ed. (Nashville: Abingdon Press, 2013), 1–35; J. R. H. Moorman, *A History of the Church in England*, 3rd ed. (Harrisburg: Morehouse Publishing, 1980), 269–89; Rack, *Reasonable Enthusiast*, 10–33.

11. Noll, *Rise of Evangelicalism*, 34–36.

when it was transferred to Great Britain.[12] In the mid-Atlantic colonies there was no state church, with a plethora of denominations and groups existing alongside one another, including Anglican, Quaker, Presbyterian, Congregationalist, Dutch and German Reformed, Mennonite, Moravian, Roman Catholic, and Judaism. Moving south the established church was Anglican in the southern colonies and the West Indies, with other groups gradually taking root as the eighteenth century progressed. Wesley's time in Georgia in the mid-1730s reflected the diversity of the American wilderness.[13] From his *Journal* we learn there were several groups active in the colony, including Anglicans, Moravians, Salzburgers (Pietists), Presbyterians, Catholics, Baptists, and a few Deists.

Anglican High Church Tradition

John Wesley read widely and traveled extensively. He therefore encountered most of the religious groups and theological traditions active in his day. The Church of England, however, deserves special attention because Wesley was a lifelong member and the Anglican tradition touched every aspect of his life, thought, and ministry. Familiarity with his Anglicanism will prove crucial to our story.

Throughout his life Wesley maintained he was a loyal son of the established church.[14] Fidelity to the church and the High Church tradition was bred into Wesley from childhood. His parents, Samuel (d. 1735) and Susanna (d. 1742), conformed from Dissent to the established church

---

12. Noll, *Rise of Evangelicalism*, 36.

13. Noll, *Rise of Evangelicalism*, 37.

14. Wesley's relationship to the Church of England has been the subject of much study. Questions remain about his faithfulness on several matters, including his practice of ordination. Besides the standard histories on Wesley, see Frank Baker, *John Wesley and the Church of England* (London: Epworth Press, 1970); Ryan Nicholas Danker, *Wesley and the Anglicans: Political Division in Early Evangelicalism* (Downers Grove, IL: IVP Academic, 2016); Harrington W. Holden, *John Wesley in Company with High Churchmen* (London: Church Press Company, 1870); Gwang Seok Oh, *John Wesley's Ecclesiology: A Study in Its Sources and Development* (Lanham, MD: Scarecrow Press, 2007); James H. Rigg, *The Churchmanship of John Wesley, and the Relations of Wesleyan Methodism to the Church of England* (London: Wesleyan-Methodist Book-Room, 1886).

during the Anglican renewal of the 1680s and became devout High Churchmen in their convictions. Later in life Wesley acknowledged his High Church upbringing, "From a child I was taught to love and reverence the Scripture . . . the primitive Fathers . . . the Church of England, as the most scriptural national church in the world."[15] So Wesley's earliest thoughts and impressions about justification before God came from his upbringing in the Anglican High Church tradition, passed down to him from his parents and inculcated in him by his education at Charterhouse and at Oxford. We will look more closely at his parents' influence in the next chapter.

High Churchmanship in Wesley's day traced its lineage back through the Caroline divines and Laudianism to classical Anglicanism and the English Reformation; and further back to the primitive church of the first four centuries.[16] Following the lead of Richard Hooker, High Churchmen looked to the threefold font of scripture, reason, and tradition to discern spiritual truth.[17] As staunch defenders of Anglican polity and discipline, with its *via media* between Rome and Geneva, High Churchmen considered the Church of England as both catholic and Reformed. Geordan Hammond listed several beliefs of High Churchmanship in the eighteenth century: apostolic succession, episcopacy, divine right monarchy, the authority of the church fathers, and a deep commitment to church tradition, including its liturgies and sacraments.[18] Rack suggested that High Church sentiments were prevalent among the lower clergy in the early decades, while Vivian Green noted the dominance of High Churchmanship at Ox-

---

15. *Farther Thoughts on Separation from the Church* §1 (*Works*, 9:538). See also *Telford*, 6:156.

16. Moorman, *A History of the Church in England*, 224–25, 229–37, 248–49, 264–73. In this study classical Anglicanism refers to the period from the late sixteenth to early seventeenth centuries when a synthesis developed among major Anglican theologians (C. FitzSimons Allison, *The Rise of Moralism: The Proclamation of the Gospel from Hooker to Baxter* [Wilton, CT: Morehouse Barlow, 1966], ix).

17. Baker, *John Wesley and the Church of England*, 14–15.

18. Hammond, *John Wesley in America*, 14.

ford, where Wesley studied.[19] Even though Wesley adopted evangelical beliefs in 1738, his High Churchmanship continued to inform his ministerial and theological approach as an evangelical, including developments in his doctrine of justification.[20]

In keeping with the historic faith of the church catholic, High Churchmen had a sacramental view of the Christian life in which justifying and regenerating grace is initially granted in baptism, nurtured through life by the sanctifying work of the Spirit, and completed at the Final Judgment when God declares the fully sanctified Christian righteous and fit to enter the eternal kingdom. The believer's justification before God therefore involved a process of spiritual renewal that included two key moments: baptism and final judgment. This is the doctrine of double justification, which will factor greatly in our story. Jeffrey Chamberlain outlined the Anglican *ordo salutis* as baptism (initial justification)—sanctification (state of justification)—final judgment (final justification)—eternal glory.[21] This *ordo*, likewise, defined and shaped the High Church *via salutis* or scriptural path of attaining salvation.[22] As a High Churchman, the early Wesley assumed the doctrine of double justification in his understanding of the

---

19. Rack, *Reasonable Enthusiast*, 26; V. H. H. Green, *The Young Mr. Wesley* (London: Edward Arnold, 1961), 27–28.

20. There are many studies on Wesley's High Churchmanship and sacramental theology after his evangelical conversion in 1738. Geordan Hammond presents one of the best summaries (*John Wesley in America*, 194–203). See also Ole E. Borgen, *John Wesley on the Sacraments: A Definitive Study of John Wesley's Theology of Worship* (Grand Rapids: Francis Asbury Press, 1972); John C. Bowmer, *The Sacrament of the Lord's Supper in Early Methodism* (London: Dacre Press, 1951); Henry H. Knight III, *The Presence of God in the Christian Life: John Wesley and the Means of Grace* (London: Scarecrow Press, 1992); Rack, *Reasonable Enthusiast*, 154, 402–20.

21. Chamberlain, "Moralism, Justification, and the Controversy over Methodism," 672.

22. *Ordo salutis* is Latin for "order of salvation." It refers to the way in which the different aspects of salvation are logically sequenced in the Christian life. *Via salutis* is Latin for "way of salvation" or the scriptural path of salvation. It should not be confused with modern notions of "spiritual journey," which are often open-ended and undefined. The High Church *via salutis* was defined by its understanding of the Christian gospel and its sequence (*ordo*) of baptism—sanctification—final judgment—glorification. In this study both *ordo salutis* and *via salutis* are used because Wesley at times logically sequenced his doctrines and at other times gave a holistic description of the Christian path of salvation. Though both approaches are similar and overlap, their purpose and function are different.

way of salvation. It was part of his embedded theology that informed his approach to the Christian life.[23]

The Anglican *via media* opened the door for Roman Catholic and Protestant perspectives to contribute to the High Church view of double justification. Alister McGrath explained that the High Church tradition assumed a Catholic definition of justification (to make righteous) in relation to final justification but rejected Rome's teaching of inherent righteousness as its formal cause.[24] Instead, High Churchmen adopted a Protestant view of Christ's imputed righteousness for present justification while affirming the need of inherent righteousness or good works for final justification.[25] This *via media* was made possible by a subtle distinction made between *condition* and *merit*. Justification is by faith in Christ alone apart from works, yet good works are necessary for final salvation. Both statements could be affirmed because faith and works were seen as not accruing merit, as Catholicism taught, but as conditions for present and final justification.[26] Following standard Reformation theology, good works prior to present justification were denied but following present justification were deemed necessary to authenticate saving faith and prepare for final justification.[27] Another concern of High Churchmen was to counter Calvinist antinomianism and its tendency to exalt salvation by faith alone at the expense of obedience to God's commands.[28] In opposition to

---

23. Embedded theology refers to a faith that is assimilated from the "countless daily encounters with their Christianity—formal and informal, planned and unplanned." Embedded theology is contrasted with deliberative theology, which refers to a faith learned through thoughtful reflection of religious beliefs. See Howard W. Stone and James O. Duke, *How to Think Theologically*, 2nd ed. (Minneapolis: Fortress Press, 2006), 13.

24. McGrath, *Iustitia Dei*, 280–81. On formal cause, see note 34 below.

25. Chamberlain, "Moralism, Justification, and the Controversy over Methodism," 659–62.

26. Chamberlain, "Moralism, Justification, and the Controversy over Methodism," 672. Present justification refers to this life, final justification to the Last Judgment.

27. Article XII, Anglican Articles of Religion.

28. Chamberlain, "Moralism, Justification, and the Controversy over Methodism," 663. The early Wesley expressed his concern over Lutheran and Reformed authors who magnified faith to the exclusion of keeping God's commandments (Journal, January 25, 1738, *Works*, 18:212n95).

Puritan Calvinism, High Churchmen of the seventeenth and eighteenth centuries leaned Arminian and held that the doctrinal standards of the church—the Prayer Book, Articles, and *Homilies*—supported an Arminian perspective.[29]

Another facet of High Churchmanship in Wesley's day was the holy living tradition. Holy living authors included both Protestants and Roman Catholics. When Wesley listed in his *Plain Account of Christian Perfection* the three authors who influenced his early views of holiness, two were Protestant (High Church Anglicans Jeremy Taylor and William Law) and the other Roman Catholic (Thomas à Kempis). Holy living authors were the Pietists of the Anglican tradition, accentuating the "life of God in the soul" through a disciplined practice of the means of grace.[30] This same goal was found in the Christian mystic tradition. Robert Tuttle explained that the mystics sought perfect union with God through purification and contemplative illumination in which a seeker would "concentrate all [their] faculties on God."[31] Many of the mystics that Wesley read were part of the Catholic Reformation and left a mark on his early views that linked justification to holy living.

Holy living theology in Wesley's day supported the notion that greater degrees of holiness would increase a believer's assurance of salvation. That is, the more holy a person became, the more confidence they would have to face final judgment. This rationale served as a powerful impetus in the early Wesley to attain salvation assurance through holy living. His failure to secure a solid assurance is an integral part of our story that helps to explain why he adopted a new doctrine of justification in 1738. Wesley's new gospel of justification by faith alone was informed by developments from the sixteenth to the eighteenth centuries. To set the stage for this part of our story, we turn to the history of the doctrine of justification.

---

29. The church's standards being her Catechism, Articles, and Homilies. Alan C. Clifford, *Atonement and Justification: English Evangelical Theology 1640–1790, An Evaluation* (Oxford: Clarendon Press, 1990), 78–80.

30. "Life of God in the soul" was a favorite expression among the Oxford Methodists and was the title of Henry Scougal's famous book.

31. Robert G. Tuttle Jr., *Mysticism in the Wesleyan Tradition* (Grand Rapids: Francis Asbury Press, 1989), 24.

Historical Review

Historians remind us it has been through the "furnace of controversy" that fundamental doctrines of the Christian faith have been "pounded out on the anvil of debate."[32] For the doctrine of justification this began in the sixteenth century. As Lutheran scholar Bernhard Lohse observed, "Prior to the sixteenth century, the doctrine of justification never assumed a significance even remotely comparable to that in Luther . . . not in Augustine or Peter Lombard or Thomas Aquinas or Bonaventure, to name a few."[33] For this reason our review begins in the sixteenth century when the Western tradition split, and the Church of England formed as an independent ecclesiastical body. The following sketch introduces the main features of various traditions, with attention given to details that pertain to our story, like formal cause,[34] Christ's imputed righteousness, double justification, and the relationship between justification, the new birth, and good works.

Roman Catholicism

The Church of Rome in the sixteenth century looked back over a thousand years to Augustine for its theological foundation on justification.[35]

---

32. Brian J. Arnold, *Justification in the Second Century* (Waco, TX: Baylor University Press, 2018), 5.

33. Bernhard Lohse, *Martin Luther's Theology: Its Historical and Systematic Development* (Minneapolis: Fortress Press, 2006), 259.

34. Formal cause addresses the question, What makes a person to stand righteous before God? Or on what basis is a person accepted by God? Christopher Allison defined formal cause as "that which made it to be what it is, as heat makes a thing hot" (Allison, *The Rise of Moralism*, 3). Rome argued it was inherent righteousness. Protestants countered it was Christ's imputed righteousness, or, as our study shows, took a view that combined elements of the Catholic and Protestant positions.

35. For studies on Rome's doctrine of justification, see James K. Beilby and Paul Rhodes Eddy, eds., *Justification: Five Views* (Downers Grove, IL: InterVarsity Press Academic, 2011); Michael Horton, *Justification*, 2 vols. (Grand Rapids: Zondervan, 2018); McGrath, *Iustitia Dei*; Roger E. Olson, *The Story of Christian Theology: Twenty Centuries of Tradition and Reform* (Grand Rapids: InterVarsity Press, 1999); Jaroslav Pelikan, *Reformation of Church and Dogma: 1300–1700* (Chicago: University of Chicago Press, 1984); Brant Pitre, "The Roman Catholic Perspective on Paul," in *Perspectives on Paul*, ed. Scot McKnight and B. J. Oropeza (Grand Rapids: Baker Academic, 2020).

Roger Olson explained that for the Bishop of Hippo "justification is the gradual process by which a sinner is made actually righteous internally by having God's own righteousness infused through the grace of baptism, faith, works of love and the entire penitential life."[36] Several features deserve our attention. Rome taught the doctrine of double justification with baptism and final judgment as the bookends of the justification process.[37] With forgiveness granted in baptism and sustained by the sacraments, final justification looked to the transformation of life as the basis for acceptance. In this system the formal cause of justification was inherent righteousness, infused in believers through their union with Christ by the indwelling presence of the Holy Spirit.[38]

Synergism was inherent in the Catholic position. Salvation is by faith, but this faith was understood as an inward virtue: "faith working through love" (Gal. 5:6). Since scripture teaches that final justification will be according to works,[39] Catholicism developed a complex theory of merit, including merit as divine gift in Christ *(congruous merit)* and as reward for good works *(condign merit)*.[40] In was in this latter sense that believers receive an infusion of righteousness to merit eternal life.[41] Justification therefore meant to *make righteous*. From the concept of accumulated merit, the practice of indulgences developed in which pardon for sin's temporal punishment in purgatory was granted in exchange for financial gifts to the church.[42] It was this practice that sparked the Protestant Reformation in October 1517,

---

36. Olson, *The Story of Christian Theology*, 389.

37. Theodore Alois Buckley, trans., *Canons and Decrees of the Council of Trent*, Session 6, chs. 6–16 (London: George Routledge, 1851), 32–42.

38. Theodore Alois Buckley, *Canons and Decrees of the Council of Trent*, 34.

39. E.g., Matt. 16:27; Rom. 2:6-11; 2 Cor. 5:10.

40. Buckley, *Canons and Decrees of the Council of Trent*, 41; McGrath, *Iustitia Dei*, 138–50.

41. Council of Trent, Session 6 Ch. 16, "Those very works which have been done in God, fully satisfied the divine law according to the state of this life, and truly to have merited eternal life, to be obtained also in its due time" (Buckley, *Canons and Decrees of the Council of Trent*, 41).

42. On indulgences, see James Buchanan, *The Doctrine of Justification: An Outline of Its History in the Church and of Its Exposition from Scripture* (Edinburgh: T & T Clark, 1867), 100–108; Olson, *Story of Christian Theology*, 357; Pelikan, *Reformation of Church and Dogma*, 134–36.

when Martin Luther nailed Ninety-Five Theses to the church door in Wittenberg, Germany.

Martin Luther

In contrast to Rome, Luther (d. 1546) understood justification in a forensic sense. Drawing on the Pauline antithesis of faith and works, Luther taught that humanity is sinful and cannot merit salvation by infused righteousness. Instead, through divine grace those who trust in Christ are *declared righteous*: their sins are forgiven, and Christ's righteousness is reckoned to their account. This declaration is based on the believer's union with Christ. Luther called it "alien righteousness." Just as a groom and bride share everything in common, so Christ assumes a sinner's sin and guilt and clothes them with his righteousness.[43] In contrast to Rome's synergism, Luther's view was inherently monergistic. Justification is an act of God alone. Justification is by faith with human works playing no role.

In recent decades scholars have recognized that Luther understood justification to mean more than a declaration of righteousness. It also signified a new creation in which the believer spontaneously does good works, triumphs over the power of sin ("Through faith a person becomes free from sin"),[44] and enjoys an assurance of salvation.[45] Even with these benefits, Luther maintained the believer remains throughout this life *simul justus et peccator*—simultaneously righteous and sinful.[46] More important

---

43. Luther, *The Freedom of the Christian*, in *Martin Luther's Basic Theological Writings*, 3rd ed., ed. Timothy F. Lull and William R. Russell (Minneapolis: Fortress Press, 2012), 409; John Trinklein, "Holiness unto Whom? John Wesley's Doctrine of Entire Sanctification in Light of The Two Kinds of Righteousness" (PhD diss., Concordia University, 2016), 178.

44. Lull and Russell, eds., *Martin Luther's Basic Theological Writings*, 79.

45. The Finnish school has highlighted this aspect of the Reformer's doctrine. See Tuomo Mannermaa, *Christ Present in Faith: Luther's View of Justification* (Minneapolis: Fortress Press, 2005); Kirsi Stjerna, "Finnish Interpretation of Luther," in *Dictionary of Luther and the Lutheran Tradition*, gen. ed. Timothy J. Wengert (Grand Rapids: Baker Academic, 2017). Other Lutheran scholars have noted this aspect of Luther's doctrine; see Paul Althaus, *Theology of Martin Luther* (Minneapolis: Fortress Press, 1966), 226, 234; Lohse, *Martin Luther's Theology*, 262–63; Trinklein, "Holiness unto Whom?" 178.

46. Althaus, *Theology of Martin Luther*, 235, 242; Lohse, *Martin Luther's Theology*, 263, 265.

for our study, Luther's ideas of justifying faith as generating a new existence permeates his *Preface to the Epistle of St. Paul to the Romans*, which was read on the night of Wesley's evangelical conversion at Aldersgate.[47] Thus, Luther did not sharply distinguish between justification and regeneration as later Protestants would do. Instead, justification encompasses a "person's total renewal up to the consummation."[48] This meant that Luther subsumed regeneration and sanctification into justification. Even though he valued good works as necessary evidence and the fruit of saving faith, Luther did not adopt the theory of double justification, leaving it to Martin Bucer (d. 1551) and other Protestants to take that stance.[49]

Calvin and Protestant Scholastics

Luther's views on forensic justification became widely accepted among Protestants of the Lutheran, Reformed, and Anglican traditions. John Calvin (d. 1564) read Luther's writings extensively and held that justification is by faith in Christ alone for the "remission of sins and the imputation of Christ's righteousness."[50] Like Luther, Calvin grounded justification on a believer's union with Christ and held that regeneration and sanctification follow justification.[51] What set Calvin apart was his views on unconditional election and absolute predestination, which will become an integral part of our story. A consensus soon developed within Protestantism on the nature of justification. Alister McGrath noted its three main features. First, justification refers to a forensic declaration of a new status rather than a process of being made righteous. Second, justification is distinguished from regeneration and sanctification. Whereas justification refers to an act of God, regeneration and sanctification involve an

---

47. Lull and Russell, eds., *Martin Luther's Basic Theological Writings*, 79.

48. Lohse, *Martin Luther's Theology*, 262.

49. Lohse, *Martin Luther's Theology*, 266.

50. John Calvin, *Institutes of the Christian Religion*, 2 vols. (Louisville: Westminster John Knox Press, 1960), 1:727.

51. Richard A. Muller, *Calvin and the Reformed Tradition: On the Work of Christ and the Order of Salvation* (Grand Rapids: Baker Academic, 2012), 212.

internal process of renewal. Third, the formal cause is the righteousness of Christ imputed or reckoned to a believer, and not inherent or infused righteousness.[52]

For most Protestants the concept of imputation rests on some form of the penal substitution theory of the atonement that stresses an objective satisfaction of divine justice. This view was deemed necessary for a juridical interpretation. Protestant scholastics distinguished between Christ's active and passive righteousness. By *active* was meant Christ's perfect human obedience to God's law, and *passive* to his atoning death on the cross. The latter purchased forgiveness and acceptance before God, whereas the former merited a legal standing of righteousness for eternal life. Both were considered essential to justification, but the accent often fell on the imputation of Christ's active righteousness. Concerning the *ordo salutis*, Richard Muller explained that Protestant scholastics tended to place justification after calling, regeneration, and conversion since these were deemed "necessary antecedents to the faith that receives God's gracious justification."[53] By doing so, they parted paths with Luther and Calvin. However, this was done to distinguish their stance from Rome's position, which Protestants considered to be Pelagian. So central was belief in justification by faith alone that many Protestants considered it the *articulus stantis vel cadentis ecclesiae*—the article upon which the church stands or falls.

English Reformation

In England the break with Rome was more about politics than doctrine since Henry VIII remained Catholic in his theology until his death in 1547. Following his death, the Church of England gravitated toward a Protestant view of justification that became part of the Thirty-Nine Articles of Religion.[54] Article XI reads:

---

52. McGrath, *Iustitia Dei*, 212–13.

53. Richard A. Muller, *Dictionary of Latin and Greek Theological Terms: Drawn Principally from Protestant Scholastic Theology* (Grand Rapids: Baker Academic, 2005), 163.

54. For more details about the development of the Anglican *Articles of Religion*, see McGrath, *Iustitia Dei*, 258–65.

> We are accounted righteous before God, only for the merit of our Lord and Saviour Jesus Christ by faith, and not for our own works or deservings. Wherefore, that we are justified by faith only is a most wholesome doctrine, and very full of comfort, as more largely is expressed in the Homily of Justification.[55]

The next two articles clarify that good works serve as evidence and fruit of justifying faith and therefore cannot be done prior to saving faith. This was standard Protestant theology, first enunciated by Luther. The mention of the "Homily of Justification" refers to Thomas Cranmer's sermon on salvation in the *Book of Homilies*. Cranmer (d. 1556) was the main architect behind the Book of Common Prayer (BCP) and is credited with the three sermons on salvation, faith, and good works in the *Homilies*. In the sermon on salvation Cranmer spelled out a doctrine of justification that essentially agrees with Luther. He began by asserting that justification cannot be earned or merited by works and is received only through the righteousness of another.[56] This gift of righteousness comes through the imputation of Christ's active and passive righteousness, who provided a penal satisfaction of God's justice:

> So that Christ is now the righteousness of all them that truly do believe in him. He for them paid their ransom by his death. He for them fulfilled the law in his life. So that now in him and by him every true Christian man may be called a fulfiller of the law; for as much as that which their infirmity lacketh, Christ's justice hath supplied.[57]

Cranmer's understanding of justification was monergistic, for he repeatedly affirmed that it is the "office of God only" to justify.[58] Nevertheless, his descriptions of the human role in exercising faith left the door

---

55. Articles of Religion, Art. XI; Book of Common Prayer (BCP), 1571 edition.

56. Thomas Cranmer, "An Homily of the Salvation of Mankind by Only Christ Our Saviour from Sin and Death Everlasting," in *The Library of Christian Classics: English Reformers,* ed. T. H. L. Parker (Louisville: Westminster John Knox Press, 2006), 262. There were two "Book of Homilies" produced in the sixteenth century; see Gerald Grey, ed., *The Books of Homilies: A Critical Edition* (Cambridge: James Clarke & Co, 2015).

57. Cranmer, "Homily of the Salvation of Mankind," 264.

58. Cranmer, "Homily of the Salvation of Mankind," 267, 269.

open for either an Arminian or Calvinist reading. Cranmer associated the gift of justification to the sacrament of baptism, which in the sixteenth century was universally administered to infants.[59] Sins following baptism are entrusted to Christ's heavenly intercession with forgiveness conditioned upon repentance. There is no discussion of losing one's justification though that interpretation is possible with his distinction between living and dead faith. Another sermon in the *Homilies* does discuss this point at large (#8 "How Dangerous a Thing it is to Fall From God").[60] There is also no discussion of justification in relation to final judgment, suggesting that the gift of righteousness is complete in its initial gift. Good works follow saving faith and serve as evidence of its authenticity. In Cranmer's view, justifying faith includes spiritual life and good works.[61] By incorporating spiritual life into his concept of justifying faith, Cranmer followed Luther by subsuming regeneration into justification. His next two sermons on faith and good works reflect the same position.

Religious sympathies in sixteenth-century England under Elizabeth I included three main groups. First, there were those who wanted the nation and church to return to Rome. This pro-Roman party included most if not all the bishops when Elizabeth came to the throne in 1658. This faction supported the Catholic position on justification. Second, there were those who wanted to purify the English Church of all remaining Catholic elements in its polity, liturgy, and doctrine. Known as Puritans, this party held Reformed views on ecclesiastical matters and on the important doctrine of justification. In between was a middle party that wanted neither "servility to Rome nor subservience to Geneva."[62] They supported the Elizabethan Settlement and the *via media* on matters of church pol-

---

59. Cranmer, "Homily of the Salvation of Mankind," 268–69. Infant baptism was so universal in the sixteenth century that no baptismal rite for adults was included in the BCP. One was added in the 1662 BCP because many born during the Commonwealth period had not been baptized. Colin Buchanan, *Historical Dictionary of Anglicanism*, 2nd ed. (New York: Rowman & Littlefield, 2015), 90–91.

60. Cranmer, "Homily of the Salvation of Mankind," 268, 270. The sermon on falling from God does not address the issues that divided Arminian and Calvinist positions, like whether those who fall away were truly regenerate Christians.

61. Cranmer, "Homily of the Salvation of Mankind," 265.

62. Moorman, *History of the Church of England*, 200.

ity, liturgy, and doctrine. In retrospect scholars call this group "Anglican" to distinguish them from the other two groups and because over time this was the tradition that became known as Anglicanism.[63] Since there were several traditions within the Church of England in the sixteenth and seventeenth centuries, there was a spectrum of views on justification. Significant to Wesley's doctrine of justification were the views held by the Anglicans and Puritans.

Classical Anglicanism

Within the Anglican wing of the established church from the late sixteenth to the early decades of the seventeenth century there developed two basic positions on justification. Mainstream Anglicans—like Richard Hooker (d. 1600), John Davenant (d. 1641), and Lancelot Andrewes (d. 1626)—held a moderate Reformed view of justification defined in opposition to Catholicism. Hooker acknowledged that Rome and the Church of England agreed that salvation was through the merits of Christ's righteousness.[64] The point of debate concerned formal cause. Rome taught justification by inherent righteousness; the Anglican Church by imputation.[65] Rome affirmed it is by faith and works, Anglicans by faith alone.[66] When Catholic cardinal Robert Bellarmine (d. 1621) pointed out that Christ's righteousness could not be the basis for justification since it was the meritorious cause, George Downame (d. 1634) countered it was not Christ's righteousness but its imputation that serves as the formal cause.[67]

---

63. Randy Maddox points out that the label "Anglican" came into regular use after the Restoration in 1660 ("Introduction to Wesley's Doctrinal and Controversial Treatises," in *Works*, 12:7). See Allison, *The Rise of Moralism*, ix. Some include more of the seventeenth century under this label (Paul Avis, *In Search of Authority: Anglican Theological Method from the Reformation to the Enlightenment* [London: Bloomsbury, 2014]).

64. John Keble, ed., *The Works of That Learned and Judicious Divine, Mr. Richard Hooker*, 3 vols., 5th ed. (Oxford: Clarendon Press, 1865), 3:486.

65. Keble, *Works of Richard Hooker*, 3:487, 490; Allison, *Rise of Moralism*, 3, 9, 25, 28.

66. Keble, *Works of Richard Hooker*, 3:530.

67. Allison, *Rise of Moralism*, 16.

Even though classical Anglicans stressed imputation as the formal cause, they also recognized the remission of sin. This is seen in their understanding of Christ's ascension to the Father's right hand. By his heavenly intercession Christ provides ongoing justification through daily forgiveness and the continual imputation of his righteousness.[68] Good works and sanctification involve inherent righteousness but cannot justify for the simple reason that sin remains in the believer throughout this life. Yet, good works do necessarily follow and give evidence and assurance of authentic faith.[69] Hooker summarized a standard Anglican perspective when he contrasted three kinds of righteousness: *justifying righteousness* is perfect and absolute, but not inherent; *sanctifying righteousness* is inherent, but neither perfect nor absolute; *glorifying righteousness* is both perfect and inherent.[70]

Even though Hooker and likeminded colleagues represented a mainstream view of justification among Anglicans, there were other perspectives that coalesced into a position somewhat closer to Rome's. Though these Anglicans held a minority viewpoint, their influence would extend down into Wesley's day, and included the likes of William Forbes (d. 1634), Thomas Jackson (d. 1640), William Laud (d. 1645), and Henry Hammond (d. 1660). At the heart of their soteriology was an Augustinian understanding of justification (to make righteous) and the Catholic doctrine of double justification.[71] They believed firmly in a causal connection between justification and holy living.[72] As William Laud suggested in the following confession:

> Christ Jesu . . . is our Redeemer, Advocate, Author and Finisher of our Faith, our Propitiation, Righteousness, and Justification; that I and all penitents may hereafter live a godly, righteous, and sober life, to the glory of Thy holy Name, and the salvation of our own souls.[73]

---

68. Allison, *Rise of Moralism*, 17.

69. Keble, *Works of Richard Hooker*, 3:508.

70. Keble, *Works of Richard Hooker*, 3:485.

71. McGrath, *Iustitia Dei*, 280; Allison, *Rise of Moralism*, 35, 37, 40, 44, 57.

72. Allison, *Rise of Moralism*, 61.

73. William Laud, *A Summarie of Devotions of William Laud* (Oxford: William Hall, 1667), 7.

Justification was therefore understood to be by faith and good works. Faith alone pertains to receiving baptismal and present justification, but good works are necessary for final justification. Rejecting the notion of imputation as the formal cause, these divines endorsed a definition of justification that included both remission of sin and inherent righteousness.[74] According to Forbes, the problem with imputed righteousness is that it suggests Christians are as righteous as Christ is before God and implies they are more righteous in this life (due to imputation) than they will be in the next as glorified believers.[75] Such notions were preposterous to these early holy living divines. Jackson concurred by arguing that good works are as integral to justification as to sanctification.[76] He also denied the idea of a formal cause for the simple reason that Christians are forgiven and never formally just in the eyes of God.[77]

Underlying the divide between the two Anglican perspectives was a difference in orienting concern—between a more Reformed or Catholic viewpoint guiding their respective theologies.[78] One area of agreement was the extent of the atonement. The Thirty-Nine Articles affirmed a general theory of atonement (Art. XXXI). Hooker articulated the same in contrast to the high Calvinism of Theodore Beza (d. 1605).[79] By the beginning of the seventeenth century, resistance toward Puritan high Calvinism led to the rise of Arminian beliefs among Anglicans that stressed predestination according to divine foreknowledge and grace-assisted human freedom.[80] These developments will have a major impact on Wesley and his doctrine of justification.

---

74. McGrath, *Iustitia Dei*, 281; Allison, *Rise of Moralism*, 34, 42, 57.

75. Allison, *Rise of Moralism*, 34.

76. Allison, *Rise of Moralism*, 49.

77. Allison, *Rise of Moralism*, 55.

78. Maddox, *Responsible Grace*, 18.

79. Keble, *Works of Richard Hooker*, 3:485.

80. Dewey D. Wallace Jr., "Puritan Polemical Divinity and Doctrinal Controversy," in *The Cambridge Companion to Puritanism*, ed. John Coffey and Paul C. H. Lim (Cambridge: Cambridge University Press, 2008), 214–15.

Puritanism

From its beginnings in the sixteenth century, Puritanism was predominantly Reformed in theology and yet reflected a spectrum of views as hyper, high, and moderate. Noted for their use of covenant theology to structure their soteriology, Puritans had a fervent interest in the spiritual dynamic of the Christian life. William Perkins's (d. 1602) *Golden Chain* exerted a major influence on Puritan thought related to causality in salvation.[81] Influenced by Theodore Beza, Perkins is credited with introducing high Calvinism into English Puritanism.[82] The high Calvinism of Perkins and John Owen (d. 1683) included a following list of beliefs: supralapsarianism, double predestination, limited atonement, final perseverance, and justification by imputation of Christ's active and passive righteousness. According to Owen, Christ's death functioned as a commercial transaction in which the debt of sinners is fully discharged. In this scheme there is no room for the concept of double justification, for once the debt is satisfied the believer stands fully and legally righteous before God.[83] Further to the fringe were antinomians who advocated an eternal justification of the elect, who were chosen and justified from eternity in the mind of God. These hyper-Calvinists denied the need of good works to serve as evidence and assurance of saving grace. Both high and moderate Calvinists rejected this notion and held that justification does not occur until a person experiences effectual calling and faith in Christ.[84]

Probably the most well-known moderate Calvinists in the seventeenth century were John Goodwin (d. 1665) and Richard Baxter (d. 1691). Both men would leave a mark on Wesley's doctrine. To the ire of the high Calvinists, Goodwin and Baxter published works attacking the implicit antinomianism in their position. In opposition to the doctrine of limited atonement, moderate Calvinists held that Christ's death was "sufficient

---

81. Wallace, "Puritan Polemical Divinity and Doctrinal Controversy," 208.

82. Clifford, *Atonement and Justification*, 78.

83. William H. Goold, *The Works of John Owen*, 16 vols. (Carlisle: The Banner of Truth Trust, 1965), 5:137–52.

84. Wallace, "Puritan Polemical Divinity and Doctrinal Controversy," 217.

for all even if efficient only for the elect."[85] Baxter argued that the high Calvinist view of the imputation of Christ's active righteousness leads inevitably to antinomianism, since it undercuts the need for obedience by the Christian. In its place he proposed that Christ's passive righteousness is imputed for forgiveness and acceptance, which is all that is needed to remove the barrier between God and the sinner. He further stressed the doctrine of double justification and the necessity of good works for final acceptance. As we will see, it was from Baxter's *Aphorismes of Justification* that Wesley derived his famous assertion in the 1770 Conference Minutes that "every believer, till he comes to glory, works *for* as well as *from* life."[86] Wesley published extracts of both Baxter and Goodwin to counter the high Calvinist doctrine of justification in his day.

Puritan beliefs about justification are spelled out in the Westminster Confession of Faith (1646) and in the Larger and Shorter Catechisms. The Westminster Confession presents a high Calvinist viewpoint on justification. From eternity God decreed to justify the elect. Christ's satisfaction includes his obedience and death, fully discharging the debt owed by the elect sinner. Consequently, justification involves the imputation of Christ's active and passive righteousness. Faith is the instrumental cause and is not imputed for righteousness. Assurance of salvation grows by degrees through the sanctifying work of the Spirit.[87] In the Shorter Catechism some important differences stand out. For starters, justification is defined as pardon and acceptance, with only a general statement about imputation. Nothing is said specifically about Christ's active and passive righteousness.[88] This shorter definition fits either a moderate or high Calvinist view of justification, which probably explains the popularity of the Shorter Catechism within various branches of Puritan and Dissenting Calvinists. Of interest is the *ordo salutis* in the Smaller Catechism. While justification follows effectual calling and union

---

85. Wallace, "Puritan Polemical Divinity and Doctrinal Controversy," 218.

86. *Annual Minutes of Some Late Conversations* 1770 (*Works*, 10:392, emphasis his); *An Extract of Mr. Richard Baxter's Aphorisms of Justification* (*Works*, 12:86).

87. Philip Schaff, *The Creeds of Christendom*, 3 vols. (Grand Rapids: Baker Book House, 1990), 3:626–28, 637–39.

88. Schaff, *The Creeds of Christendom*, 3:683.

with Christ, a final acquittal takes place at the Last Judgment.[89] Thus, the ambiguity of the Catechism allows for the idea of double justification, which some moderate Calvinists affirmed. Moreover, the description of justification in the Small Catechism was quite adaptable to the Anglican perspective, which possibly explains why Wesley chose to publish an extract of this Catechism in the 1750s.

Caroline Divines

The Caroline divines refer to Anglican theologians, writers, and church leaders during the reigns of Charles I and Charles II (1625–85). These divines derived their name from *Carolus*, Latin for Charles. The early Carolines overlap with classical Anglicanism and later merge with the High Churchmen of Wesley's day. This period saw greater polarization between Anglicans and Puritans, politically and theologically. The Carolines leaned Arminian in doctrine and High Church in soteriology, following the lead of William Laud.[90] McGrath commented that the later Carolines were deeply influenced by holy living theology.[91] Fearing antinomianism, these Anglicans rejected the Reformed view of justification as complete at initial faith for the Catholic doctrine of double justification. Yet, they rejected Rome's position on formal cause, as we saw above.[92]

Within the Carolines *via media* between Catholicism and Reformed, there remained a spectrum of views on justification. Some affirmed the imputation of Christ's righteousness, reflecting a more Reformed viewpoint, while others leaned Catholic and considered justification to include the blotting out of guilt and the inward renewal of righteousness—without endorsing the Catholic position on formal cause. The former view was

---

89. The *ordo* in the Small Catechism is effectual calling—union with Christ—justification—adoption—sanctification—assurance—perfection at death—acquittal at final judgment—glory.

90. Buchanan, *Historical Dictionary of Anglicanism*, 133.

91. McGrath, *Iustitia Dei*, 282.

92. Mark Langham, *The Caroline Divines and the Church of Rome: A Contribution to Current Ecumenical Dialogue* (London: Routledge, 2018), 134.

represented by churchmen like William Beveridge (d. 1708) and the latter by the holy living theologian Jeremy Taylor (d. 1667).[93] Both men would have an impact on Wesley. George Bull (d. 1710) argued that James subsumes Paul on the matter of justification and 1 Peter 1:2 represents the correct *ordo salutis*, with sanctification preceding (final) justification. Yet, Bull rejected Rome's view of formal cause and insisted that faith and repentance are accepted on account of Christ's righteousness as the meritorious cause.[94] In agreement with standard Protestant theology, the Carolines agreed that good works spring from and bear witness to saving faith and in this sense do not merit salvation; yet some held they do in secondary sense merit more grace since God rewards believers for their good works.[95] We will later see the same perspective taken up by Wesley in the 1770s. This brings up another important difference with Puritanism. The Carolines understood assurance to pertain to the present forgiveness of sin and not to final perseverance. Yet, for these holy living divines such assurance was bound to the sanctification process.[96] As we will see in the next chapter, such views will have an immense influence on the early Wesley's understanding of justification.

Pietism

Another movement that would influence Wesley's views on justification was Pietism. Its beginnings are usually identified with the publication of *Pia Desideria* by Philipp Jakob Spener (d. 1705) in 1675, though its roots go back to Johann Arndt (d. 1621) and his influential work *True Christianity*.[97]

---

93. Beveridge taught that Christ's active and passive righteousness is imputed to believers and also affirmed the doctrine of double justification (*Private Thoughts upon Religion and the Christian Life, Volume I* (London: John Hatchard & Son, 1834, repr. BiblioLife, LLC), 57–72. Taylor linked justification and sanctification as a single path of progression in one's salvation (Langham, *Caroline Divines and the Church of Rome*, 133).

94. Allison, *Rise of Moralism*, 118, 124–25, 128, 132.

95. Langham, *Caroline Divines and the Church of Rome*, 137–39.

96. Langham, *Caroline Divines and the Church of Rome*, 129. Allison, *Rise of Moralism*, 64–73.

97. For an excellent overview of Arndt's life, theology, and influence, see Johannes Wallmann, "Johann Arndt," in *The Pietist Theologians*, ed. Carter Lindberg (Malden, MA: Blackwell Publishing, 2005), 21–37.

Chapter One

Five years prior to the *Pia Desideria*'s publication, Spener began his *collegia pietatis* (pious groups) as a means of promoting vital Christian living.[98] Whereas Lutheran Orthodoxy stressed *Christus pro nobis* (Christ for us), Pietism put the accent on *Christus in nobis* (Christ in us). Like other German Pietists, Spener accepted Luther's teaching on alien righteousness and believed justification to be the heart of true Christian faith. But his emphasis on the new birth led him to subsume justification into regeneration.[99] As McGrath pointed out, this became a chief mark of Pietism.[100]

Count Nikolaus Ludwig von Zinzendorf (d. 1760) of the Moravians held similar views. Following Luther, Zinzendorf focused on Christ and the cross. Although Zinzendorf affirmed an objective atonement and the imputation of Christ's active and passive righteousness, the overall thrust of his gospel message highlighted the subjective work of inward transformation. Although Christ's entire life, from birth to death, is meritorious, the accent was put on its appropriation.[101] How this is accomplished is by looking to the wounds of Jesus, especially his "Side Wound" from which salvation flows.[102] What seekers must do is to passively gaze on Christ as the Spirit draws them. There is no need to practice the means of grace or to do any works of preparation, because salvation is received solely by God's free grace.[103] The quietism of the Moravians would cause Wesley in 1740 to sharply disagree with this morphology of conversion and consequently their justification doctrine.

Another group associated with Pietism was the Quakers, who defined justification as the fruit of the new birth. Robert Barclay (d. 1690) argued that the formal cause of justification is the "inward birth" of "Jesus

---

98. K. James Stein, "Philipp Jakob Spener," in *The Pietist Theologians*, 84.

99. Stein, "Philipp Jakob Spener," 90.

100. McGrath, *Iustitia Dei*, 294.

101. Peter Vogt, "Nicholas Ludwig von Zinzendorf," in *The Pietist Theologians*, 213.

102. Vogt, "Nicholas Ludwig von Zinzendorf," 212.

103. Arthur J. Freeman, *An Ecumenical Theology of the Heart: The Theology of Count Nicholas Ludwig von Zinzendorf* (Bethlehem: The Moravian Church in America, 1998), 176–78.

brought forth in the heart."[104] Since the Son is accepted by the Father, believers share in this acceptance by having been brought to life in Christ.[105] This led to an emphasis on good works since they bear witness to the reality of the divine life within. In other words, good works follow the new birth and justification as heat radiates from fire.[106] Barclay and the Quakers were therefore skeptical of the Protestant emphasis on justification apart from good works.[107]

Calvinism and Arminianism

The shadow of the prior two centuries continued to spread over Wesley's day with sharp differences separating Protestants over the doctrine of justification. One of these divides was the Calvinist-Arminian Controversy that began in the seventeenth century. For a little background, the dispute began when the Dutch Reformed theologian Jacob Arminius (d. 1609) objected to the high Calvinism of Theodore Beza (Calvin's successor at Geneva) and of Dutch Reformed theology in general. Arminius and his followers challenged the high Calvinism of unconditional election, double predestination, limited atonement, irresistible grace, and final perseverance. In their place they advocated conditional election, general atonement, resistible grace, and the possibility of apostasy.[108]

On English soil the Calvinist-Arminian Controversy contributed to the divisive politics of the seventeenth century. Puritan dominance during the interregnum ended abruptly with the restoration of King Charles II in 1660. With the *Act of Uniformity* in 1662, Puritans were forced into

---

104. Robert Barclay, *An Apology for the True Christian Divinity*, 11th ed. (London: Edward Marsh, 1849), 194.

105. Barclay, *Apology for True Christian Divinity*, 194.

106. Barclay, *Apology for True Christian Divinity*, 196.

107. Barclay, *Apology for True Christian Divinity*, 195.

108. On the Calvinist-Arminian Controversy, see Clifford, *Atonement and Justification*; W. Stephen Gunter, "From Arminius to the Synod of Dort," in *Perfecting Perfection: Essays in Honour of Henry D. Rack*, ed. Robert Webster (Cambridge: James Clark & Co, 2016), 8–28; Olson, *The Story of Christian Theology*, 454–72. For an overview of Calvin and Wesley, see Don Thorsen, *Calvin vs. Wesley: Bringing Belief in Line with Practice* (Nashville: Abingdon Press, 2013).

Nonconformity so that by the end of the century the established church was for the most part Arminian in theology.[109] However, regarding justification the dispute continued into the eighteenth century as Calvinists and Arminians sparred over the doctrine. Wesley and the Methodists, the majority of Anglican clergy (mainstream and High Church), and the General Baptists were Arminian while Calvinism dominated elsewhere. This included the Calvinistic forms of Methodism led by George Whitefield (d. 1770), the Countess of Huntingdon Selina Hastings (d. 1791), Howell Harris (d. 1773), and others. In addition, there were evangelicals in the established church that leaned Reformed but remained loyal to the church and its polity. Apart from the General Baptists, most of Dissent were Calvinist, including Particular Baptists, Presbyterians, and Independents. The exceptions included Romans Catholics, Pietists, and other fringe groups.

The Calvinists were not a monolithic party in the eighteenth century. The three classifications of moderate, high, and hyper continued to nuance their respective positions on justification. Allen Coppedge noted the boundaries between the three groups were not fixed, for individuals often moved between the three classifications.[110] Although denominations and groups were often characterized by one form of Calvinism, in the eighteenth century it was common for individuals to hold a different view from their denomination. This was especially true of the Church of England and its *via media*.

Moderate Calvinists followed in the footsteps of Richard Baxter and included evangelicals both within and without the established church. Coppedge summarized their central tenets as total depravity, the preparatory purpose of the Law, and justification by faith alone through Christ's

---

109. On the demise of Puritan dominance in the latter half of the seventeenth century, see John Coffey and Paul C. H. Lim, eds., *The Cambridge Companion to Puritanism* (Cambridge: Cambridge University Press, 2008); G. R. Cragg, *From Puritanism to the Age of Reason* (Cambridge: Cambridge University Press, 1966); Danker, *Wesley and the Anglicans*, 225–30; Moorman, *History of the Church in England*, 243–68.

110. Allen Coppedge, *John Wesley in Theological Debate* (Wilmore: Wesley Heritage Press, 1987), 40. He presents Whitefield as an example of a moderate Calvinist who during the controversy with Wesley in the early 1740s appeared to align himself with the views of high Calvinism.

imputed righteousness.[111] Their resistance toward Calvinistic antinomianism led to an accent on good works as evidence of salvation. Well-known moderates included George Whitefield, Jonathan Edwards (d. 1758), John Newton (d. 1807), and Henry Venn (d. 1873). *High Calvinists* embraced the views of Theodore Beza and the Synod of Dort (1618). Being "Five-Point" Calvinists, they accentuated the imputation of Christ's active and passive righteousness within a framework of federal theology and limited atonement. High Calvinists included John Edwards (d. 1716) of Cambridge, the Baptist Andrew Fuller (d. 1815), and Anglican evangelicals Augustus Toplady (d. 1778), Richard Hill (d. 1808), and Rowland Hill (d. 1833). The last three would become strident opponents of Wesley during the Minutes Controversy in the 1770s. The third classification was *Hyper-Calvinists*, who so stressed the divine decrees and the eternal covenant of grace that the elect was seen as eternally justified. As a result, personal holiness and good works were negated as well as a passion for evangelism. The majority of hyper-Calvinists in Wesley's day were Baptists, like John Gill (d. 1771) and John Brine (d. 1765).

In the other camp were the Arminians. Within the Church of England Bishop Spencer Madan (d. 1813) probably expressed the sentiment of most Arminian clergy when he stated that believers are justified in a threefold sense: "meritoriously by Christ, instrumentally by faith, declaratively by works."[112] Alexander Garden (d. 1791) agreed that saving faith is always accompanied with good works, so that it is proper to say we are justified by faith and works.[113] This made sense to many Anglicans because of their Arminian convictions and belief in double justification. As Josiah Tucker (d. 1799) noted, the gospel covenant of salvation remains conditional through this life and is only secured by a life of obedience to the end when God formally declares the believer righteous.[114] John Fletcher

---

111. Coppedge, *John Wesley in Theological Debate*, 39.

112. Spencer Madan, *Justification by Works, and Not by Faith Only, Stated, Explained, and Reconciled with Justification by Faith, without Works* (London, 1761), 22.

113. Alexander Garden, *The Doctrine of Justification . . . in a Letter to A. Croswell* (Charles-Town: Peter Timothy, 1742), 31–34.

114. Josiah Tucker, "A Short and Familiar Way of Explaining the Doctrine of Justification," *Methodist History* 44, no. 3 (April 2006): 168.

(d. 1785) developed the Anglican position further by teaching there have been distinct dispensations of grace since the fall of Adam that culminated in the gospel covenant. He aligned these dispensations to the spiritual states that a person passes through—natural, legal, and evangelical.[115] He went further and taught there are four degrees of justification in the Anglican *via salutis*: a universal justification for infants by prevenient grace, an imputed justification by saving faith in Christ, a declarative justification by good works, and a public justification at the Final Judgment. With each degree Fletcher stressed that Christ alone is the meritorious cause.[116] As we will see later, Fletcher's views will have a marked influence on Wesley's mature perspective regarding degrees of acceptance.

To conclude, Protestants agreed that Rome's definition of justification—*to make righteous*—was unscriptural and Pelagian. And most Protestants believed the Greek word *dikaioō* refers to the law court and means *to declare righteous*. But from there the unity dissipated into a wide range of views that divided Protestants into competing camps, often within the same denominational tradition. Throughout his life Wesley would engage most of the various views on justification to form his own beliefs on the subject. With this introduction we are now ready to begin our story with the early Wesley's quest to attain a righteous standing before God.

---

115. Jeffrey Wallace, ed., *The Works of John Fletcher*, 5 vols. (Brookfield: Apprehending Truth Publishers, 2011–21), 3:4–5.

116. Wallace, ed., *Works of John Fletcher*, 1:160–61.

CHAPTER TWO

SEEKING RIGHTEOUSNESS AS AN ANGLICAN HIGH CHURCH DIVINE: 1703–37

Theology is embedded in the practices of the faith. The way most Christians learn their faith is by the "countless daily encounters with their Christianity."[1] These encounters include both planned and unplanned ways in which an individual, family, or congregation worships and lives out their faith. So, our story begins long before Wesley was a leader of the Methodist movement. His initial beliefs about justification were first formed in the Epworth parsonage and nurtured through his education at Charterhouse and Oxford. Wesley later came to a point of crisis over these beliefs at the end of his Georgian mission and this led to a tectonic shift in his understanding of the gospel and a Christian's present standing before God. To explore these developments and their contribution to his doctrine of justification, we begin with his childhood before moving to his time at Oxford and Georgia.

---

1. Stone and Duke, *How to Think Theologically*, 13.

Early Years

When Wesley decided to record his evangelical conversion in May 1738, he began by stating that he had lost his baptismal regeneration by age ten.[2] He added that he had been "strictly educated and carefully taught" that he "could only be saved by universal obedience, by keeping all the commandments of God." He explained that as a child he "gladly received" the instruction of his parents, though he did not yet grasp the meaning of "inward obedience or holiness."[3] That would come later. But during his time at Charterhouse (1714–20) he remembered becoming more negligent of "outward duties" and feeling the pinch of his sin. Yet he still hoped to be finally saved because he was not as bad as other people. A similar pattern continued during his time at Christ Church, Oxford (1720–24), but now with stronger convictions over his sinful failures, especially "before and after the Holy Communion."[4]

On the surface these comments might suggest the young Wesley had a works-based religion.[5] But this conclusion fails to consider the religious context behind these remarks. If we look more closely at what Wesley wrote, considering his High Church culture, we can detect the Anglican doctrine of double justification and its sacramental view of the Christian life. In chapter 1 we learned that High Church Anglicans understood justification to be initially granted in baptism and formally declared at the Last Judgment. Their Arminian theology led them to emphasize the conditionality of the gospel covenant for final salvation with Holy Communion serving as a primary means for sustaining grace in the Christian life. As we will now see, the early Wesley developed his initial notions of justification through his "countless daily encounters" with his High Church faith in the Epworth parsonage.

---

2. On the question of when Wesley wrote the Aldersgate Memorandum, see Olson, *Wesley and Aldersgate*, 36–37.

3. *Journal*, May 24, 1738 §1 (*Works*, 18:243).

4. *Journal*, May 24, 1738 §§2–3 (*Works*, 18:243).

5. This is a common assessment of the early Wesley, even by scholars. William Ragsdale Cannon's assessment in his *Theology of John Wesley, with Special Reference to the Doctrine of Justification* (London: University Press of America, 1974), 63.

Samuel Wesley

In chapter 1 we noted that a sacramental view of the Christian life was inculcated in Wesley at an early age.[6] This becomes evident when we survey his parents' writings. Besides their Anglican High Churchmanship, Samuel and Susanna's religious beliefs were imbued with Puritanism from their upbringing in Nonconformity and influenced by German Pietism through their contact with Anthony Horneck (d. 1697).[7] A basic outline of Samuel's High Church views on salvation are found in his manual to his parishioners *The Pious Communicant Rightly Prepar'd*.[8] Samuel's soteriology was grounded on the Puritan concept of two covenants and in agreement with other Anglicans he did not conflate the covenant of works with the Mosaic Law.[9] God's covenant with Adam as our federal head was based on works, but Adam broke that covenant and along with his descendants came under the sentence of death, both temporal and eternal. Therefore, God instituted a covenant of grace, which was foreshadowed in the protoevangelium of Genesis 3:15 and revealed through Abraham and the Mosaic Law. However, its "full and complete discovery" awaited the "times of the Gospel."[10] As Samuel explained, the new covenant in Christ contains the "most perfect revelation of the divine will, the promises of God, and those conditions on which he accepts and forgives us."[11]

---

6. On his parents' influence, see Baker, *John Wesley and the Church of England*; Kenneth J. Collins, *John Wesley: A Theological Journey* (Nashville: Abingdon Press, 2003); Heitzenrater, *Wesley and the People Called Methodists*; Green, *The Young Mr. Wesley*; Robert C. Monk, *John Wesley: His Puritan Heritage* (Nashville: Abingdon Press, 1966); Rack, *Reasonable Enthusiast*.

7. Monk, *John Wesley: His Puritan Heritage*. Arthur Alan Torpy, *The Prevenient Piety of Samuel Wesley, Sr.* (Lanham, MD: Scarecrow Press, 2009), 72–74. Samuel and Horneck held the same theology of sacramental justification. See Scott Thomas Kisker, *Foundation for Revival: Anthony Horneck, the Religious Societies, and the Construction of Anglican Pietism* (Lanham, MD: Scarecrow Press, 2008), 173–97.

8. Samuel Wesley, *The Pious Communicant Rightly Prepar'd; Or, A Discourse Concerning the Blessed Sacrament* (London: Charles Harper, 1700).

9. On Puritan views of covenant theology and the conflation of the covenant of works with the Mosaic Law, see Stanley J. Rodes, *From Faith to Faith: John Wesley's Covenant Theology and the Way of Salvation* (Eugene, OR: Pickwick Publications, 2013). See also Monk, *John Wesley: His Puritan Heritage*.

10. Samuel Wesley, *Pious Communicant*, 29.

11. Samuel Wesley, *Pious Communicant*, 29.

Christ's role as our representative is to provide a "sacrifice for us to atone his Father's anger," while our part is to repent, believe, and offer sincere obedience.[12]

At this point Samuel's High Churchmanship comes to the forefront when he described how the benefits of Christ's saving work are applied to the believer. The new covenant in Christ is initiated in baptism wherein the baptizand is regenerated and forgiven for the "damning guilt" of original sin.[13] Although no one perfectly keeps their baptismal vows, the baptized child assumes responsibility for their baptismal covenant at confirmation.[14] These baptismal vows are renewed each time the sacrament of communion is taken.[15] So central was the Lord's Supper to Samuel that he called it the "substance of all other Christian duties."[16] He believed the sacrament not only serves to express one's vows to God, it confers covenant benefits to worthy communicants. Quoting the Anglican *Homilies*, Samuel reiterated that worthy communicants receive "not only the outward sacrament, but the *spiritual thing* also, not the *figure*, but the *truth*, not the *shadow* only, but the *body*."[17] In this way worthy communicants partake of Christ's body and blood after a spiritual manner and receive grace for forgiveness and sanctification.

The importance of the sacrament to the Christian life is seen in Samuel's emphasis on "faithful receivers."[18] He claimed the apostles, primitive church, and Church of England agree that only worthy communicants receive the sacrament's saving benefits. Communicants must examine themselves before partaking, using the Ten Commandments as a guide.

---

12. Samuel Wesley, *Pious Communicant*, 29.

13. Samuel Wesley, *Pious Communicant*, 29. "Of Baptism" §§6, 9, in *Pious Communicant*, 197–99, 204–5.

14. Samuel Wesley, *Pious Communicant*, 29. In the BCP, confirmation is for children who reach the age of discretion and can recite "the [Apostles'] Creed, the Lord's Prayer, and the Ten Commandments; and can also answer to such Questions, as in the short Catechism are contained" ("The Order of Confirmation").

15. Samuel Wesley, *Pious Communicant*, 29.

16. Samuel Wesley, *Pious Communicant*, 38.

17. Samuel Wesley, *Pious Communicant*, 23, emphasis his.

18. Samuel Wesley, *Pious Communicant*, 24.

Samuel realized that such stern warnings might cause parishioners to stay away from the Table. To counter this tendency, he devoted an entire chapter to the "perpetual obligation" of communicating "frequently."[19] He encouraged his parishioners to focus on the benefits while at the same time warning them of the dangers of neglecting the Holy Meal. On the plus side, both baptism and the Lord's Supper offer grace and an assurance of salvation. They are the "seals of God's covenant with us."[20] Samuel is worth quoting since he connected faithful reception of the sacraments to assurance of justification and sanctification:

> The *Holy Symbols*, when duly received, do exhibit and convey unto us divine *virtue* and assistance, and all the inestimable *benefits* which were purchas'd for us, and reached out unto us by the death of a Redeemer; as justification or *actual pardon* of our sins, the reinstating us in God's favour, and assuring us that he is *reconciled* to us, and that we are accounted righteous before him; as well as *sanctification*, or actual strength and grace to conquer our Sins and to obey his *commands*.[21]

From Samuel's *Pious Communicant* we gain important insights into John's early religious formation. Given Samuel's strong stand on partaking in a worthy manner, John's remarks in the Aldersgate Memorandum about his youthful struggles "before and after Holy Communion" make sense.[22] Similarly, his father's emphasis on frequent communicating probably contributed to John's later commitment to "constant communion."[23] And it appears the young Wesley learned from his father that the sacrament was central to sustaining his justification since it confers forgiveness and sanctifying grace. John acknowledged as much to his mother in 1725, "When I communicated worthily, i.e., with faith, humility, and thankfulness, my preceding sins were *ipso facto* forgiven me."[24] What begins to

---

19. Samuel Wesley, *Pious Communicant*, 42.

20. Samuel Wesley, *Pious Communicant*, 36.

21. Samuel Wesley, *Pious Communicant*, 36–37, emphasis his.

22. *Journal*, May 24, 1738 (*Works*, 18:243).

23. See Wesley's sermon "The Duty of Constant Communion" (*Works* 3:427), originally written during his Oxford period.

24. Letter, June 18, 1725 (*Works*, 25:170).

emerge from this sketch of Samuel's teachings is that the young Wesley was nurtured in a sacramental view of justification, initially granted in baptism, and sustained by the Lord's Supper.

Susanna Wesley

From the surviving correspondence between John and his mother, we know Susanna left a definite mark on her son's faith and theology.[25] Her works consist of letters, journals, and a variety of educational, catechetical, and controversial writings.[26] Her views on justification are scattered throughout her writings, with the fullest account found in her exposition of the Apostles' Creed. Written as a letter to her daughter of the same first name, Susanna explained in detail her beliefs about the gospel and salvation. From her exposition we can deduce that what she wrote in this letter is what she taught all her children, including John. Just as the creed is organized around the Trinity, Susanna's exposition incorporates an economic Trinitarian perspective of salvation. God initiated a covenant of works with Adam, the "first general head of mankind," which he transgressed and brought guilt and punishment to his posterity.[27] In its place a covenant of grace was instituted that promised salvation through the "seed of the woman" (Gen. 3:15).[28] The conditions of this new covenant were no longer "perfect obedience," but "faith in Christ Jesus and sincere though imperfect obedience to the laws of God."[29]

As the "second general head" of the human race, Jesus Christ fulfills the three offices of prophet, priest, and king. Susanna's grasp of Christ's office as priest reveals her theological acuity:

---

25. This is evident from the degree of confidence Wesley had in his mother's counsel (e.g., *Works*, 25:159–90).

26. Charles Wallace Jr., *Susanna Wesley: The Complete Writings* (Oxford: Oxford University Press, 1997).

27. Wallace, *Susanna Wesley*, 382.

28. Wallace, *Susanna Wesley*, 384.

29. Wallace, *Susanna Wesley*, 384.

> Now I would fain know which way his justice could be satisfied, since 'tis impossible for a finite being as man is to do it . . . unless some other were substituted in our stead that would undergo the punishment we have deserved and thereby satisfy divine justice and purchase pardon and favour from God, the merit of whose perfect obedience should atone for the imperfection of ours, and so obtain for us title to those glorious rewards, to that eternal happiness.[30]

In this compressed statement, Susanna expressed her understanding of justification. She subscribed to a penal substitution theory of the atonement and inferred the imputation of Christ's active and passive righteousness as the basis for pardon, restoration to God's favor, and title to the eternal kingdom. Digressing into a fairly long description of Christ's passion in her letter, Susanna affirmed Christ's death as an "actual, real, separation of his soul and body" and that he did "actually descend into hell" and there proclaim his victory over the principalities and powers.[31] Drawing on the Apostle Paul's statement in Romans 4:25, Susanna held that Christ was raised from the dead for our justification and now reigns in heaven with absolute "power and dominion." From there he will return to publicly judge every person "according to what they have done on earth."[32]

For the third article of the creed, Susanna drew on the Nicene Creed and Anglican John Pearson to stress that the Holy Spirit is the "author of all holiness in us by sanctifying our natures, illuminating our minds, rectifying our wills and affections," and by "conveying grace into the soul" through the "word and sacraments."[33] Besides these benefits, the Holy Spirit "assures us of our adoption."[34] Baptism is the "first remission" of sin and repentance serves to maintain "constant forgiveness" in the Christian

---

30. Wallace, *Susanna Wesley*, 381.
31. Wallace, *Susanna Wesley*, 391.
32. Wallace, *Susanna Wesley*, 392.
33. Wallace, *Susanna Wesley*, 392.
34. Wallace, *Susanna Wesley*, 392.

life.³⁵ Her views on the Lord's Supper mirror that of her husband's. The sacrament conveys pardon and grace to worthy communicants.

Sacramental Justification

More space has been devoted to Samuel and Susanna's writings because of their parental influence on John's early religious formation. Their views illustrate the High Church perspective that John was nurtured in. Even though he was only a child, their writings infer he was taught a High Church sacramental view of the Christian life that included basic knowledge of the economic Trinity, covenant theology, original sin, double justification, and holy living. He likewise was taught an elementary understanding of justification as pardon and acceptance along with a rudimentary concept of Christ's atonement purchasing salvation. These truths were further instilled in John by the Anglican Catechism that he learned for confirmation. For it too taught an economic Trinitarian view of salvation by grace through a penal substitution view of the atonement. Justification involves the forgiveness of sin (initially received in baptism) and the Lord's Supper is a primary means of grace in the Christian life.³⁶ To summarize, then, we can conclude from his High Church upbringing in the Epworth home that the young Wesley was taught a *sacramental view of justification* that was inculcated in him by the "countless daily encounters" he had with his Anglican faith.³⁷

Confirmed at the age of nine (July 15, 1712), John left Epworth two years later for Charterhouse, London, to continue his education.³⁸ He lived with his older brother Samuel Jr., who was a committed High Churchman like their parents. After six years Wesley entered Christ Church, Oxford, and completed his undergraduate studies in 1724. Under the tutorship of George Wigan and Henry Sherman, both conventional High Church-

---

35. Wallace, *Susanna Wesley*, 394.

36. The Anglican Catechism and Rite of Ordination used the Apostles' Creed, Ten Commandments, and the Lord's Prayer to instruct pupils in a sacramental view of the Christian life (BCP, 289–98).

37. Stone and Duke, *How to Think Theologically*, 13.

38. Baker, *John Wesley and the Church of England*, 10.

men, Wesley's education continued to ground him in the Anglican High Church view of justification. Frank Baker perceptively noted that at age twenty-one Wesley's religion seemed to have been only an "older version of the boy of ten who left Epworth for Charterhouse."[39] That would begin to change the next year.

Oxford

The year 1725 would prove pivotal for Wesley in several ways. He made the momentous decision to follow in his father's footsteps and pursue a clerical calling in the Church of England. Seeking his parents' counsel on the matter, John was advised by Samuel on matters of academics and the right reasons for entering holy orders, whereas Susanna directed her son to weigh his spiritual character and whether he had a "reasonable hope of salvation by Jesus Christ."[40] In response, John began to read devotional works that challenged his religious commitment and opened his eyes to the necessity of inward holiness for salvation.[41] Years later he recalled being "exceedingly affected" on the matter of purity of intention and saw for the first time that "true religion was seated in the heart."[42] The spiritual awakening that followed altered the direction of Wesley's religious life and led to important developments in his doctrine of justification.

Holy Living Divines

On the heels of his religious awakening in 1725, Wesley's interest turned to the Anglican holy living tradition and to Christian mysticism. By the early 1730s he was digging into patristics, ancient liturgies, and

---

39. Baker, *John Wesley and the Church of England*, 12.

40. Letters, January 26 and February 23, 1725 (*Works*, 25:157–60).

41. Letter to Countess of Huntingdon, June 19, 1771 (*Telford*, 5:258–59). "On Laying the Foundation for the New Chapel," I.1, 5; April 21, 1777 (*Works*, 3:580–81, 583). "The General Spread of the Gospel" §13, April 1783 (*Works*, 2:490–91).

42. *A Plain Account of Christian Perfection* §2 (*Works*, 13:136); *Journal*, May 24, 1738 (*Works*, 18:243).

Anglican sacramentalism.[43] Sermons by popular Anglican divines and other Pietist works were passed between Wesley and his friends. He read the Greek New Testament and ancient classics, with his interests reaching into other areas, like natural philosophy. Our interest is with those authors who contributed to his doctrine of justification at this time. Of these authors, two stand out as representative and influential: Jeremy Taylor (d. 1667) and William Law (d. 1761). Both were Anglican High Churchmen, yet each had a distinct emphasis that supplied important concepts to Wesley's early understanding of objective righteousness.

Jeremy Taylor was a prolific author and influential churchman of the Restoration era. Wesley read several of Taylor's works but the one that caught his attention the most was *The Rule and Exercises of Holy Living and Holy Dying*. Originally published as separate volumes in 1650 and 1651, *Holy Living and Holy Dying* is best described as a discipleship manual in which Taylor advocated a "rule and method" approach to the Christian life. Richard Heitzenrater explained that Wesley adopted this "distinctive approach" during his spiritual awakening in 1725 and over the next several years mentored others in the method.[44] Taylor's gospel stressed evangelical repentance, holy living, and the conditionality of salvation within the Anglican *ordo salutis*. One of Taylor's fullest statements on justification in *Holy Living and Holy Dying* is found in the section on repentance:

> [God] changes also upon man's repentance, that he alters his decrees, revokes his sentence, cancels the bills of accusation, and throws the records of shame and sorrow from the court of heaven, and lifts up the sinner from the grave to life, from his prison to a throne, from hell and the guilt of eternal torture to heaven, and to a title to never-ceasing felicities.[45]

---

43. On Wesley's interest in patristics and Anglican High Church sacramentalism during his Oxford period, see Geordan Hammond's *John Wesley in America: Restoring Primitive Christianity* (Oxford: Oxford University Press, 2014).

44. Richard P. Heitzenrater, *Mirror and Memory: Reflections on Early Methodism* (Nashville: Kingswood Books, 1989), 69–77.

45. Jeremy Taylor, *Holy Living and Holy Dying: With Prayers Containing the Whole Duty of a Christian* (New York: Cosmo Classics, 2007), 233–34.

Justification here includes a cluster of blessings, with the central idea that it alters one's standing before God and puts the believer on the path of salvation. However, contrary to standard English Reformed theology, Taylor did not believe these blessings were fully completed at any point in this life. As did other High Church Anglicans, he held a progressive view of repentance. It begins in baptism and continues through life. Since repentance is a condition for forgiveness and maintaining justification, Taylor concluded that pardon for sin is partial and progressive throughout life:

> In the Old Testament pardon of sins was nothing but removing the punishment... in the gospel pardon of sins is another thing; pardon of sins is a sanctification... As we hate sin, and grow in grace, and arrive at the state of holiness... in the same degree we are to judge concerning the forgiveness of sins... forgiveness of sins is not a secret sentence, a word, or a record; but it is a state of change, and effected upon us.[46]

To illustrate his point, Taylor pointed to Israel when time and again God forgave their idolatry. In each instance, forgiveness applied to past commissions of sin.[47] When Israel committed idolatry again, God brought punishment that required fresh pardon. In the same way, evangelical forgiveness remains partial and progressive in life. God forgives Christians when they repent of past sin. Future sin will require future pardon. A second related point concerns the gift of pardon in a Christian's sanctification. Taylor held that through the pardon of sin God effectually works to bring about greater deliverance from sin. Evangelical forgiveness therefore does not consist merely of a "secret sentence, a word, or a record," as the Calvinists taught, but effects a "state of change" that ultimately prepares a Christian for final justification and eternal life. In the end, Taylor presented a High Church Arminian alternative to the Puritan view of justification as complete and finished at initial faith in Christ.

However, Wesley initially questioned Taylor's concept of progressive pardon having grown up believing that when he communicated in a

---

46. Taylor, *Holy Living and Holy Dying*, 488–89.
47. Taylor, *Holy Living and Holy Dying*, 239.

worthy manner his "preceding sins were *ipso facto* forgiven."[48] On this point he misread Taylor, who also believed the sacrament confers forgiveness.[49] But by 1730 Wesley would commend Taylor's association of forgiveness with sanctification and believed it represented one of the clearest explanations of pardon he had come across.[50] Holy living was now firmly wedded to justification in the early Wesley's soteriology.

From his diary we learn that Wesley probably began to read William Law's *Serious Call to a Holy and Devout Life* (1729) in late 1730. Two years later he perused Law's prior work *A Practical Treatise upon Christian Perfection* (1726).[51] Law was a non-juror and gained notoriety through his involvement in the Bangorian Controversy. His influence on Wesley was immense over the next several years, to the point that Wesley sought his counsel on spiritual matters and tailored his ministry after Law's principles outlined in the above two writings.[52] In both works Law presents a strong Pietist impulse, with justification subsumed into the new birth. Law's gospel was based on the meta-narrative of humanity's creation, fall, and recovery of the divine image. Christ's death is a "full, perfect, and sufficient sacrifice" that ended the Old Testament sacrificial system and "fully reconciles God to accept us upon the terms of the new covenant."[53] The new covenant is premised on "two great truths, the deplorable corruption of human nature, and its new birth in Christ Jesus."[54]

It was here that Law's Pietist impulse comes to the forefront. He accepted the Anglican *ordo salutis* and took seriously the church's teachings

---

48. Letter, June 18, 1725 (*Works*, 25:170).

49. Taylor, *Holy Living and Holy Dying*, 243–52.

50. Letter, February 28, 1730 (*Works*, 25:245).

51. Wesley claimed to have read Law several years earlier, in 1727–28. His extant diary points to 1730 and 1732. On this point, see the exchange between Frank Baker and Fredrick Hunter in the *Proceedings of the Wesley Historical Society* 37 (Oct. 1969, June 1970, Oct. 1970): 78–82, 143–50, 173–77. For Wesley's remarks, see Journal, May 24, 1738 (*Works*, 18:244); *The Principles of a Methodist* §16 (*Works*, 9:56); *A Plain Account of Christian Perfection, As Believed and Taught by the Rev. Mr. John Wesley, From the Year 1725 to 1765* §4 (*Works*, 13:137).

52. Letters, June 26, 1734; May 14, 1738 (*Works*, 25:386, 540).

53. William Law, *A Practical Treatise upon Christian Perfection* (Eugene, OR: Wipf and Stock, 2001), 80.

54. Law, *A Practical Treatise upon Christian Perfection*, 13.

on baptism. In *Christian Perfection* Law outlines his views regarding the baptismal covenant:

> No sooner are we baptized, but we are to consider ourselves as new and holy persons, that are entered upon a new state of things, that are devoted to God, and have renounced all, to be fellow-heirs with Christ, and members of his kingdom.[55]

From this quote we see that Law considered a true Christian to be wholly devoted to God.[56] This led to his next point:

> Whenever we yield ourselves up to the pleasures, profits, and honours of this life, that we turn *apostates*, break our covenant with God, and go back from the express conditions, on which we were admitted into the communion of Christ's church.[57]

With this one statement Law declared baptized Christians to have lost their salvation when they turn to worldly pleasures. To be saved these nominal believers must renew their baptismal vow of full devotion evidenced by an asceticism of self-denial and renunciation of the world. This rededication or single intention Law called the "new birth," a "new creature," and a "conversion of the heart to God."[58] Those converted are true Christians and on the path of renewal in the image of God. Law's pietism stands out in that there are very few references to justification in *Christian Perfection* and *Serious Call*. In the few comments he did make, justification is defined as pardon and acceptance, which were standard terms among Anglican divines. Toward the end of life, Law published a work in which he expressed in clear terms a mainstream Anglican view of double justification.[59]

---

55. Law, *A Practical Treatise upon Christian Perfection*, 23.
56. William Law, *A Serious Call to a Devout and Holy Life* (Alachua: Bridge-Logos, 2008), 5.
57. Law, *A Practical Treatise upon Christian Perfection*, 24, emphasis his.
58. Law, *A Practical Treatise upon Christian Perfection*, 25–27, 35.
59. William Law, *Of Justification by Faith and Works: A Dialogue between a Methodist and a Churchman* (London: J. Richardson, 1760).

Law's impact on Wesley was in several areas, but three deserve notice. First, it was probably around this time that Wesley began to reinterpret his spiritual journey that he had "sinned away" his baptismal regeneration as a child.[60] This meant that his spiritual awakening in 1725 was reinterpreted as his conversion and new birth. Although his views on conversion will change once more in 1738, Law's influence was instrumental to Wesley's growing belief in adult conversion as a necessary component of authentic faith.[61] Second, it follows from the first point that Wesley could no longer rely on his baptism for an assurance of present acceptance before God. This led him to begin advocating a non-sacramental view of present justification for adults that over time will increase in prominence until it becomes a distinct category in his theology. Finally, Law's pietism influenced Wesley to subsume justification into regeneration and the single intention. Years later Wesley recounted that during this time he "confounded [justification] with sanctification" and held "confused" notions about forgiveness.[62] To be fair, his confused notions began earlier with his reading of Taylor. But Law's writings stood out by presenting an argument so forceful and compelling that inward holiness became the "one thing needful." It practically absorbed all of Wesley's attention, as is seen in his Oxford sermons.[63]

Oxford Sermons

The sermons serve as the primary source for Wesley's early views on salvation and the Christian life. The *Bicentennial Edition* contains sixteen sermons from his Oxford period, spread over a ten-year span (1725–35). In these sermons righteousness is primarily inward, it pertains to developing godly and holy character, and not about the objective righteousness of

---

60. *Journal,* May 24, 1738 (*Works,* 18:243).

61. See Wesley's Oxford sermon on adult conversion, written in 1731, "The Wisdom of Winning Souls" (*Works,* 4:305–17). For a fuller discussion of this point, see Olson, *Wesley and Aldersgate,* 137–39; "The New Birth in the Early Wesley," *Wesleyan Theological Journal* 52, no. 1 (2017): 79–99.

62. *A Further Appeal to Men of Reason and Religion,* Pt. I, VI.1, 1745 (*Works,* 11:176).

63. The phrase was a favorite of Wesley and is found in Law's *Christian Perfection,* 37, 45.

justification. This is to be expected given the influence of Taylor, Law, and other holy-living divines. To set up Wesley's remarks on justification we first need to look at his larger themes.

Wesley followed Law by centering his soteriology on the meta-narrative of humanity's creation, fall, and recovery. Albert Outler noted that Wesley held a "Christian-Platonic vision of the *imago Dei*—created, defaced, restored."[64] The divine image in Adam was perfect until the day he sinned and became a "mortal, foolish, vicious, enslaved creature."[65] The core issue was original sin, that "innate disease" that had "effaced the image of God" in human nature.[66] The good news, however, is that God has provided redemption in Christ. All things our Lord did, from his birth to his death, were "miracles of love" to heal "every spiritual sickness of our nature" and to "restore us to health, to liberty, to holiness" in the love of God.[67] Therefore, the "renewal of our fallen nature" is the "one thing needful"—a phrase taken from Luke 10:42. From this recap we can see that for Wesley Christ is more than an *exemplar* for holy living. The Son of God lived and died to merit redemptive grace for the believer's renewal in righteousness. From this we can conclude that the early Wesley was no Pelagian, nor even a semi-Pelagian. Every aspect of salvation requires divine grace, from beginning to end.

This meta-narrative of the restored *imago Dei* informed Wesley's early beliefs on justification. In the landmark sermon "The Circumcision of the Heart" (1733),[68] Wesley opened by proclaiming that the "true follower of Christ . . . is in a state of acceptance with God" (§3). The present tense ("is") clearly refers to a believer's current standing before God, their present justification. Wesley further explained that a Christian's "acceptance" is not conditioned on anything external, like baptism or "any other

---

64. *Works*, 4:352. Wesley's soteriology has been labeled semi-Augustinian for good reasons. See Christopher T. Bounds, "How Are People Saved? The Major Views of Salvation with a Focus on Wesleyan Perspectives and Their Implications" (*Wesley and Methodist Studies*, vol. 3, 2011).

65. "The Image of God" II.3, 5 (*Works*, 4:298–99).

66. "The Image of God" IV.1; "The One Thing Needful" I.2 (*Works*, 4:301, 354).

67. "The One Thing Needful" II.3, 5 (*Works*, 4:356–57).

68. *The Circumcision of the Heart* (*Works*, 1:401–14).

outward form," but on a "right state of soul" (§3). His Protestant leanings become evident when he later stated that this "right state of soul" is attained by faith. For it is by faith that God's "children" see their "calling" is to "glorify God" who "bought" them by the redemption of Christ, and in response offer themselves "entirely 'unto God, as those that are alive from the dead'" (I.7-8).[69] Having been made alive, believers are "born of God" and "now do, through [God's] grace, the things which are acceptable in his sight" (I.9). Moreover, faith does not leave Christians without hope in their assurance of salvation, for it gives them a "joyous prospect of that 'crown of glory' which is 'reserved in heaven'" (I.9). So, faith produces hope, and both lead to love in which "every affection, and thought, and word, and work" terminates in God, who is the "sole end as well as source" of the Christian's "being" (I.12).

In this sermon present justification is linked to faith, new birth, assurance, and holy living. Since saving faith produces a holy life—a life that is acceptable to God—Wesley could say that the believer is justified by faith. In this way he could express a High Church view of the Protestant faith. Regarding influences, an Augustinian paradigm is evident in that a believer's "state of acceptance" follows from an inherent righteousness produced by the Spirit of God.[70] Other influences include George Bull and the Caroline divines, though William Law's fingerprints are everywhere. Notably, the believer's present justification ("state of acceptance") is conditioned not on their baptism but on a "right state of soul." This confirms a shift in emphasis from a sacramental to a non-sacramental view of justification had already begun in his soteriology and would come to fruition in 1738. Wesley also followed Law by subsuming justification into the meta-

---

69. When Wesley decided to publish *The Circumcision of the Heart* in 1748, he added a section to his definition of faith in section I.7 to bring it in line with his evangelical understanding of saving faith (*Works*, 1:405a). As published, the first half of section I.7 represents his early definition of faith as receiving God's inward transforming power. Keeping this earlier definition of faith in the published edition suggests that Wesley did not abandon his earlier view of saving faith, but added onto it his evangelical view.

70. On the Holy Spirit infusing righteousness, see "Seek First the Kingdom" §6 (*Works*, 4:219). Albert Outler noted that Wesley was echoing Richard Hooker's "distinction between the Anglican and Roman doctrines of infused righteousness and grace" (*Works*, 4:219n14).

narrative of inward transformation (humility—faith—hope—love).[71] As we will soon see, within a couple years this Pietist impulse will move him toward the Moravian gospel when his holy living gospel failed to give him assurance in the face of imminent death.

After discussing present justification, Wesley quickly transitioned to final justification. The Last Judgment is when the "true follower of Christ" will receive God's public declaration of approval. Quoting Matthew 25:23 ("Well done, good and faithful servant!"), Wesley encourages believers to "be content to wait for thy applause till the day of thy Lord's appearing" when everyone will receive their "praise from God" before the "great assembly of men and angels" (§3). As scripture abundantly teaches, this final pronouncement will be conditioned on good works.[72] Toward the end of the sermon Wesley repeats the Anglican position that faith is the "foundation of good works" and that the Holy Spirit is the "inspirer and perfecter both of our faith and works" (II.4).

The account of present and final justification in *The Circumcision of the Heart* represents the only discussion of the subject in his extant sermons of the Oxford era.[73] To find a much fuller presentation we turn to Wesley's devotional and sacramental writings.

Collection of Forms of Prayer

Around 1730 Wesley began to compile prayers and psalms in a notebook for personal use, which was common practice in Anglican piety.[74] The psalms came from the BCP and the prayers from Anglican divines. This manuscript prayer manual then became the primary source for Wesley's first publication in 1733, *A Collection of Forms of Prayer for Every*

---

71. In the sermon these four qualities serve as stages in Wesley's *via salutis*. On this point, see Olson, *Wesley and Aldersgate*, 74–75.

72. NT texts teach that final judgment will be according to works (Matt. 25:35-36; Acts 17:31; Rom. 2:1-16; 1 Cor. 3:10-15; 2 Cor. 5:10; Rev. 20:12).

73. Wesley briefly discussed final justification in a letter to Richard Morgan on March 15, 1734 (*Works*, 25:382). See Olson, *Wesley and Aldersgate*, 53.

74. Randy L. Maddox, ed., "John Wesley's Manuscript Prayer Manual, c. 1730–1734" (The Wesley Works Editorial Project-Online Resources, 2018; www.wesley-works.org).

Day in the Week.[75] The *Collection of Forms* was designed for his students and fellow Methodists at Oxford, and over the years nine editions were produced.[76] Both the prayer manual and the *Collection of Forms* include morning and evening prayers that are organized around a Christian virtue for each day of the week. The *Collection of Forms* also includes a list of questions on each day for self-reflection. Just as renewal in the divine image is the "one thing needful" in the sermons, this same leitmotif is the orienting concern in this devotional work. One feature that stands out in the *Collection of Forms* is the economic Trinity effectually working our restoration in the *imago Dei*, including our justification before God.

The opening prayer of the *Collection of Forms* sets the Trinitarian agenda for the entire work, "Glory be to thee, O holy, undivided Trinity, for jointly concurring in the great work of our redemption, and restoring us again to the glorious liberty of the sons of God."[77] Here, Wesley suggested there is a "perichoretic coactivity" in which the three divine persons interpenetrate one another's redemptive work.[78] A corollary is Wesley's use of the law of appropriation to underscore the roles of the Father, Son, and Holy Spirit in the economy of salvation. There are numerous examples, like this short prayer of consecration, "To thee, O God, Father, Son, and Holy Ghost, my Creator, Redeemer, and Sanctifier, I give up myself entirely. May I no longer serve myself, but thee, all the days of my life."[79] Although our redemption is the work of the one

---

75. *A Collection of Forms of Prayer for Every Day in the Week* (*Works*, Jackson, 11:203–37; see preface for 6th ed. in *Works*, Jackson, 14:270–72).

76. Frank Baker, *A Union Catalogue of the Publications of John and Charles Wesley*, 2nd ed. (Stone Mountain, GA: 1991). See also, Richard Green, *The Works of John and Charles Wesley: A Bibliography*, 2nd ed. (London: Methodist Publishing House, 1906), 9. Fellow Oxford Methodist Benjamin Ingham mentions using the *Collection* in his diary. See Richard P. Heitzenrater, *Diary of an Oxford Methodist: Benjamin Ingham, 1733–1734* (Durham, NC: Duke University Press, 1985), 105–6.

77. *Collection of Forms of Prayer* (*Works*, Jackson, 203).

78. Elmer M. Coyer, *The Trinitarian Dimension of John Wesley's Theology* (Nashville: New Room Books, 2019), 81n9.

79. *Collection of Forms of Prayer* (*Works*, Jackson, 226). Other examples of Wesley listing the individual roles are found on pages 235 and 237. The distinction of roles by the divine persons informs the prayers throughout the entire work.

"undivided Trinity," the *Collection of Forms* follows the pattern set by the Apostles and Nicene creeds and assigns roles to the divine persons that distinguish their activity—Father as Creator, Son as Redeemer, and Spirit as Sanctifier. A closer look at these roles offers insights into Wesley's early doctrine of justification.

The Father is known as the "Almighty and everlasting God," from whom the Son eternally generates and the Spirit proceeds.[80] Regarding the Spirit's procession, Wesley followed the Western tradition by affirming the *filioque*, the Spirit's procession from the Father and the Son (more on this point below).[81] As the Creator and Sustainer of all things, the Father is the beginning and end of redemption.[82] The Father therefore provides for our justification in Christ, "Almighty God, who hast given thine only Son to die for our sins, and to rise again for our justification."[83] Besides providing for our redemption, the Father is assigned the primary role of pardoning sin, for nearly every petition for forgiveness is addressed to the Father.[84] This authority also pertains to final justification. For it is the Father who will grant "merciful acceptance in the last day, through the merits of thy blessed Son."[85] That day will certainly be "dreadful," yet believers will be shown "mercy" by the Father through the "mediation and satisfaction of thy blessed Son, Jesus Christ."[86] So, within the economic Trinity it is the prerogative of the Father to pardon sin and on the last day to grant access to the "everlasting kingdom."[87]

Whereas the cross receives little attention in Wesley's sermons, the atonement emerges as central to the believer's justification in the *Collection*

---

80. *Collection of Forms of Prayer* (*Works*, Jackson, 203, 214, 221, 223, 228); Maddox, "Wesley's Prayer Manual," 14, 31.

81. *Collection of Forms of Prayer* (*Works*, Jackson, 218–19).

82. *Collection of Forms of Prayer* (*Works*, Jackson, 203, 232–34); Maddox, "*Wesley's Prayer Manual,"* 1, 4, 18.

83. Maddox, "Wesley's Prayer Manual," 20.

84. *Collection of Forms of Prayer* (*Works*, Jackson, 205, 209, 210, 214, 221, 234); Maddox, "Wesley's Prayer Manual," 16, 18, 23.

85. *Collection of Forms of Prayer* (*Works*, Jackson, 225).

86. *Collection of Forms of Prayer* (*Works*, Jackson, 218).

87. *Collection of Forms of Prayer* (*Works*, Jackson, 228).

of Forms (and the manuscript prayer manual).[88] The Son offered a "full, perfect, and sufficient sacrifice for the sins of the whole world" whereby he merits for his people mercy, forgiveness, acceptance, and title to the eternal kingdom.[89] In the prayer manual Wesley repeatedly referred to the cross in substitutionary terms that procures and merits pardon and sanctifying grace.[90] In the Friday morning prayer of the *Collection of Forms* Wesley opens the meditation on the Redeemer's life and passion by first offering praise to his divine personage, "O Saviour of the world, God of God, light of light, thou art the brightness of thy Father's glory, the express image of his person. . . . Be thou my light and peace."[91] By beginning with Christ's deity before contemplating the depths of his passion, Wesley suggested that the sufficiency of the atonement is grounded on the intrinsic worth of the Son's divine person. That is, the merit and value of Christ's passion rests on who he is that poured out his life for our redemption.

The same prayer proceeds to reflect on the redemptive power of Jesus's healing ministry before digressing into a lengthy meditation on his passion. Such contemplations inspire humility and a confession of sinfulness ("I, miserable sinner . . . am altogether unworthy"), and lead to deeper consideration of the believer's death to sin.[92] In the Wednesday prayer on mortification, Wesley includes a meditation on what it means to be "planted together with thee in the likeness of thy death" in order to be raised in the "likeness of thy resurrection."[93] Participation in Christ's death and resurrection puts to death the old life and imparts new life in Christ.[94] The Holy Spirit, as the Spirit of Christ's passion and resurrection, enables believers to "utterly destroy the whole body of sin" so that they "no

---

88. Maddox, "Wesley's Prayer Manual," 88–103.

89. *Collection of Forms of Prayer* (*Works*, Jackson, 203, 215, 221, 223, 225, 228). On the early Wesley's understanding of the atonement in relation to the sacraments, see Hammond, *John Wesley in America*, 41, 51–54.

90. Maddox, "Wesley's Prayer Manual," 88–103.

91. *Collection of Forms of Prayer* (*Works*, Jackson, 228). Implicit in these remarks is the doctrine of eternal generation.

92. *Collection of Forms of Prayer* (*Works*, Jackson, 229).

93. *Collection of Forms of Prayer* (*Works*, Jackson, 222). The scripture text is Romans 6:5.

94. *Collection of Forms of Prayer* (*Works*, Jackson, 222). Union with Christ is also stressed in the Prayer Manual (Maddox, "Wesley's Prayer Manual," 90, 99).

longer live to the desires of men" and instead pursue the "will of God."[95] The indwelling Spirit enables believers to declare, "I am crucified with Christ. Nevertheless I live; yet not I, but Christ liveth in me" (Gal. 2:20).[96]

Wesley's statements on the believer's union with Christ show that he rejected any notion of works righteousness. Instead, his soteriology was rooted in the Augustinian paradigm of salvation as a lifelong journey enabled by divine grace. Richard Heitzenrater's summary of Wesley's (and Oxford Methodist's) soteriology is worth quoting:

> Salvation is not a momentary event but involves a process of restoration and becoming holy, of cultivating the love of God in such a way as to draw closer to the goal of having the mind of Christ. The emphasis of the Christian life then was on sanctification as one pressed on, with the assistance of God's grace, toward perfection in love and final justification.[97]

Yet, there is more to consider about Wesley's doctrine of justification in the *Collection of Forms*. We saw above that he appealed to Romans 4:25 that linked the believer's justification to Christ's resurrection. By ascending to the Father's right hand, the Son continually intercedes to bring forgiveness and other covenant blessings to his people. Wesley praised the Lord Jesus for his disposition to forgive and redeem, "O, how easy is it for thee to forgive! For that is thy nature. How proper is it for thee to save! For it is thy name."[98] As our mediator, Christ's advocacy is significant in two ways. First, as a merciful high priest, believers can be assured of their pardon and acceptance by God. Second, and related to the first point, Christ's exaltation assures his people of his presence in the sacraments to confer grace.[99] For instance, by partaking of the holy meal, Christ dwells in his people and they in him.[100] From this

---

95. In this prayer Wesley identifies the Holy Spirit as the Spirit of Christ ("thy Holy Spirit"). Implicit here is the *filioque*. It is the Spirit's procession from the Son that makes him the Spirit of Christ and the agent of the Christian's participation in Christ's death and resurrection.

96. *Collection of Forms of Prayer* (*Works*, Jackson, 222).

97. Heitzenrater, *Mirror and Memory*, 100.

98. *Collection of Forms of Prayer* (*Works*, Jackson, 231).

99. Maddox, "Wesley's Prayer Manual," 20, 27, 40, 41, 42, 51, 55, 65.

100. Maddox, "Wesley's Prayer Manual," 88, 91.

union believers receive the "refreshing graces" of forgiveness and inward strength, which in turn furthers their sanctification and renewal in the *imago Dei*.[101]

The Lord's Supper therefore serves as a primary means for the benefits of the atonement to be dispensed to believers and thereby maintain their justification before God. For this reason, Wesley practiced the discipline of constant communion, and even wrote a sermon to encourage the practice among his fellow Methodists.[102] Just as the High Church sacramentalism of his parents informed his earliest theology about justification, these same convictions continued to guide his beliefs and practices during his Oxford era. Anglican works that contributed to his sacramentalism at this time were Daniel Brevint's *The Christian Sacrament and Sacrifice* (1673) and Robert Nelson's *The Great Duty of Frequenting the Christian Sacrifice* (1706).[103] Another influential source was John Johnson's two-volume *Unbloody Sacrifice* (1714, 1718), which Wesley studied during his voyage to America.[104]

Turning to the Holy Spirit, whereas the Father's role is to pardon sin and grant access to the eternal kingdom, and the Son's part is to purchase redemption by his death and in his resurrection to perpetually plead his people's cause, the Holy Spirit's work is to testify and impart these redemptive benefits to God's people. Hence, all three persons of the "holy, undivided Trinity" are involved in our justification that begins in baptism, continues through life, and is finalized at the Last Judgment. Fundamental to the Spirit's role as Sanctifier is his procession from the

---

101. Maddox, "Wesley's Prayer Manual," 103.

102. *The Duty of Constant Communion*, 1732, pub. 1787 (*Works*, 3:427–39). The sermon is based on Robert Nelson's *Companion for the Festivals and Fasts of the Church of England . . .* (1704).

103. Daniel Brevint, *The Christian Sacrament and Sacrifice; by Way of Discourse, Meditation, and Prayer upon the Nature, Parts, and Blessings of the Holy Communion* (Oxford: Sheldonian Theatre, 1673); Robert Nelson, *The Great Duty of Frequenting the Christian Sacrifice* (London: W. Boyer, 1706). For a discussion of these authors' influence on Wesley, see Geordan Hammond, *John Wesley in America*, 62–66.

104. John Johnson, *The Unbloody Sacrifice, and Altar, Unvail'd and Supported* (London: Robert Knaplock, 1714, 1718). See Geordan Hammond, *John Wesley in America*, 50–53.

Father and the Son (the *filioque*). In the *Collection of Forms* Wesley used a variety of verbs to describe the Spirit's salvific activity—enables, inspires, assists, breathes, guides, aides, comforts, assures, unifies, and sanctifies.[105] These activities bring the objective work of the Father and the Son to fruition in the lives of God's people. As the Spirit of God and the Spirit of Christ, the Holy Spirit effectually applies the justifying, redemptive work of the Father and the Son to the hearts and lives of believers, effecting their recovery in the divine image. Thus, the Spirit's role in the "perichoretic coactivity" of the economic Trinity is to internalize the promises and benefits of the new covenant established by the Father and mediated through the Son.

More space has been devoted to the *Collection of Forms* because it offers a panoramic view of Wesley's early doctrine of sacramental justification. Wesley's gospel was not shallow, nor did he consider salvation merited by good works. Firmly anchored in the Anglican High Church tradition, Wesley held that grace empowers a believer's renewal in righteousness and holy love, with eternal fellowship and happiness in God as the *terminus ad quem*—the final goal of the restored *imago Dei*. The holy living divines opened Wesley's eyes to see the necessity of inward holiness for this renewal to take place, and for a believer's justification to be finalized at the Last Judgment. Justification and holiness were intertwined in his soteriology. His current doctrine of present justification was subsumed in the renewal process. Only later would it become a distinct category in his theology. At the same time, Wesley employed the economic Trinity to explain in detail his doctrine of justification. Following the pattern set in scripture, the ancient creeds, and his own Anglican standards, Wesley recognized specific roles for the triune persons in our justification: the Father *loves* and *declares*, the Son *procures* and *intercedes*, the Spirit *testifies* and *imparts*. This Trinitarian pattern is found in the closing doxology of the *Collection of Forms*:

Now, to God the Father, who first loved us, and made us accepted in the Beloved;

---

105. *Collection of Forms of Prayer* (*Works*, Jackson, 203, 204, 207, 209, 212, 218, 219, 222, 226, 230, 234, 235, 237).

to God the Son, who loved us, and washed us from our sins in his own blood; to God the Holy Ghost, who sheddeth the love of God abroad in our hearts, be all love and all glory in time and to all eternity. Amen.[106]

Georgia

On the eve of his departure to America, Wesley shared in a letter to John Burton that his chief motive for going was the "hope of saving my own soul."[107] Wesley believed that Georgia would be a more pristine environment for him to pursue the "one thing needful"—his renewal in the *imago Dei*.[108] However, his two-plus years at the "ends of the earth" turned out very different from the way he planned.[109] Georgia became a transition period in how he understood justification. Whereas from childhood Wesley held a sacramental view that was later infused with notions of inward holiness, during his two years in America he openly began the shift toward a non-sacramental view that would define justification as a perceptible assurance of present forgiveness received instantaneously by faith in Christ alone. This seismic shift is the focus of our story now.

Loss of Assurance

The primary factor for this abrupt change in Wesley's soteriology was his doubts in the face of imminent death. Wesley's lifelong fear of the sea got the best of him on several occasions during his voyage to America.[110]

---

106. *Collection of Forms of Prayer* (*Works*, Jackson, 237). This doxology is also found at the end of Wesley's sermon "The Love of God," written about three months before he published the *Collection*.

107. Letter, October 10, 1735 (*Works*, 25:439). On Wesley's ministry in Georgia, see Collins, *John Wesley: A Theological Journey*; Hammond, *John Wesley in America*; Heitzenrater, *Wesley and the People Called Methodists*, 64–80; Rack, *Reasonable Enthusiast*, 107–36.

108. Wesley stresses throughout his letter that Georgia was more conducive to his goal of attaining inward holiness (*Works*, 25:439–42). See Hammond, *John Wesley in America*, 13.

109. *Journal*, February 1, 1738 (*Works*, 18:215).

110. For Wesley's lifelong fear of the sea, see his *Journal*, February 3, 1738 (*Works*, 18:222). Wesley recorded four episodes of fear during the voyage (*Works*, 18:139, 140, 141, 142).

Then on January 25, 1736, a powerful hurricane battered the ship for hours and left the English passengers screaming in terror while the German Moravians "calmly sung." When Wesley asked a Moravian if he or the women and children were afraid to die, he replied, "I thank God, no . . . our women and children are not afraid to die."[111] In the face of imminent death, a felt sense of assurance became the "one thing needful."

This point was driven home when Wesley arrived in Georgia. Soon after landing, he discussed the matter with Moravian leader August Spangenberg (d. 1792). Spangenberg asked a series of questions about Wesley's assurance of salvation. Although Wesley stammered out "I do," he later confessed his inner doubts, "I fear they were vain words."[112] The seeds of doubt were now planted. In July Wesley experienced more apprehensions during a severe thunderstorm, "This voice of God, too, told me I was not fit to die; since I was afraid rather than desirous of it!"[113] In contrast to his own experience, Wesley witnessed at this time two people who faced death with confidence.[114] Then, a couple weeks later a similar episode happened while traveling by boat to Charleston. Crossing St. Helena Sound, the wind became so violent that even the sailors became apprehensive. Although Wesley sought to calm everyone, in his heart he chastised himself, "How is it that thou hadst no faith?"[115]

Wesley's nagging lack of assurance was eroding his confidence. Struggles with doubt came to a head during his return trip to England in January 1738. Reflecting on his life, Wesley acknowledged the "most infallible of proofs," namely "inward feeling," that he lacked "a faith as implies peace in life or death."[116] His memorable words two weeks later tell the story of what transpired in his soul over the past two years:

---

111. *Journal,* July 10, 1736 (*Works,* 18:143).

112. *Journal and Diary,* February 8, 1736 (*Works,* 18:146, 352).

113. *Journal,* July 10, 1736 (*Works,* 18:165).

114. Mr. Lascelles and Rebecca Bovey. Wesley, *Journal,* May–July 1736 (*Works,* 18:159–61, 164–65).

115. *Journal,* July 27, 1736 (*Works,* 18:169).

116. *Journal,* January 8, 1738 (*Works,* 18:208–9).

> I went to America to convert the Indians; but Oh! Who shall convert me? Who, what is he that will deliver me from this evil heart of unbelief? I have a fair summer religion. I can talk well; nay, and believe myself, while no danger is near: but let death look me in the face, and my spirit is troubled. . . . O who will deliver me from this fear of death?[117]

His lack of peace in the face of imminent death convinced Wesley that he needed a new gospel, one that would give him solid assurance when facing death.[118] For a committed High Churchman like Wesley, help came from an unlikely source—the Pietists.

Pietist Tutors

One of the first Pietist authors Wesley read was August Hermann Francke (d. 1727), professor of theology at the University of Halle and renowned for his charitable work with orphans. Wesley read several of Francke's works in the early 1730s, including *Nicodemis: Or, Treatise against the Fear of Man*. In this work Francke presented a desire for the world's acceptance as a leading cause for nominal faith among Christians. The cure is a "true conversion of the heart to God" in which a person moves from a "false and imaginary faith, to a true living faith, that works by love."[119] Genuine faith overcomes the world and its attractions, and thus frees a person from the "fear of man."[120] Faith unites a person to Christ and brings the Spirit's testimony of their adoption in Christ.[121] Like other Pietists, Francke stressed faith as a perceptible assurance of salvation as a core component of conversion. And he appealed to Hebrews 11:1 to

---

117. *Journal*, January 24, 1728 (*Works*, 18:210–11).

118. Kenneth Collins includes an excellent discussion on the fear of death as a test of Christian experience in Wesley's theology (*John Wesley: A Theological Journey*, 58–62).

119. August Hermann Francke, *Nicodemis: Or, A Treatise against the Fear of Man* (London: Joseph Downing, 1706), 78–79.

120. Francke, *Nicodemis*, 3–7, 94.

121. Francke, *Nicodemis*, 80, 108.

describe saving faith, as did other Pietists, which Wesley will later do as an evangelical.[122]

In Georgia Wesley's bond with the Moravians grew stronger. Their interest in primitive Christianity appealed to Wesley because of his interest in early Christian spirituality. He admired their Christian demeanor, and regularly attended their meetings. He sought their counsel in personal matters, translated their hymns, and conversed often with them about their beliefs and ecclesiology. Johann Töltschig (d. 1764) explained to Wesley and his friends their beliefs on grace and justification by faith.[123] In an exchange of letters, Count Zinzendorf summarized his faith to Wesley on the Trinity, Christ's redemption, the sacraments, and the marks of the church.[124] It is notable that Zinzendorf's comments on the atonement reflect the Pietist emphasis on inward renewal. As we learned in chapter 1, the Pietists tended to subsume justification into the new birth. For Zinzendorf, justification was essentially the same thing as regeneration.[125] The linking of justification to the new birth led the Moravians to connect justifying faith to assurance of salvation. Wesley also interacted with the Salzburgers, a group of Lutheran Pietists who lived north of his residence in Savannah. They probably introduced Wesley to a foundational work of German Pietism, Johann Arndt's four-volume *True Christianity*. The immense popularity of this work is seen in its 125 printings by the end of the eighteenth century.

Arndt's work appealed to Wesley because of his meta-narrative of the restored *imago Dei*. He began with our creation in the image of God, now defaced by Adam's sin. The recovery of the image takes place through the new birth, described as the inward work of the Spirit whereby a person transitions from a "child of wrath and damnation" to a "child of grace

---

122. Heb. 11:1 first appears in *An Earnest Appeal to Men of Reason and Religion* §6 (*Works*, 11:46).

123. Martin Schmidt, *John Wesley: A Theological Biography*, 3 vols. (Nashville: Abingdon Press, 1962, 1972, 1973), 1:161.

124. Letter, October 23, 1736 (*Works*, 25:479–83). For a synopsis of the letter, see Schmidt, *John Wesley*, 163–66.

125. *Journal*, July 12, 1738 (*Works*, 18:261).

and blessedness."[126] When describing this inward change, Arndt explained it in christological terms, "We are once again renewed to eternal life in Christ, born anew out of Christ, and become new creatures in Christ."[127] The sufferings of Christ accomplished both a "payment for all our sins and a renewal of man through faith and true repentance."[128] Regarding saving faith, Arndt appealed to Hebrews 11:1 that it involves both assurance and conviction of belief.[129] For Arndt, then, faith is personal and experiential, it involves "deep trust," and unites a person to Christ and God.[130]

What is notable about the Pietist gospel is its non-sacramental character. Saving faith comes by direct personal encounter with Christ, which is perceptible and felt by a person. This was in sharp contrast to Wesley's High Church tradition that understood faith more as a theological virtue that was nurtured through the sacraments and other means of grace.[131] Assurance in the Anglican sacramental tradition was deduced from being a worthy communicant or by keeping the covenant obligations. In contrast, Pietists associated assurance of salvation with the experience of heartfelt trust in Christ. Assurance was immediately felt when a person broke through to faith in Christ, as Francke's conversion testimony exemplifies:

> In . . . such great dread I fell once more upon my knees on this Sunday evening, and I appealed to God . . . for salvation from such a miserable state. Then the Lord, the living God, heard me from his throne while I was still on my knees. . . . Then all my doubt vanished as quickly as one turns one's hand; I was assured in my heart of the grace of God in Christ Jesus.

---

126. Johann Arndt, *True Christianity*, trans. Peter Erb (New York: Paulist Press, 1979), 37.

127. Arndt, *True Christianity*, 39.

128. Arndt, *True Christianity*, 40.

129. Arndt, *True Christianity*, 45.

130. Arndt, *True Christianity*, 45, 47.

131. Letter, March 15, 1734 (*Works*, 25:382). The theological virtues serve as a framework for Wesley's soteriology in the landmark sermon "The Circumcision of the Heart" (*Works*, 1:402–9).

. . . All sadness and unrest of the heart was taken away at once. . . . I arose a completely different person from the one who had knelt down.[132]

During Wesley's time in Georgia the Pietist message of perceptible assurance introduced him to a new understanding of the gospel as it pertains to a Christian's present standing before God. This "new gospel" eventually led Wesley to adopt a non-sacramental view of justification in addition to his sacramental view. The story of this transition is recorded in Wesley's writings of the period.

Georgia Writings

On the eve of his departure Wesley preached at St. Mary's Cathedral in Oxford. Titled *The Trouble and Rest of Good Men*, Wesley set out to show the hope that the Anglican faith offers. His premise is that this present life is one of spiritual conflict due to the reign of sin, with final deliverance at death. Wesley explained that Christians are born of the Spirit and follow Christ in varying degrees. Those who are strong in the faith are "truly renewed" and "full of the knowledge and love of God." They have found the "one thing needful" and continue to wage war against sin.[133] For these single-minded Christians, the next life promises rest from the troubles of this life. In that day their new birth will be fully realized,[134] when the cross has cleansed them from all their sin.[135] For his Anglican audience, death offered hope of final justification and the restored *imago Dei*. In this sermon Wesley presented a mainstream Anglican doctrine of assurance, but it is more of a future hope than a present reality.

---

132. Quoted from Markus Matthias, "August Hermann Francke," in *The Pietist Theologians*, ed. Cater Lindberg (Malden, MA: Blackwell Publishers, 2005), 102–3.

133. *The Trouble and Rest of Good Men* I.2–3 (*Works*, 3:535–37).

134. "O happy day, wherein I begin to live, wherein I taste my native freedom!" *Trouble and Rest* II.6 (*Works*, 3:540–41).

135. "The blood of the Lamb hath healed all their sickness, 'hath washed them thoroughly from their wickedness, and cleansed them from their sin.'" *Trouble and Rest* II.5 (*Works*, 3:539).

In anticipation of his safe arrival in Georgia, Wesley wrote an inaugural sermon titled *A Single Intention*. The sermon builds on the message of the last one by calling upon his audience to have a faith that is strong in God. The central theme is that one cannot serve God with so many distractions in this life unless their intention is singularly focused on pleasing God. So, at the end Wesley exhorted his audience, "Behold, all things about you are become new! Be ye likewise new creatures! From this hour at least let your eye be single: whatever you speak, or think, or do, let God be your aim, and God only!"[136] And the promise is that the Holy Spirit with purify your heart and firmly establish your hope in God. Wesley here restated the holy living view of assurance. As the indwelling Spirit replaces "every unholy affection" with "peace, and joy, and love," the sanctified believer experiences greater degrees of assurance through their deepening union with God.

From these two sermons we learn that at the start of his mission in Georgia, Wesley's central aim remained as before—the restored *imago Dei*. By subsuming justification and assurance into the single intention and the renewal process, Wesley was ill-equipped for the fears that would overtake him during the voyage. As a result, he questioned the singularity of his intention and his lack of fitness to face God.[137] Even though his ministry in Georgia was more successful than what his comments suggest, his troubles with parishioners and local authorities and his failed romance with Sophia Hopkey only deepened his inner struggles.[138] As we saw above, it all came to a head during his return voyage to England when Wesley had time to reflect on his need for a different kind of faith.

However, Wesley's struggles do not tell the whole story. During this period, he began to learn a new gospel. From his reading of Pietist works and his interactions with the Moravians and Salzburgers, Wesley came to a new understanding of assurance as a gift of Christ's justifying righteousness. When he passed through Darien, a settlement of Scottish highlanders, on New Year's Day, 1737, the Presbyterian minister John

---

136. *A Single Intention* II.9 (*Works*, 4:377).

137. *Journal*, November 23, 1735; January 17 and January 23, 1736 (*Works*, 18:140–42).

138. Geordan Hammond correctly points out that Wesley's ministry was upon the whole far more successful than what many scholars and historians suggest (*John Wesley in America*, 190–94).

Macleod gave him a copy of *The Memoirs of the Life of the Reverend Mr. Thomas Halyburton* (1714). Over the next two weeks Wesley pored over its pages.[139] He prized the *Memoirs* for its detailed account of God imparting a perceptible assurance of justification through faith alone.[140] The *Memoirs* put Wesley in touch with Reformed soteriology in a way that resonated with his spiritual needs and corroborated what he was learning from the Pietists. Four months later Wesley went to Charleston to take care of business. Due to bad weather, he stayed longer than expected and was able to attend the annual meeting of clergy in South Carolina. For several hours the clergy discussed the subject of "Christ our Righteousness." Feeling deeply impressed by the discussion, Wesley jotted down in his journal that he had not heard "such a conversation . . . in England, or hardly on any other occasion."[141]

Collection of Psalms and Hymns

It was probably on this visit to Charleston that Wesley contacted the printer Lewis Timothy to publish his new hymnal, *Collection of Psalms and Hymns* (1737). The hymnal follows the outline of the *Collection of Forms of Prayers* by organizing the hymns in three sections according to the days of the week (Sunday, Wednesday/Friday, and Saturday). More than a third of the hymns come from the non-Conformist minister Isaac Watts (d. 1748), and several are translations of German hymns. As for themes, the *Collection of Psalms and Hymns* accents the restored *imago Dei* and the economic Trinity, but also includes motifs that within a year will inform his new doctrine of justification. Hymns are included that speak of being "justified by grace" through the "purchase of [Christ's] death."[142] The cross is depicted as a vicarious, meritorious expression of God's love, purchasing

---

139. *Diary,* January 3–15, 1737 (*Works,* 18:461–63).

140. Joel R. Beeke, ed., *Memoirs of the Rev. Thomas Halyburton* (Grand Rapids: Reformation Heritage Books, 1996). For further discussion on Wesley's interest in the Memoirs, see Olson, *Wesley and Aldersgate,* 60–62.

141. *Journal,* April 22, 1737 (*Works,* 18:179).

142. *Collection of Psalms and Hymns* (Charles-town: Lewis Timothy, 1737), 55.

"pardon and life for dying souls."[143] In the hymn "The Names of Christ," the benefits of Christ's death are succinctly stated, "Of wrath appeased, of sins forgiven; of hell subdued, and peace with heaven." A couple stanzas down, the hymn celebrates the saving work of Christ:

> Jesus my great high priest has died, I seek no sacrifice beside;
> Thy blood did once for all atone, and now it plead before thy throne.[144]

In a similar fashion, saving faith is defined in evangelical terms as trust and reliance on Christ alone for salvation. Here are three stanzas from the hymn "Faith in Christ":

> But there's a voice of sovereign grace, sounds from thy sacred word;
> Here ye despairing sinners come, and trust upon the Lord.
>
> To the blest Fountain of thy Blood, incarnate God, I fly;
> Here let me wash my spotted soul, from Crimes of deepest die.
>
> A guilty, weak, and helpless Worm, into thy Arms I fall;
> Be Thou my Strength and Righteousness, My Jesus and my All.[145]

The concept of "Christ our righteousness"—the title of hymn nineteen—now finds expression in several places:

> Our guilty Spirits dread, to meet the Wrath of heaven;
> But in thy Righteousness array'd, we see our Sins forgiven.[146]
>
> Our guilty Souls are drown'd in Tears, till thy atoning Blood appears;
> Then we awake from deep distress, and sing, the Lord our Righteousness.[147]

The *Collection of Psalms and Hymns* points to important developments in Wesley's understanding of justification. Particularly significant is the

---

143. *Collection of Psalms and Hymns*, 36, 44–47.
144. *Collection of Psalms and Hymns*, 30, emphasis his.
145. *Collection of Psalms and Hymns*, 52, emphasis his.
146. *Collection of Psalms and Hymns*, 56.
147. *Collection of Psalms and Hymns*, 35.

idea that Christ's righteousness is the ground of the believer's justification. This suggests a shift had begun toward an objective understanding of righteousness in contrast to his prior inward focus. Yet, Wesley does not yet speak in explicit terms of imputed righteousness. That will come later. Another development is the introduction of "sovereign grace."[148] Humanity's sinful impotence is contrasted to the Triune God's unlimited ability and willingness to save. As "poor helpless worms," worshippers proclaim that they possess in Christ "grace, wisdom, power, and righteousness."[149] Christ is an all-sufficient Savior, who is "Almighty to redeem."[150] The concept of sovereign grace will soon lead to his proclamation of "free grace."[151]

Even though Wesley did not yet grasp the full implications of what he was learning from his Pietist friends, he was well on his way to adopting a non-sacramental view of justification as a distinct category in his theology and religious experience. The next step would be for him to connect his view of justification in the *Collection of Psalms and Hymns* to the Pietist doctrine of instantaneous conversion through direct encounter with the living Savior. The person who would mentor Wesley in this next step was the Moravian missionary Peter Böhler. This is the subject of our next chapter.

---

148. *Collection of Psalms and Hymns*, 35, 41, 52, 56.

149. *Collection of Psalms and Hymns*, 36.

150. *Collection of Psalms and Hymns*, 12.

151. On Wesley's notion of sovereign grace, see Kenneth J. Collins, *The Theology of John Wesley: Holy Love and the Shape of Grace* (Nashville: Abingdon Press, 2007), 160–64.

CHAPTER THREE

ALDERSGATE AND EARLY CONTROVERSIES OVER JUSTIFICATION: 1738–49

The year 1738 stands out as the most famous in the life of John Wesley. The reason is simple. On May 24 he experienced evangelical conversion at a religious meeting on Aldersgate Street, London. His memorable words, "I felt my heart strangely warmed," introduced what he experienced that evening when he trusted in Christ alone for salvation—"an assurance was given me that he had taken away *my* sins, even *mine*, and saved *me* from the law of sin and death."[1] It was not by chance that Wesley framed his testimony around the theme of assurance. For as we saw in the last chapter, it was the lack of assurance that drove him to listen to a "new gospel" that promised a felt sense of forgiveness and freedom from sin as a gift of free grace. By describing his conversion in terms of perceptible assurance, Wesley conveyed he had embraced a doctrine of justification in sharp contrast to what he had believed before.

---

1. *Journal*, May 24, 1738 (*Works*, 18:250, emphasis his). For Wesley's interpretation of his Aldersgate conversion, see Mark K. Olson, *Wesley and Aldersgate: Interpreting Conversion Narratives* (London: Routledge, 2019). Studies on Aldersgate are legion. Here are some recent studies: Kenneth J. Collins and John H. Tyson, eds., *Conversion in the Wesleyan Tradition* (Nashville: Abingdon Press, 2001); Hindmarsh, *The Evangelical Conversion Narrative*; Randy L. Maddox, ed., *Aldersgate Reconsidered* (Nashville: Kingswood Books, 1990); Rack, *Reasonable Enthusiast*.

The years 1738 to 1749 probably represent the most fruitful period for Wesley's doctrine of justification. At this time the doctrine became a staple in his writings, marking a new category in Wesley's theology. While he continued to define justification in standard Anglican terms (pardon and acceptance), he expanded its meaning to include the Pietist concept of perceptible assurance. There is much to unpack here about his "new doctrine" of justification and its development over the next decade. The chapter is divided into four sections. The first part covers the Moravian/Lutheran phase that lasted into the early 1740s, followed by his alignment with a moderate Reformed view in the mid-1740s. The final two sections examine the influence of his High Church sacramentalism and his views on assurance in his justification doctrine.

Moravian/Lutheran Period

By the spring of 1738 Wesley was convinced he had been on a wrong path regarding his salvation. For thirteen years he had rigorously pursued inward holiness and faithfully practiced sacramental piety. He was devout and sincere, committed to good works and keeping with exactness the rubrics of his church. Nevertheless, he now considered it all rubbish, nothing more than a system of works righteousness. Wesley confessed he had been "ignorant of the righteousness of Christ" and instead had "sought to establish [his] own righteousness."[2] Despite all his personal and religious goodness, none of these made him "acceptable to God" or could "abide [God's] righteous judgment."[3]

At this time Wesley embraced a "new gospel."[4] Wherever he preached he proclaimed "free salvation by faith in the blood of Christ."[5] This "new doctrine," as he and his friends called it, was that by "faith in or through Christ" a person receives "in a moment" the twin fruits of a "sense of

---

2. *Journal,* May 24, 1738 (*Works,* 18:246).
3. *Journal,* February 1, 1738 (*Works,* 18:214–15).
4. *Journal,* May 24, 1738 (*Works,* 18:248).
5. *Journal,* May 14, 1738 (*Works,* 18:239–40).

pardon for all past, and freedom from all present sins."⁶ Thus saving, justifying faith reconciles a person to the favor of God through the merits of Jesus Christ, and frees them from the enslaving power of sin and its servile fear. It also unites them to Christ and the fullness of his love, joy, and peace.⁷ This was the essence of Wesley's new doctrine of justification in the spring of 1738. Some aspects of his beliefs had not changed, like his basic definition of justification as pardon and acceptance. But much was new, and the tone and emphasis were fundamentally at odds with his prior position. Whereas the Pietists in Georgia had planted the seed for Wesley's "new gospel," it was Peter Böhler and Martin Luther who watered that seed and converted Wesley to the "new faith."⁸

Böhler and Luther

When Wesley met Peter Böhler (d. 1775) on February 7 he jotted down in his journal, "A day much to be remembered."⁹ Böhler proclaimed a gospel of free grace that subsumed justification into the new birth.¹⁰ At the University of Jena he experienced instantaneous conversion under the direction of August Spangenberg and expected the same with his converts. Central to conversion and justification was the gift of perceptible assurance, whereby "through the merits of Jesus . . . poor sinners receive forgiveness and are set free from the dominion of sin."¹¹ The twin fruits

---

6. On "new doctrine," see *Journal*, March 6, 1738 (*Works*, 18:228); and Daniel Benham, ed., *Memoirs of James Hutton: Comprising the Annals of His Life and Connection with the United Brethren* (London: Hamilton, Adams, and Co., 1856), 29. On instantaneous salvation with the two accompanying fruits, see *Journal*, April 22 and May 24, 1738 (*Works*, 18:234, 248).

7. *Journal*, February 1, 1738 (*Works*, 18:215–16).

8. Wesley used three labels for his evangelical gospel: "new doctrine," "new gospel," and "new faith" (*Journal*, May 1, 1738 [*Works*, 18:236]). See footnotes 4 and 6 above.

9. *Journal*, February 7, 1738 (*Works*, 18:223).

10. Primary sources for Böhler's gospel message in the spring of 1738 are his diary (in German), Wesley's *Journal*, and Benham's *Memoirs of James Hutton*. For secondary sources, see Martin Schmidt, *John Wesley: A Theological Biography*, 3 vols, trans. Norman Goldhawk (Nashville: Abingdon Press, 1962, 1972, 1973), 1:224–45.

11. Lockwood, *Memorials of Peter Bohler*, 74–75.

of pardon and freedom were repeatedly impressed on Wesley.[12] Following standard Moravian soteriology, Böhler downplayed any need for preparation to receive the gift of faith, including a protracted season of spiritual struggle. The concept of a preparatory struggle (*Busskampf*) was taught by August Francke and his followers at Halle. Instead of *Busskampf,* Böhler and his Moravian colleagues emphasized unbelief as the fundamental problem and conversion as an "abrupt change from not having faith to possessing faith."[13] Frederick Dreyer explained Böhler and the Moravian's theology of justifying faith:

> Whoever lacks faith struggles against sin in vain; whoever has faith struggles no more. With faith comes power over sin; further struggle is needless. The gift of faith is immediate. There are no degrees, no gracious preliminaries or stages in which the unbeliever may imagine that he possesses the very thing he lacks.[14]

Böhler's triumphant gospel left no room for doubt and placed little value on the means of grace. It was a gospel of *sola fides in solus Christus*—faith alone in Christ alone. In fact, Böhler considered Anglican reliance on the means of grace at best a stumbling block or at worst a system of works righteousness. In a letter to Count Zinzendorf, Böhler summarized his sentiments about the English Christians:

> Our mode of believing in the Saviour is so easy to Englishmen that they cannot reconcile themselves to it.... They justify themselves; therefore they always take it for granted that they believe already, and would prove their faith by their works; and thus so plague and torment themselves that they are at heart very miserable.[15]

With his emphasis on free grace, it is interesting that Böhler did not teach Wesley a clear doctrine of imputed righteousness. Christ's righ-

---

12. E.g., *Journal,* March 23, April 22, May 24, 1738 (*Works,* 18:232, 234, 248).

13. Frederick Dreyer, *The Genesis of Methodism* (Bethlehem: Lehigh University Press, 1999), 41.

14. Dreyer, *Genesis of Methodism,* 41.

15. Lockwood, *Memorials of Peter Bohler,* 68–69. See Schmidt, *John Wesley,* 1:229.

teousness purchases reconciliation to God and thus saves from sin's guilt and power, but Böhler stopped short of saying it is imputed. Instead, he implored Wesley to affectionally bond to the cross as an expression of Christ's love, "That you may taste, and then see, how exceedingly the Son of God has loved you, and loves you still, and that so you may continually trust in him, and feel his life in yourself."[16] In saying this, Böhler expressed a concept of union with Christ with a sentimentalism that would later become exaggerated in Moravian theology.[17] It also suggests how the Moravians applied Luther's teachings in his *Preface to the Epistle of St. Paul to the Romans.*

By the eighteenth century Luther's *Preface* had become the "classical text for evangelical conversion."[18] It was highly prized by the Moravians and other Pietists and was instrumental to Wesley's conversion at Aldersgate. The *Preface* opens with the sinner's plight under God's law. As the sinner attempts to fulfill God's law by works, either through fear of punishment or hope of reward, they fail because their heart is not in it. The sinner therefore feels condemned under the law. The problem is the sinner does not freely love God or God's law since they are sinful at heart. Luther diagnosed the core issue to be unbelief, which he considered "the root, the sap, and the chief power of all sin."[19] The remedy is a living faith in Christ:

> Faith . . . is a divine work in us which changes us and makes us to be born anew of God, John 1:12-13. It kills the old Adam and makes altogether different men, in heart and spirit and mind and powers; and it brings with it the Holy Spirit. . . . Faith is a living, daring confidence in God's grace, so sure and certain that the believer would stake his life on it a thousand times.[20]

---

16. *Journal,* May 13, 1738 (*Works,* 18:238–39). Whether Böhler believed in imputed righteousness is likely, but there is no record of him teaching it to Wesley in the latter's *Journal.*

17. W. R. Ward, *The Protestant Evangelical Awakening* (Cambridge: Cambridge University Press, 1992), 155–59. Clifford W. Towlson, *Moravian and Methodist: Relationships and Influences in the Eighteenth Century* (London: Epworth Press, 1957), 129–30.

18. W. R. Ward, *Early Evangelicalism: A Global Intellectual History, 1670–1789* (Cambridge: Cambridge University Press, 2006), 43.

19. Lull and Russell, *Martin Luther's Basic Theological Writings,* 76–78.

20. Lull and Russell, *Luther's Basic Theological Writings,* 79.

Luther understood faith to be the instrumental cause of justification because God "counts [faith] as righteousness for the sake of Christ." Having been restored to God's favor, faith "brings the Spirit" who imparts a genuine love for God and his truth. Saving faith spontaneously generates desires to do good works and to "take pleasure in God's commandments." Thus "faith alone makes a person righteous and fulfills the law."[21] Yet, Luther acknowledged throughout the *Preface* the ongoing struggle between flesh and Spirit in the life of the Christian even though their sins are forgiven and their adoption in Christ assured.[22]

Given his stature as the reformer who rediscovered justification by faith alone, Luther's *Preface* served as an authoritative source for Wesley.[23] It is notable that Luther did not stress Christ's imputed righteousness in the *Preface*, as he did in other writings, but put the accent on Christ's imparted righteousness. Several themes from the *Preface* influenced Böhler's message to Wesley: unbelief as the primary sin that condemns, justification as assurance of forgiveness and new life, faith as the immediate condition and its perceptibility, and the transition from unbelief to faith as instantaneous. Finally, Luther's description of justifying faith as "killing the old Adam" appeared to support Böhler's claim that faith "cancels the corruption and condemnation entailed by the first Adam."[24] Coming from the Anglican tradition, Wesley understood such statements to say that justifying faith sanctifies entirely. The expectation of a pure heart will contribute to Wesley's post-conversion doubts throughout the remainder of 1738.[25]

---

21. Lull and Russell, *Martin Luther's Basic Theological Writings*, 78–79.

22. Lull and Russell, *Martin Luther's Basic Theological Writings*, 78, 79, 81, 83.

23. For further study on Luther's influence on Wesley's doctrine of justification, see Mark K. Olson, "Martin Luther's Contribution to John Wesley's Doctrine of Justification," *Wesley and Methodist Studies* 13, no. 2 (2021): 130–53.

24. Wesley, *Journal*, May 13, 1738 (*Works*, 18:239n10).

25. Wesley records in his journal and letters that a major source for his post-conversion doubts was that he lacked a full deliverance from sin. See Olson, *Wesley and Aldersgate*, 76–81, 93–95. It would take until the end of 1739 for Wesley to formulate the doctrine of Christian perfection as a second, post-justification blessing.

Aldersgate Writings

Turning to Wesley's earliest evangelical documents in the spring of 1738, we see Böhler and Luther's influence in several areas. In the Aldersgate memorandum, written over a two-week period following his evangelical conversion, Wesley followed his mentors' lead by grounding justification on our absolute need for grace and the Pauline antithesis of faith and works.[26] He likewise reflected Böhler's negative attitude toward Anglican sacramentalism by ascribing his prior pursuit of inward holiness to seeking salvation by works.[27] This represented a 180-degree change in attitude toward his past religious life. Just as Luther stressed the accusatory function of the law, Wesley confessed his condemnation under the law:

> I was now properly "under the law"; I knew that "the law" of God was "spiritual." . . . Yet was I "carnal, sold under sin" . . . I was indeed fighting continually, but not conquering. Before, I had willingly served sin: now it was unwillingly, but still I served it.[28]

Feeling chained to this "vile, abject state of bondage to sin," Wesley acknowledged that his fundamental problem was unbelief.[29] Applying what Böhler taught him, Wesley confessed to being "wholly void" of a "true, living faith in Christ," because he lacked a perceptible assurance of this faith.[30] The "one thing needful" is a "true, living faith" in Christ, which is

---

26. The *Aldersgate Memorandum* represents the eighteen numbered paragraphs in the *Journal* entry for May 24, 1738 (*Works*, 18:242–51). Wesley wrote the *Memorandum* immediately following his evangelical conversion (*Works*, 18:242n30). See Olson, *Wesley and Aldersgate*, 36–37, for a discussion on when Wesley wrote the *Memorandum*.

27. The works Wesley spoke of included setting aside time daily for devotional purposes, partaking of communion each week, watching against every sin, keeping the stationary fasts of the ancient church, and striving to the "utmost of [his] power" to keep God's law. His meaning is that he had trusted in these works to make himself acceptable to God (Wesley, *Journal*, May 24, 1738 §§4–9 [*Works*, 18:244–46]).

28. Wesley, *Journal*, May 24, 1738 §§9–10 (*Works*, 18:246–47).

29. Wesley, *Journal*, May 24, 1738 §10 (*Works*, 18:247).

30. Wesley, *Journal*, May 24, 1738 §§11–12 (*Works*, 18:247–48).

defined as a "full reliance on the blood of Christ shed for *me*; a trust in him as *my* Christ, as *my* sole justification, sanctification, and redemption."[31]

Then, on May 24 Wesley listened to Luther's description of the "change which God works in the heart through faith in Christ."[32] Böhler taught that justifying faith instantaneously generates a new existence, not just a new standing. Wesley now testified to a perceptible assurance of faith in Christ for salvation, even marking down the exact time ("about a quarter before nine"). Appealing to John 1:29 and Romans 8:2, Wesley stated that Christ had "taken away *my* sins, even *mine*, and saved *me* from the law of sin and death."[33] These gospel promises succinctly expressed his current understanding of justification, based on Böhler's mentorship. That is, the gift of justifying, saving faith in Christ gave him a perceptible assurance of forgiveness and power over sin. Wesley now knew he was justified and born again.

The same themes and message are found in Wesley's evangelical manifesto *Salvation by Faith*, preached three weeks after his Aldersgate conversion.[34] Wesley began by attributing all of God's works to his free grace, which is defined as "free, undeserved favour" (§1). Although free grace did not formally become part of Wesley's theological terminology until 1738, he was exposed to the concept from his mother who used the term occasionally to reference God's universal love and goodwill.[35] Wesley agreed with his mother's Arminian viewpoint, but now associated free grace with the gospel of salvation by faith alone to highlight the sheer gratuity of gospel justification.[36] This same sentiment was expressed in the

---

31. Wesley, *Journal*, May 24, 1738 §§11, 12 (*Works*, 18:247, 248–49, emphasis his).

32. Wesley, *Journal*, May 24, 1738 §14 (*Works*, 18:250).

33. Aldersgate Memorandum §14 (*Works*, 18:250, emphasis his). Wesley repeatedly appealed to John 1:29 to refer to justification as an assurance of forgiveness and acceptance before God. On this point, see Olson, *Wesley and Aldersgate*, 48–50.

34. *Salvation by Faith* (*Works*, 1:117–30).

35. Wallace, *Susanna Wesley*, 113, 173, 190; Wesley, *Letters*, August 18, 1725 (*Works*, 25:180).

36. Kenneth Collins pointed out the phrase "underscores the activity of God *alone*" by excluding all human merit in Wesley's soteriology (Collins, *Theology of John Wesley*, 162–63).

sermon "Free Grace," when Wesley asserted that grace is "free in all" and "free for all."[37] These remarks suggest an element of monergism in Wesley's doctrine of justification.[38]

Regarding the law of God, Wesley followed Luther by referring to its accusatory function and omitting its other two uses.[39] Quoting Romans 3:20, Wesley inserted the word *only* into the biblical text to make it clear that "by the law is *only* the knowledge of sin" (II.3).[40] He next defined justification to be according to grace through faith in the merits of Christ's "life, death, and resurrection" (I.5, II.3). By "merit" Wesley understood Christ's atonement to be the "only sufficient means of redeeming man from death eternal" (I.5). It removed the "curse of the law" and "blotted out" our guilt so that "no condemnation" remains for those who believe in Jesus (II.3). In these remarks, Wesley followed both Böhler and Luther by stressing the non-imputation of sin, but not of the imputation of Christ's active righteousness. Even more explicit is Wesley's statement that justification in the "largest sense" includes the new birth and "deliverance from the whole body of sin" (II.7).[41] Here, he clearly expressed Böhler and Luther's views on regeneration linked to justification. Throughout the sermon Wesley treats justification as a synonym for "present salvation" and everything it signifies (I.5, III.1).

An entire section in *Salvation by Faith* is devoted to defining saving faith. After exposing the deficient faiths of the heathen (general belief in God), devils (mere intellectual assent), and the pre-Pentecost disciples (weak, powerless faith), the faith that justifies involves a "disposition of the heart" that exercises a "full reliance" and "trust" in Christ's life, death,

---

37. *Free Grace* §§2–4 (*Works*, 3:544–45).

38. That Wesley endorsed a degree of monergism in his theology, see *Journal*, August 24, 1743 (*Works*, 19:331).

39. Luther taught there were two uses (civil and accusatory). After Luther, Melanchthon and Calvin taught three uses of the law. Wesley later agreed with Calvin and the Puritans. See his sermon "The Original, Nature, Properties, and Use of the Law" (*Works*, 2:1–19).

40. *Works*, 1:122, emphasis mine. Wesley later expressed a threefold use of the law, in a manner similar to Calvin and Melanchthon ("The Original, Nature, Properties, and Use of the Law," *Works*, 2:1–19).

41. This is found in the 1738 edition of the sermon. See *Works*, 1:124n64.

and resurrection as the only means for salvation and eternal life (I.1-5).[42] But before a person can exercise saving faith in Christ, they first must renounce all reliance in their own works and goodness (III.5).[43] This was how Wesley understood the "alone" in justification by faith alone. It is faith in Christ alone for salvation. Another essential feature of saving faith is the gift of perceptible assurance. Wesley adopted the Moravian view that the Spirit witnesses directly to the believer's pardon and acceptance upon faith in Christ. Perceptible assurance was now a feature of justifying faith.[44]

A couple points follow. First, Wesley's "new gospel" was essentially Pietistic Lutheran and non-sacramental. Initially, Wesley was astonished by Böhler's claim that faith could be given in a moment—"as lightning falling from heaven." It took the witness of scripture and the testimonies of converts to convince him otherwise.[45] Justification now signified an *experience* for Wesley.

Second, Wesley apparently dismissed the theory of a twofold justification at this time. Harald Lindström noted that the "idea of final salvation is pushed into the background [and] present salvation now becomes the object of his central, if not exclusive, interest."[46] In 1739 Wesley rejected the teaching of double justification on two occasions. In September he conversed with a "serious clergyman" on justification and sanctification. When asked, Wesley summarized the position of many Anglican clergy: they conflate justification with sanctification, consider holiness and good works the cause and condition of justification, and associate the new birth

---

42. For further discussion on Wesley's definition of saving faith, see Collins, *Theology of John Wesley*, 165–69.

43. This was an important aspect of Wesley's testimony at Aldersgate, "I felt I did trust in Christ, Christ alone for salvation" (*Works*, 18:250). See Olson, *Wesley and Aldersgate*, 48.

44. Wesley referenced the Spirit's witness in *Salvation by Faith* III.6 (*Works*, 1:127–28) and in the Aldersgate Memorandum §10 (*Works*, 18:247). On perceptible assurance in Wesley's theology, see Joseph W. Cunningham, *John Wesley's Pneumatology: Perceptible Inspiration* (Burlington: Ashgate, 2014).

45. *Journal*, April 22 and 28, 1738 (*Works*, 18:234–35).

46. Harald Lindström, *Wesley and Sanctification* (Nappanee, IN: Francis Asbury Press, 1980), 207.

with baptism.[47] What is notable about this summary is that each point expresses an aspect of the double-justification theory. Likewise, when he was told in December that "many wise and learned men" in the Church of England teach a twofold justification by faith and good works, Wesley replied that justification is not twofold but a single event ("present remission of sins"). He added that the merits of Christ's death are its "sole cause" and faith alone its only condition.[48] On both occasions Wesley asserted that his position represented the official teachings of the Church of England in its founding documents.[49]

English Reformation Writings

In November 1738 Wesley began "more narrowly to inquire" into the Church of England's contested doctrine of justification by faith, located in its Articles, *Homilies*, and Prayer Book.[50] That this was not his first inquiry into the *Homilies* on the subject is almost certain given that only a year prior he completed a reading of these sermons while assessing Pietist teachings on justification.[51] His intent now was probably to examine the subject more closely to discern his church's official position. Wesley's investigation surely included the Articles of Religion and Prayer Book, but his attention turned particularly to Thomas Cranmer's three sermons on salvation in the *Book of Homilies* and later to Robert Barnes's (d. 1540) essay on justification. Wesley published extracts of both men's writings in 1738 and 1739.

Both Cranmer and Barnes were deeply influenced by Luther's teachings on justification, as was the English church in the sixteenth century.

---

47. *Journal,* September 13, 1739 (*Works,* 19:96–97).

48. *Journal,* December 13, 1739 (*Works,* 19:128).

49. Wesley supported his position by appealing to the Church of England's Articles, Homilies, and Prayer Book (*Journal,* September 13, 1739; December 13, 1739 (*Works,* 19:96, 128).

50. *Journal,* November 12, 1738 (*Works,* 19:21). Wesley says "controverted" doctrine, which meant disputed or contested (Wesley, *Complete English Dictionary,* 2nd ed. [Bristol: William Pine, 1764]).

51. *Journal,* September 30, 1737 (*Works,* 18:193).

They both traveled to Germany in the 1530s and interacted with Lutherans and other reformers. Michael Whiting describes Barnes as a "Lutheran theologian" after his trip to Wittenberg.[52] Anglican scholars acknowledge Lutheran influence on the doctrinal standards of the English church, as is evident in Article XI on justification:

> We are accounted righteous before God, only for the merit of our Lord and Saviour Jesus Christ by Faith, and not for our own works or deserving: Wherefore, that we are justified by Faith only is a most wholesome Doctrine, and very full of comfort, as more largely is expressed in the Homily on Justification.[53]

Wesley's extract of Cranmer's three sermons, titled *The Doctrine of Salvation, Faith, and Good Works*,[54] moves beyond the themes found in the Aldersgate memorandum and *Salvation by Faith* to endorse a clear forensic view of justification. Since everyone is a sinner by transgressing God's law, they are "constrained to seek for another righteousness or justification" (I.1). To meet this need "God sent his only Son into the world to fulfil the law for us," so that by the merits of his death he could "make satisfaction to the Father for our sins" (I.1). Therefore, justification is due "not only to God's mercy and grace, but his justice also" (I.5). Wesley then explained:

> Christ is now the righteousness of all them that truly believe in him. *He for them paid their ransom by his death. He for them fulfilled the law in his life*; so that now in him and by him every Christian may be called a fulfiller of the law, forasmuch as that which their infirmity lacked Christ's righteousness has supplied. (I.7)

By affirming the imputation of Christ's active and passive righteousness, Wesley was restating in Anglican terms Luther's doctrine of "alien

---

52. Michael S. Whiting, *Luther in English: The Influence of His Theology of Law and Gospel on Early English Evangelicals, 1525–35* (Eugene, OR: Pickwick Publications, 2010), 309, 315.

53. Paul Avis, *Anglicanism and the Christian Church* (Edinburgh: T & T Clark, 1989), 28; Chapman, *Anglican Theology*, 33, 66, 71; Moorman, *A History of the Church in England*, 163; McGrath, *Iustitia Dei*, 228; Whiting, *Luther in English*, 161–337; *Book of Common Prayer*, 1662 edition.

54. *The Doctrine of Salvation, Faith, and Good Works* (*Works*, 12:32–43).

righteousness." Even though Wesley had been exposed to imputation teachings from his parents and Anglican authors like William Beveridge, the concept did not find expression in his theology until now.[55] The doctrine of imputation is also inferred as the formal cause of justification in other writings. In March 1739 Wesley mentioned Christ's "righteousness and blood"—his obedience and sufferings—as the "cause of our salvation" in a letter to James Hervey, and made the same point in journal entries on August 27 and September 13.[56] In October he reissued Robert Barnes's treatise on justification that taught the doctrine of imputation. For example, Barnes stated, "Wherefore, we say with blessed St. Paul, that faith only justifieth by imputation; that is, all the merits and goodness, grace and favour, and all that is in Christ to our salvation, is imputed and reckoned unto us, because we hang and believe on him."[57] Three years later Wesley advocated the same position in *The Principles of a Methodist*:

> Christ therefore is now the righteousness of all them that truly believe in him. "He for them paid the ransom by his death. He for them fulfilled the law in his life." So that now in him, and by him, every believer may be called a fulfiller of the law.[58]

Continuity and Discontinuity

From Wesley's early evangelical writings it becomes evident that from 1738 to 1742 he taught a doctrine of justification by the imputation of Christ's active and passive righteousness. Christians are not only forgiven their past sin due to Christ's penal sufferings; they are reckoned legally

---

55. Beveridge clearly taught justification by imputation in his *Private Thoughts* and sermons, which Wesley began to read as early as 1726 (sermons) and 1731 (*Private Thoughts*). In none of his extant early writings does Wesley mention the concept of imputation. It first appears in his 1738 tract *The Doctrine of Salvation, Faith, and Good Works* (*Works*, 12:27).

56. Letter, March 20, 1739 (*Works*, 25:610); *Journal*, August 27 and September 13, 1739 (*Works*, 19:89, 96).

57. Robert Barnes, *On Justification by Faith Only, according to the Doctrine of the Eleventh Article of the Church of England*, in *Writings of Tindal, Frith, and Barnes*, ed. W. M. Engels (Philadelphia: Presbyterian Board of Education, 1842), 124.

58. *The Principles of a Methodist* §5 (1742, *Works*, 9:51). The quotations are from the *Book of Homilies*, "Sermon of the Salvation of Mankind," pt. 1.

righteous based on Christ's perfect obedience to God's law. This suggests the imputation of Christ's active and passive righteousness was the formal cause of justification in his soteriology, along with Christ's death as the meritorious cause and faith the instrumental cause.[59] His position was similar to that of classical Anglicans Hooker and Downame. However, Wesley was unaware at this time of the antinomian implications of the imputation doctrine. As we will soon see, his views will change with his fallout with the Moravians and Calvinists in the early 1740s.

Wesley also came to a new appreciation of his church's official statements on faith and good works. Article XII clarified that good works cannot go before present justification, nor can they "put away our sins, and endure the severity of God's judgment." Instead, good works "spring out necessarily of a true and lively faith" in Christ.[60] The same points were made by Cranmer and Barnes. Fred Sanders aptly expressed Wesley's position, "No sanctification precedes justification, and the sinner brings nothing to the bargaining table."[61] From Cranmer's sermon on salvation Wesley found what would become his new standard for justifying faith—a "sure trust and confidence in God that by the merits of Christ his sins be forgiven and he reconciled to the favour of God."[62] Implicit in this definition is an evangelical understanding of faith as perceptible assurance. Scholars have correctly noted Wesley's early statements on faith as assent and yet failed to consider his early remarks on faith as trust and reliance.[63]

---

59. *Journal,* August 27, 1739 (*Works,* 19:89).

60. *Book of Common Prayer,* 555.

61. Fred Sanders, *Wesley on the Christian Life: The Heart Renewed in Love* (Wheaton: Crossway, 2013), 132.

62. *Doctrine of Salvation, Faith, and Good Works* I.15 (*Works,* 12:37). The quotation is from the *Book of Homilies,* "Sermon of the Salvation of Mankind," pt. 3.

63. Collins, *The Scripture Way of Salvation: The Heart of John Wesley's Theology* (Nashville: Abingdon Press, 1997), 74; W. Stephen Gunter, *The Limits of "Love Divine": John Wesley's Response to Antinomianism and Enthusiasm* (Nashville: Kingswood Books, 1989), 70–71; Maddox, *Responsible Grace,* 124–25. Most of Wesley's expressions of faith as trust and reliance are found in his sacramental writings. This is to be expected given his beliefs that the sacraments confer justifying and sanctifying graces. For example, in his manuscript prayer manual Wesley renounces all trust in his own righteousness and expresses "reliance on the merits of thy crucified Son" (Maddox, Manuscript Prayer Manual, 89, 92).

The real change was the shift from a predominantly sacramental to non-sacramental view of justification. Faith as trust became associated with instantaneous conversion and the Spirit's direct testimony of acceptance. Consequently, the means of grace were no longer seen as necessary to receive justification before God. Justifying faith was a gift of free, sovereign grace.

In the same way, the atonement became more pronounced in Wesley's "new gospel." Throughout his life Wesley held standard Anglican views of the penal substitution theory. Traditional terms like oblation, ransom, sacrifice, satisfaction, and propitiation were regularly employed by Wesley to explain the atonement.[64] So, it might be asked, what changed in his theology of the cross? The answer is found in his "new doctrine" of free grace. By excluding all human works, justification became a work of sheer gratuity on God's part, with Christ's death as its "whole and sole cause."[65] Wesley's "new doctrine" of instantaneous conversion incorporated a monergistic element.[66] Writing to Lady Cox two months prior to Aldersgate, Wesley considered the Spirit's work in conversion as "equivalent to all outward miracles."[67] He repeated the same idea in his *Earnest Appeal to Men of Reason and Religion*, where the gift of saving faith is a "work of omnipotence." He added, "It requires no less power thus to quicken a dead soul than to raise a body that lies in the grave."[68] With the believer's justification and new birth attributed solely to God, with the seeker pas-

---

64. Collins, *Theology of John Wesley*, 99–108. For other studies on Wesley's atonement theology, see Kiyeong Chang, *The Theologies of the Law in Martin Luther and John Wesley* (Lexington, KY: Emeth Press, 2014); Clifford, *Atonement and Justification*; John Deschner, *Wesley's Christology: An Interpretation* (Dallas: Southern Methodist University Press, 1960, 1985); Maddox, *Responsible Grace*; Herbert B. McGonigle, *John Wesley: The Death of Christ* (Ilkeston, UK: Moorleys Print & Publishing, 2014); Thomas C. Oden, *John Wesley's Teachings: Christ and Salvation* (Grand Rapids: Zondervan, 2012).

65. *Journal*, September 13, 1739 (*Works*, 19:96).

66. On monergism in Wesley's soteriology, see Collins, *Theology of John Wesley*, 160–64. See also, Gunter, *The Limits of Love Divine*.

67. Letter, March 7, 1738 (*Works*, 25:534).

68. *An Earnest Appeal to Men of Reason and Religion* §9 (*Works*, 11:48). Compare with Wesley's journal comment on August 24, 1743 (*Works*, 19:332). For further discussion on Wesley's theology of instantaneousness, see Olson, *Wesley and Aldersgate*, 154–57.

sive in the instant of reception, the cross as the sole procuring cause was clearly underscored in Wesley's "new gospel."[69]

A new view of the atonement solidified a Trinitarian foundation to his "new doctrine." The Trinitarian pattern of the ancient ecumenical creeds expressed in Anglican theology and worship continued to form the backbone of his justification doctrine. As the fountain of all grace, the Father sent the Son and grants forgiveness and acceptance to all who believe.[70] The Son, for his part, procured forgiveness and righteousness by satisfying divine justice through his perfect obedience and atoning death.[71] The Holy Spirit applies the saving benefits of the Father and Son by removing "all servile fear" of God's wrath because of the Son's "satisfaction to his Father."[72] Elmer Colyer appropriately summarized Wesley's Trinitarian soteriology:

> Justification refers to God's pardon or forgiveness of our sins and our guilt because of the love of God the Father that comes to us through Christ's life, death, and resurrection and is made real in our lives by the Holy Spirit.[73]

A final area of continuity and discontinuity concerns Wesley's *ordo salutis*. The consensus among scholars has been that with his "new faith" Wesley altered his *ordo* by placing justification before sanctification.[74] However, this conclusion fails to consider his prior High Church doctrine of double justification. In the last chapter we saw that during his Oxford period Wesley began to stress the necessity of adult conversion. This was largely due to the influence of William Law on the loss of baptismal

---

69. A feature of Wesley's Aldersgate testimony was his passivity in the event. God was the primary agent; Wesley simply felt the work of God in his heart. On this point, see Olson, *Wesley and Aldersgate*, 159.

70. Wesley, *Journal*, May 24, 1738 §6 (*Works*, 18:245); *Salvation by Faith* I.5 (*Works*, 1:121); *Doctrine of Salvation, Faith, and Good Works* I.12 (*Works*, 12:36).

71. *Doctrine of Salvation, Faith, and Good Works* I.5 (*Works*, 12:34).

72. *Salvation by Faith*, II.4 (*Works*, 1:122–23); *Doctrine of Salvation, Faith, and Good Works*, I.1 (*Works*, 12:32).

73. Colyer, *Trinitarian Dimension of John Wesley's Theology*, 167.

74. E.g., Collins, *Theology of John Wesley*, 169–70; Colyer, *Trinitarian Dimension of John Wesley's Theology*, 140.

regeneration after one turns to worldly living. From that time Wesley began to teach the necessity of adult conversion for present salvation. In 1738 Wesley did not alter his *ordo* but redefined adult conversion according to his new evangelical gospel. His "new doctrine" initially led to the dismissal of final justification, though this proved short-lived. As we will see, by the mid-1740s Wesley will once again promulgate his double-justification theory. So, Wesley's evangelical *ordo* was as follows:

baptism—present justification—sanctification—final justification—eternal glory

This evangelical *ordo salutis* would remain a permanent feature of Wesley's soteriology except for the addition of a second sanctifying moment in 1740.[75] Pertinent to our study is that Wesley's evangelical *ordo* continued to reflect his Anglican heritage with its sacramental view of the Christian life.

Moderate Reformed Period

In 1739 two controversies began to brew that led to the formation of three main branches in the new evangelical movement. The first debate was between Wesley and George Whitefield (d. 1770) over predestination. Known as the Free Grace Controversy, the dispute became so sharp that Methodism split into two camps, Wesleyan (Arminian) and Calvinist (Reformed),[76] with both sides publishing tracts and letters against each other.[77] The second controversy took place between Wesley and the Moravians over degrees of justifying faith and the role of the means of grace in

---

75. The first published record of Wesley teaching Christian perfection as a second, post-justification event is in the preface of *Hymns and Sacred Poems*, 1740 (*Works*, 13:42–48). There are hints of it earlier in his *Journal* (see January 25, 1739; *Works*, 19:32).

76. Heitzenrater, *Wesley and the People Called Methodists*, 117–19; Joel Houston, *Wesley, Whitefield, and the "Free Grace" Controversy: The Crucible of Methodism* (New York: Routledge, 2020); Rack, *Reasonable Enthusiast*, 198–202.

77. The controversy began with Wesley's sermon "On Free Grace" in the spring of 1739. He then published several works, including Baxter's *Aphorisms* in 1745. Whitefield in turn published an open letter against Wesley (*A Letter to the Reverend Mr. John Wesley, in Answer to His Sermon Entitled Free-Grace* (London: W. Strahan, 1741).

evangelical conversion. This led to formal separation in July 1740, but tensions reverberated for several years leading Wesley to publish three apologetic tracts against the Moravians in 1745.[78] One outcome of both controversies was that Wesley became convinced the Calvinists and Moravians were advocating antinomianism and this led him to define his justification doctrine more precisely.[79]

1744 Annual Conference and Farther Appeal

At the first annual conference in June 1744 the subject of justification was front and center.[80] The doctrine was defined in standard Anglican terms as pardon and divine favor, with justifying faith to include a perceptible assurance of present salvation. To support this definition Wesley appealed to Hebrews 11:1 ("divine supernatural *elenchus*" or evidence of "things not seen"), which he had first done the prior year in his *Earnest Appeal to Men of Reason and Religion*.[81] The question of Christ's imputed righteousness was raised but Wesley now claimed the phrase to be unscriptural and that Paul referred to faith as being imputed for righteousness.[82] To the claim that Romans 5:19 suggests the imputation of Christ's righteousness, Wesley explained that "by the merits of Christ all men are cleared from the guilt of Adam's sin."[83] He then elaborated on what Christ's obedience and death provide, and surprisingly the answer dealt with the subjective work of inward righteousness and the future resurrection. The objective work of the cross is not even mentioned. Instead, Wesley stated the

---

78. *A Short View of the Difference between the Moravian Brethren . . . and John and Charles Wesley* (London: W. Strahan, 1745); *A Dialogue Between an Antinomian and His Friend* (London: W. Strahan, 1745); *Second Dialogue between an Antinomian and His Friend* (London: W. Strahan, 1745).

79. One of the better studies on Wesley's response to antinomianism is Gunter, *The Limits of Love Divine*.

80. For the 1744 Conference Minutes on justification, see *Works*, 10:126–31.

81. *Works*, 11:46. Wesley was first exposed to Hebrews 11:1 as a definition for justifying faith years earlier from the Moravian August Spangenberg (Manuscript Journal, July 31, 1737 [*Works*, 18:532]).

82. E.g., Rom. 4:5.

83. Conference Minutes, 1744 Q.16 (*Works*, 10:129).

Methodists had inadvertently "leaned too much toward Calvinism" and toward "antinomianism."[84] Implicit in these discussions was Wesley's concern that the imputation doctrine was being used by the Calvinists and Moravians to undercut the necessity of holy living in the Christian life.

During this period Wesley gravitated back to his prior belief in double justification. We saw above that in 1739 he had twice dismissed the doctrine and insisted justification to be a single work. But the threat of antinomianism awakened Wesley to the dangers of a strong imputation doctrine. Just days after his critique of Luther as the source of the Moravian errors, Wesley once more read George Bull's *Harmonica Apostolica* and this time without any noted criticism.[85] He simply stated Bull's position on double justification and his views regarding faith and good works. The lack of criticism possibly suggests the beginning of a shift in Wesley's perspective.[86] At the annual conference in June 1744 Wesley acknowledged that Paul and James refer to two different moments of justification in Abraham's life, when he was age seventy-five and twenty-five years later when Isaac was offered on the altar.[87] This biblical example refuted the idea of justification as a single work at initial faith. By December Wesley was once again espousing the notion of a twofold justification. In part 1 of his *Farther Appeal of Men of Reason and Religion*, Wesley clarified that justification "sometimes means our acquittal at the last day," though in the Anglican Articles and *Homilies* it refers to "present forgiveness, pardon of sins, and consequently acceptance with God."[88] From this point forward the doctrine of double justification would remain a permanent feature of Wesley's soteriology.

In the *Farther Appeal* Wesley restated his beliefs about justification and salvation. The source of justifying faith is "God alone" (I.6), Christ's life and death serve as the meritorious cause (II.8), Hebrews 11:1 defines

---

84. Conference Minutes, 1740 QQ.17–20 (*Works*, 10:130).

85. *Journal*, June 24, 1741 (*Works*, 19:202).

86. *A Farther Appeal of Men of Reason and Religion* part I §5 (*Works*, 11:113).

87. Conference Minutes, 1744 Q.14 (*Works*, 10:128).

88. *Farther Appeal* part 1 I.2 (*Works*, 11:105). Double justification is repeatedly affirmed in the *Farther Appeal* part 1 (see II.1, 2, 4, 8, 10).

justifying faith as a "sure trust and confidence that Christ died for *my* sins, that he 'loved *me* and gave himself for *me*'" (I.4), repentance serves as a condition if there be time and opportunity (I.2; II.7, 11), and good works and holiness cannot go before present justification but do prepare for final justification (II.4, 8, 10). Salvation is defined comprehensively as not merely "deliverance from hell, or going to heaven, but a present deliverance from sin, a restoration of the soul to its primitive health, its original purity . . . the renewal of our souls after the image of God in righteousness and true holiness" (I.3). He noted that its "first sowing" is instantaneous when the Spirit witnesses to our "pardon or justification" and from there increases gradually (I.4–5). Finally, Wesley took the time to demonstrate his doctrinal agreement with his Church's Liturgy, Articles, and *Homilies* (II.4–8). At one point, he reaffirmed baptismal justification, "Infants indeed our Church supposes to be justified in baptism, although they cannot then either believe or repent" (II.4, also I.5).[89] As we will see below, Wesley did not abrogate his belief in sacramental justification but instead interweaved it with his "new gospel" of evangelical justification to form a comprehensive theology of objective righteousness with several degrees of acceptance.

Richard Baxter's Aphorisms

Wesley's views on imputed righteousness were about to change even more. While researching the subject in January 1745, a bookseller sent Wesley a copy of Richard Baxter's *Aphorismes of Justification*. As we saw in chapter 1, Baxter was a popular Presbyterian minister and theologian who held moderate Reformed views in contrast to the high Calvinism found among many English Puritans. The central aim of the *Aphorismes* was to refute antinomian teaching on justification within the Calvinist tradition, which suited Wesley's purpose following the Free Grace Controversy. Wesley was so impressed with Baxter's work that he immediately published two abridgments, the first in April and a slightly revised edition in July, just before the annual conference in August 1745. Titled *An Extract of Mr.*

---

89. The quotations and references in this paragraph can be found in *Works*, 11:105–17.

Richard Baxter's Aphorisms of Justification,[90] Wesley reduced the eighty theses to forty-five, yet retained the substance of Baxter's arguments. Besides reading the extract at several Methodist conferences, the *Aphorismes* left a lasting mark on Wesley's doctrine of justification by contributing critical ideas to several of his writings. This would include his two dialogues "between an Antinomian and His Friend" (1745),[91] his sermon "Justification by Faith" (1746),[92] and the 1770 Conference Minutes.[93]

The most significant contribution Baxter made was to provide a series of arguments against the Calvinist claim regarding the imputation of Christ's active righteousness. This went to the heart of Wesley's controversies with the Calvinists (and Moravians). Baxter showed that justification requires either keeping the law's precepts or satisfying its penalty, but not both.[94] Since scripture affirms that Christ died in the place of sinners, it is his passive righteousness that is reckoned to believers.[95] This alone is sufficient to merit justification before God. To suggest otherwise, that Christ obeyed in the place of believers, is nothing short of a "monstrous piece of antinomian doctrine," which "every Christian should abhor as unsufferable."[96] Wesley's new position on imputed righteousness is summarized by the following quotation of Baxter:

> God the Father doth accept the sufferings and merits of his Son as a full satisfaction to his violated law, and as a valuable consideration upon which he will wholly forgive the offenders themselves, and receive them again into his favour, and give them the addition of a more excellent happiness also, so that they will but receive his Son upon the terms expressed in the gospel.[97]

---

90. Wesley, *An Extract of Mr. Richard Baxter's Aphorisms of Justification* (*Works*, 12:54–88). Wesley dropped the final *e* in the title.

91. For the two dialogues, see *Works*, Jackson, 10:266–83.

92. *Works*, 1:181–99.

93. Conference Minutes, 1770 (*Works*, 10:392–94).

94. *Extract of Baxter's Aphorisms* IV, XIII (*Works*, 12:57, 66).

95. *Extract of Baxter's Aphorisms* XV, XX (*Works*, 12:68, 72).

96. *Extract of Baxter's Aphorisms* XVII (*Works*, 12:69).

97. *Extract of Baxter's Aphorisms* IV (*Works*, 12:58).

Another contribution of Baxter was on covenant theology. We saw earlier that Wesley was taught the basics of Anglican covenant theology from his parents. During his Oxford and Georgian periods, little interest was shown to the subject, even though the economic Trinity in his sacramental theology presupposes it. This changed with Wesley's "new gospel" because it drew a sharp line between the covenants of works and grace. Throughout the 1740s Wesley began to examine more closely Puritan views on the subject.[98] Baxter's contribution reiterated that the moral law in the covenant of works was not completely abolished in the new covenant.[99] This was another pillar of antinomianism in Wesley's day. Baxter provided several arguments, but his central thesis was the distinction between a repeal of the law and its relaxation.[100] The law is not fully repealed under the gospel because "the sins even of the justified are still breaches of that law." This means the law has been relaxed and the gospel standard for obedience is "far more easy than the old conditions" under the law.[101] Salvation no longer requires perfect obedience, but repentance and faith in Christ.[102] Therefore, the covenant of works continues in some force even in the new covenant. For although that covenant had formally ceased when Adam sinned, "it is not so abolished but that it will stand, in some measure, even to the end of the world."[103] As a proof, scripture teaches that everyone will be judged according to their works at the Final Judgment.

We saw above that Wesley focused almost exclusively on present salvation when he adopted his "new gospel" of justification by faith alone. But his fallout with the Calvinists and Moravians over their antinomianism led Wesley to gravitate back to his Anglican heritage, which taught that full justification includes both present pardon and final acquittal. Baxter's contribution included scriptural and rational arguments for this position. Drawing on numerous scripture texts, like Matthew 25:31-46;

---

98. Rodes, *From Faith to Faith*, 37–58.
99. *Extract of Baxter's Aphorisms* XXIII (*Works,* 12:73).
100. *Extract of Baxter's Aphorisms* IX (*Works,* 12:62).
101. *Extract of Baxter's Aphorisms* VII (*Works,* 12:60–61).
102. *Extract of Baxter's Aphorisms* XI (*Works,* 12:64).
103. Conference Minutes, 1746 Q.25 (*Works,* 10:174).

2 Corinthians 5:10; and 1 Peter 1:17, Baxter showed that works do more than validate the sincerity of one's faith in Christ, they serve as a condition for final acceptance on the last day.[104] He added that removing good works as a condition for final salvation tends to "confirm the world in their imagery faith" and plays into the hands of the "papists" who have turned "many learned men from the Protestant religion to popery."[105] In the end, Baxter considered it "antinomian doctrine" to say "we must not work or perform our duties *for* life and salvation, but only *from* life and salvation."[106] We will return to this statement when we discuss Wesley's 1770 Conference Minutes in chapter 5. "Full justification" therefore involves more than the "first moment of justification," as the antinomians and high Calvinists claimed, it includes "final justification at the bar of Christ."[107] By publishing an extract of Baxter's *Aphorismes*, Wesley presented a strong case for his doctrine of double justification.

Wesley's Sermons

The next year Wesley gathered his current thoughts for a summative presentation in the sermon "Justification by Faith." At this point we need only to note those motifs that contribute to our study of his justification doctrine. The doctrine is grounded on the biblical concept of the first and second Adam, "By the sin of the first Adam . . . we all became 'children of wrath;'" by the "second Adam . . . we are 'justified freely by his [God's] grace.'" With his focus on present justification, Wesley gave only a nod to final justification in the entire sermon.[108] Likewise, his definition of present justification emphasized the non-imputation of sin with Christ's passive righteousness as its meritorious cause.[109] His explanation

---

104. *Extract of Baxter's Aphorisms* XLV (*Works*, 12:85).

105. *Extract of Baxter's Aphorisms* XLV (*Works*, 12:87).

106. *Extract of Baxter's Aphorisms* XLV (*Works*, 12:86).

107. *Extract of Baxter's Aphorisms* XLIII, XLV (*Works*, 12:84, 88).

108. *Justification by Faith* II.5 (*Works*, 1:190).

109. *Justification by Faith* II.5 (*Works*, 1:189). His comments at IV.5 express the same sentiments on imputation as found in the 1744 Conference Minutes (*Works*, 1:196).

that present justification deals with the law's condemnation but not with Satan's accusation is a restatement of Baxter, who made the same point to contrast the purposes of present and final justification.[110] More well known was Wesley's distinction between "what God *does for us* through his Son" and "what he *works in us* by his Spirit."[111] The former refers to justification and the latter to sanctification. Not only is the economic Trinity apparent in the distinction, but the contrast settles an issue that initially was unclear in his "new gospel." To recall, when Wesley adopted his new faith in 1738 he essentially held a Pietistic Lutheran view of justification that incorporated both the objective and subjective aspects of salvation.[112] By the autumn of 1739 he was drawing a clear line between justification and sanctification.[113] Now, seven years later, Wesley reiterated that point while acknowledging there are "rare instances" in scripture where present justification includes the inward work of the Spirit, but for all practical purposes the two must be kept theologically distinct to avoid confusion between the two works of free grace.[114]

At the same time Wesley published his latest thoughts on federal theology in the sermon "The Righteousness of Faith."[115] Since covenant theology served as a framework for his justification doctrine, Wesley's views are worth noting at this time. What we find is that his perspective had not materially changed over the years. For starters, his explanation of the two covenants matches what his parents affirmed. His position also mirrored the covenant theology of William Beveridge in his influential work *Private Thoughts upon Religion and the Christian Life*, which Wesley read

---

110. *Extract of Baxter's Aphorisms* XXV (*Works*, 12:74). Baxter claimed present justification answers the law's accusations while final justification clears from Satan's accusations.

111. *Justification by Faith* II.1 (*Works*, 1:187). Restated in the 1748 sermon "The Great Privilege of those that are Born of God" §2 (*Works*, 1:431–32).

112. *Salvation by Faith* II.1–7 (*Works*, 1:121–24).

113. *Journal*, July 31 and September 13, 1739 (*Works*, 19:84–85, 96).

114. A similar evolution took place with the new birth in Wesley's thought. After 1738 he continued to speak of degrees of the new birth/regeneration, with the highest degree linked to Christian perfection (Conference Minutes 1744 [*Works*, 10:131–32]; *Journal*, January 25, 1739 [*Works*, 19:32]). By the 1750s Wesley distinguished the new birth from sanctification (*The New Birth* IV.3 [*Works*, 2:198]).

115. "The Righteousness of Faith" (*Works*, 1:202–16).

while at Oxford. As did Baxter, Beveridge, and his parents, Wesley did not conflate the covenant of works with the Mosaic Law, as was common in Puritan theology.[116] The one area in which his perspective did change concerned the "righteousness which is of faith" (I.11). Whereas before he held a sacramental view that identifies this "righteousness" with our inward renewal in the *imago Dei*, Wesley now stated it refers to the "condition of salvation" that does not "require us to *do* anything ... but only to believe in him" who justifies the "ungodly" and "imputes his faith to him for righteousness" (I.7–8). In Wesley's "new gospel," righteousness begins as a gift of divine grace purchased by Christ's death as a "propitiation for our sins" (I.13). Propitiation is defined as to "appease the wrath of God, or to avert the punishment we have justly deserved" (II.6). Thus, "Christ makes compensation and satisfies the justice of God precisely by standing in the place of sinful humanity ... and in the end by bearing the penalty, the very wages of sin."[117] Throughout his writings Wesley employed a rich vocabulary of terms to express what Christ accomplished at the cross.[118] Scholars have recognized several atonement theories in Wesley's thought, with penal satisfaction as the dominant theme.[119] Randy Maddox summarized that Wesley held a "Penalty Satisfaction *explanation* of the Atonement which has a Moral Influence *purpose*, and a Ransom *effect*."[120]

The thirteen discourses on the "Sermon on the Mount" also reflect the influence of Baxter. Once again, Wesley stressed the passive righteousness of Christ as imputed for pardon and reconciliation.[121] This gift of righteousness brings the "peace of God," defined as a "sweet repose in the

---

116. For Samuel and Susanna Wesley's views, see above, pp. 31–36. For Beveridge's views, see *Private Thoughts*, Articles IX and X. On Puritan views and Wesley's amendment of them, see Rodes, *From Faith to Faith*, 37–76.

117. Collins, *Theology of John Wesley*, 102.

118. See Maddox, Manuscript Prayer Manual, 88–104; *A Companion for the Altar: Extracted from Thomas à Kempis*, 3rd ed. (London: W. Strahan, 1744); John and Charles Wesley, *Hymns on the Lord's Supper* (Bristol: Felix Farley, 1745).

119. See Chang, *Theologies of Law in Luther and Wesley*, 97–103; Collins, *John Wesley's Theology*, 99–110; Deschner, *Wesley's Christology*, 150–57, 165–69; Maddox, *Responsible Grace*, 101–9; Oden, *John Wesley's Teachings*, 2:52–53.

120. Maddox, *Responsible Grace*, 109, emphasis his.

121. Discourse I (I.11) and IX (§21) (*Works*, 1:481, 643).

blood of Jesus, which leaves no doubt of our acceptance" and gives an "earnest of our inheritance" that the "Lord, the righteous Judge, will give at that day."[122] This example shows how Wesley could weave present and final justification into a seamless affirmation of "full justification."[123] Even so, the central concern of the sermon series is with "inward righteousness," that "holiness of heart" that is properly called "God's righteousness" and involves the "work" of the "almighty Spirit."[124] Recalling the famous line of the holy living divine, Henry Scougal, Wesley claimed that this divine righteousness is the "life of God in the soul" and "every holy and heavenly temper in one; springing up from and terminating in the love of God as our Father and Redeemer, and the love of all men for his sake."[125] In the end, the *gift* of imputed righteousness and the *work* of imparted righteousness compose the full, present righteousness of God's kingdom.[126]

Evangelical Sacramentalism

In the last chapter we saw that justification was embedded in Wesley's sacramental theology. In the 1740s Wesley published his thoughts on the means of grace and two other works that spell out his eucharistic theology.[127] Of the two works, the first was an extract of the fourth book of Thomas à Kempis's *The Imitation of Christ*, which Wesley appropri-

---

122. "Upon Our Lord's Sermon on the Mount," Discourse I I.11 (*Works*, 1:481).

123. *Extract of Baxter's Aphorisms* LXIII (*Works*, 12:84).

124. "Upon Our Lord's Sermon on the Mount," Discourse IX §21 (*Works*, 1:643). The subject of inward righteousness is also found in Discourses I, II, III, IV, V, and VII (*Works*, 1:481, 495–97, 521, 551, 592). The same focus on inward righteousness is found in the 1748 sermons "The Marks of the New Birth" and "The Great Privilege of Those That Are Born of God" (*Works*, 1:415, 431). Thus, the work of inward righteousness or holiness was foremost in his mind when writing these sermons.

125. "Upon Our Lord's Sermon on the Mount," Discourse I I.11 (*Works*, 1:481), Discourse II II.2 (*Works*, 1:495).

126. "Upon Our Lord's Sermon on the Mount," Discourse IX §§21–23 (*Works*, 1:643–44).

127. For studies on Wesley's eucharistic theology, see Ole Borgen, *John Wesley on the Sacraments;* John C. Bowmer, *The Sacrament of the Lord's Supper in Early Methodism* (London: Dacre Press, 1951); Geordan Hammond, *John Wesley in America*.

ately titled *A Companion for the Altar*. Wesley had published an edition of à Kempis's *Imitation* in 1735 and an extract in 1741. The *Companion* was released in early 1742 and went through eight editions over his lifetime. The second work was a collaboration with Charles titled *Hymns on the Lord's Supper*, with an extract of Daniel Brevint's *Christian Sacrament and Sacrifice* serving as the preface. Published nine times during Wesley's lifetime, the hymnal was widely used among the early Methodists. From the popularity of this hymnal and their High Church views on the sacrament, Geordan Hammond concluded that the "Wesleys led a revival that was sacramental and evangelical."[128] It is important to understand the sacramental character of Wesley's evangelical doctrine of justification.

The place to begin is with Wesley's High Churchmanship. His views on baptism and Holy Communion did not materially change with the adoption of his "new gospel" in 1738.[129] In this chapter we explore Wesley's views on the Lord's Supper and in the next chapter his writings on baptism. The Eucharist serves several purposes for believers. First, the sacrament is a "memorial" or remembrance of Christ's sufferings on the cross; then, a "means" to convey the "first fruits" of his passion in the present; and finally, a "pledge" to "assure us of glory to come."[130] The Lord's Table is the "altar somewhat like the sacrifice of my Saviour" where the "Bread of Life was broken" and the "Lamb of God was slain."[131] Thus, Wesley reminded his followers the main purpose for the sacrament is not the "bare remembrance" of Christ's passion, but to "invite us to his sacrifice" to receive "grace and mercy, still lasting, still new, still the same as when it was first offered for us."[132] By serving as a sign of Christ's propitiation for sin that now "continues to all ages," the sacrament functions as an

---

128. Hammond, *John Wesley in America*, 65.

129. Rack, *Reasonable Enthusiast*, 154; Hammond, *John Wesley in America*, 199.

130. John and Charles Wesley, *Hymns on the Lord's Supper, with a Preface concerning the Christian Sacrament and Sacrifice* (Bristol: Felix Farley, 1745), 4.

131. *Hymns on the Lord's Supper*, 6.

132. *Hymns on the Lord's Supper*, 6.

instrumental means by which grace is conferred to worthy recipients.[133] Wesley explained:

> As bread and wine keep up our natural life, so doth our Lord Jesus by a continual supply of strength and grace, represented by bread and wine, sustain that spiritual life which he hath procured us by his cross. The first breath of spiritual life in our nostrils, is the first purchase of Christ's blood. But alas! How soon would this first life vanish away, were it not followed and supported by a second? Therefore the sacrifice of Christ procures also grace, to renew and preserve the life he has given.[134]

From these remarks it is easy to understand why Wesley and the early Methodists, who were Arminian in theology, considered the sacrament a powerful means to sustain their justification before God. For each time they partook, they spiritually encountered the living Christ and received grace to live holy for God. In this way they preserved the favor of God on their lives. Those believers who had sinned found "forgiveness and new strength to live the life of faith."[135] However, it was at this point that Wesley's evangelical gospel altered his sacramentalism. Ole Borgen showed that Wesley believed the Lord's Supper to provide forgiveness to communicants in two different spiritual conditions. The first for believers who had sinned and the second for sinners seeking present justification. In Georgia, Wesley restricted participation to baptized believers who live a holy life.[136] By 1740 his views had changed. In response to the Moravian position that narrowed the sacrament to a confirming ordinance, Wesley proclaimed that it conveys not only sanctifying grace but also preventing and justifying grace:

> Fri. (June) 27. I preached on "Do this in remembrance of me." In the ancient church everyone who was baptized communicated daily. . . . But in later times many [e.g., the Moravians] have affirmed that the Lord's Supper is not a *converting*, but a *confirming* ordinance. . . . But experience shows

---

133. *Hymns on the Lord's Supper*, 6, 9; "The Means of Grace" II.1 (*Works*, 1:381).
134. *Hymns on the Lord's Supper*, 10.
135. Borgen, *John Wesley on the Sacraments*, 197–99.
136. Hammond, *John Wesley in America*, 122.

the gross falsehood of that assertion that the Lord's Supper is not a *converting* ordinance. Ye are the witnesses. For many now present know, the very beginning of your *conversion* to God (perhaps, in some, the first deep *conviction*) was wrought at the Lord's Supper. Now one single instance of this kind overthrows that whole assertion.[137]

Examples abound of early Methodists who experienced the Spirit's witness to their present justification while partaking of the sacrament. Sarah Ryan felt overwhelmed by the power of God when Wesley offered her the cup. Instantly, her heart was pierced, and she felt the love of Christ.[138] Against the counsel of the Moravians, Mrs. Couch pressed ahead and partook. "In that moment," noted Wesley in his journal, "she felt her load removed; she knew she was accepted in the Beloved."[139] Then there is the testimony of Wesley's mother, Susanna, who "felt her sins forgiven" when the bread was broken.[140] For these early Methodists, Holy Communion served not only to maintain their state of justification but also as a means to receive the gift of present, evangelical justification that includes a perceptible assurance of pardon and acceptance.

One other point bears mentioning. In the *Companion for the Altar* the question of merit is raised. In his extract Wesley kept à Kempis's statement that affirmed all merit belongs to the Lord Jesus.[141] The believer brings no merit to the Table. He made the same point in the sermon "The Means of Grace," "Every believer in Christ is deeply convinced that there is no *merit* but in [Christ]; that there is no *merit* in any of his own works."[142] Even in the maintenance of justification, which includes good works and holy living, Wesley affirmed the believer brings no merit to the Table. Salvation is by grace alone.

---

137. *Journal*, June 27, 1740 (*Works*, 19:158, emphasis his).

138. Paul W. Chilcote, ed., *Early Methodist Spirituality: Selected Women's Writings* (Nashville: Kingswood Books, 2007), 78–79.

139. *Journal*, September 20, 1739 (*Works*, 19:98).

140. *Journal*, August 1, 1742 (*Works*, 19:283–84).

141. Thomas à Kempis, *The Imitation of Christ*, book 4, chapter 2 (New York: Cosimo Classics, 2007), 119–20; John Wesley, *A Companion for the Altar: Extracted from Thomas à Kempis*, 3rd ed., chapter 2 (London: W. Strahan, 1744), 7.

142. *The Means of Grace* II.4 (*Works*, 1:382–83, emphasis his).

Justification and Assurance, Part One

One of the more important developments in the 1740s was the relationship between justification and assurance in Wesley's soteriology. The story behind this development is complex and Kenneth Collins correctly stated that Wesley's views on assurance "underwent more modification over time than any of his other major teachings."[143] Space allows only for a short recap before detailing what changed in his position. Even after seven decades, one of the best summaries covering this evolution is by Arthur Yates.[144] When Wesley adopted his "new gospel" in early 1738, present justification meant a perceptible assurance of pardon and acceptance. This is what he received at Aldersgate. Yates showed upon a close reading of the primary sources that by late 1738 Wesley began to distinguish between assurance and justifying faith while still associating assurance with evangelical salvation (present justification and new birth).[145]

By the mid-1740s Wesley was acknowledging the reality of degrees of faith and assurance while maintaining that the Spirit's witness is necessary for present salvation. Since faith is the condition of salvation, this meant that assurance serves to *confirm* one's faith as justifying and regenerating. For example, at the 1744 Conference Wesley stated that the "moment" a person exercises faith in Christ, the Spirit "immediately . . . bears witness" to their pardon and redemption.[146] The next year Wesley explained to Thomas Church that assurance can become "clouded with doubt or fear," but added that a "plerophory or full assurance" as "excludes all doubt and fear is available" so that the difference between the two degrees is "between the light of the morning and that of the midday sun."[147]

---

143. Collins, *Theology of John Wesley*, 131.

144. Arthur S. Yates, *The Doctrine of Assurance: With Special Reference to John Wesley* (London: Epworth Press, 1952). For more recent surveys, see Collins, *Theology of John Wesley*, 131–36; Heitzenrater, *Mirror and Memory*, 106–49; Maddox, *Responsible Grace*, 124–27.

145. Yates, *Doctrine of Assurance*, 61–62.

146. Conference Minutes, June 25, 1744, QQ. 2–8 (*Works*, 10:126–27); Yates, *Doctrine of Assurance*, 63.

147. *An Answer to Rev. Mr. Church's "Remarks"* II.8 (*Works*, 9:100); Yates, *Doctrine of Assurance*, 64.

With converts experiencing various degrees of assurance and hence justifying faith, Wesley acknowledged there are exceptions to the rule that justification always includes a felt certainty of God's pardoning love.[148] During this time the Anglican "John Smith" pressed Wesley on the matter, which probably nudged him to reconsider the matter.[149] When we turn to the minutes of the early Conferences, an important insight stands out. At none of these Conferences did Wesley separate perceptible assurance from the new birth, which constitutes "the proper Christian faith."[150] This became Wesley's permanent position, even though he did reconsider the relationship between assurance and justification.

A month following the 1747 Conference Wesley wrote to his brother Charles to clarify his position on justification and a felt certainty of salvation. "Justifying faith" is defined to mean "not under the wrath and the curse of God." By contrast, a "sense of pardon" is described as a "distinct, explicit assurance that my sins are forgiven." This "explicit assurance" is the "common privilege of real Christians," those who are born again and have "the proper Christian faith." Wesley then walks through several scriptures to show it is absurd to require an "explicit assurance" to receive "justifying faith."[151]

Four points follow from his remarks. First, Wesley altered what had been his standard definition of justifying faith since 1738: a "sure trust and confidence that Christ died for my sins, that he loved *me* and gave himself for *me*."[152] This could be shortened to "a divine assurance that Christ loved *me*, and gave himself for *me*," as he recently did at the 1747

---

148. Conference Minutes August 2, 1745 QQ. 1, 4; June 16, 1747 QQ. 1, 10 (*Works*, 10:149–50, 192, 194). Yates, *Doctrine of Assurance*, 65–67.

149. *Works*, 10:139, 171, 240–41. "John Smith" is a pseudonym for an Anglican leader who entered an extended dialogue with Wesley from 1745 to 1748. An exchange of twelve letters, six from each author, passed between them. For Frank Baker's comments on the identity of John Smith, see *Works*, 26:138.

150. Conference Minutes, May 13, 1746, 10 AM Q. 1; June 16, 1747 QQ. 3–6, 10 (*Works*, 10:174, 192–94).

151. Letter, July 31, 1747 (*Works*, 26:254–55).

152. *Farther Appeal*, part I I.4 (*Works*, 11:107); see *Journal*, February 1, 1738 (*Works*, 18:215–16); *Doctrine of Salvation, Faith, and Good Works* I.15 (*Works*, 12:37).

Conference.[153] In his letter to Charles this standard definition is applied to "the proper Christian faith" of born again believers, but not to "justifying faith."

Second, Wesley defined "justifying faith" in reference to God's wrath and curse. While this language can refer to this present life, it ultimately points to the Last Judgment and eternal damnation. The Anglican Articles of Religion and Wesley's sermon "Salvation by Faith" associate God's wrath with torment, divine punishment, and servile fear.[154] Collins agreed and added that the term denotes God's just and holy opposition toward sin.[155] Thus, "justifying faith" in this letter involves a deliverance from divine wrath and servile fear yet falls short of a perceptible assurance of present salvation. The experience of Jonathan Reeves was a case in point. He had "peace with God" before he received a "sense of pardon."[156]

Third, "justifying faith" is distinguished from the new birth and "the proper Christian faith." This follows since Wesley described two degrees of spiritual attainment. "Explicit assurance" is associated with the new birth, here identified as a "real Christian." Consequently, "justifying faith" signifies a lower degree of saving faith. This lower degree includes those who lack a felt certainty of their pardon. Wesley is confident that God will not condemn these believers simply because they do not have an "explicit assurance" of their pardon and salvation.

Finally, behind these developments stood Wesley's doctrine of double justification. Since our full justification involves two salvific moments, Wesley could apply each degree of justification to a different stage of saving faith. Final justification pertains to "justifying faith" and deliverance from God's wrath, while present justification is enjoyed by "real Christians" who have a perceptible assurance of salvation. The foundation is now set for Wesley to later distinguish between the *faith of a servant* and the *faith of a son*, which will prove important to his mature doctrine of

---

153. Conference Minutes, June 16, 1747 Q. 1 (*Works*, 10:192).
154. *Salvation by Faith* II.3 (*Works*, 1:122).
155. Collins, *Theology of John Wesley*, 64, 72, 105, 173.
156. *Letters* II, July 31, 1747 (*Works*, 26:255).

justification. Another lesson is how Wesley was led to adjust his justification doctrine to fit Christian experience.

In the next chapter we will return to the subject of justification and assurance in Wesley's soteriology. The way that he correlated them is critical to understanding his doctrine of justification. When asked at the 1746 Conference about what changed in his views from when he was at Oxford, Wesley replied, "We then knew nothing of that righteousness of faith in justification; nor of the nature of faith itself as implying consciousness of pardon."[157] Wesley's response confirms a seismic shift took place in his soteriology in 1738 and that it included a new understanding of the relationship between assurance and justification.

---

157. Conference Minutes, May 13 (10 o'clock), 1746 Q.4 (*Works*, 10:175).

CHAPTER FOUR

EXPLANATORY NOTES AND DEBATES OVER CHRIST'S RIGHTEOUSNESS: 1750–69

By 1750 the essentials of Wesley's doctrine of justification were firmly in place. What was distinctive had developed out of his spiritual journey. As Wesley was raised and educated an Anglican High Churchman who became a Pietist evangelical, his message of justification contained elements of both traditions. It was visibly Protestant and evangelical with its emphasis on faith in Christ alone and perceptible assurance yet infused with High Church sacramentalism and its doctrine of double justification. In addition, Richard Baxter established for Wesley that Christ's passive righteousness is imputed and not his sinless obedience. This countered perceived antinomian tendencies among the Calvinists and Moravians. Lastly, Wesley's Anglicanism led him to maintain that good works and holy living are a necessary fruit of present justification and preparatory for final justification. In this way Wesley held in tandem objective and subjective righteousness in his soteriology of free grace.

There was, however, no shortage of critics. Whether they were Anglican, Moravian, or Calvinist, there was something for everyone to pick apart. Critics repeatedly charged Wesley with inconsistency. From their perspective, the different strands of his theology of objective righteousness could not be held together with consistency. Wesley, however, continued to defend his position and to articulate an Arminian version of justifying righteousness to his Methodist followers. Over the next two decades he would continue to flesh out his position through publications, dialogue, and debate. First, he published a commentary on the New Testament that spelled out the biblical foundations of his doctrine. Next, Wesley issued an extract of his father's treatise on baptism that restated his High Church views on sacramental justification. Then, his debates with the Calvinists over imputed righteousness offered an opportunity to further nuance his position. Finally, Wesley's interactions with Richard Tompson and others led to continued refinement of his understanding of assurance in relation to justification.

Explanatory Notes upon the New Testament

Wesley always kept a busy schedule but in November 1753 his health deteriorated to the point he had to stop his travels and seek relief in the countryside. This turn of events provided him the opportunity to begin a project he had long desired to pursue—a commentary on the New Testament. Five editions of *Explanatory Notes upon the New Testament* were issued in Wesley's lifetime. The intended audience was not the educated classes, but "plain, unlettered" people who knew only the English language, yet reverenced God's word and desired to "save their souls."[1]

Scott Jones explained that God's word was for Wesley the primary authority for Christian faith and practice.[2] As Wesley stated in the preface, Holy Scripture is the "word of the living God" and composes the "most solid and precious system of divine truth." There is "no defect, no excess" in its pages; instead, it provides a "fountain of heavenly wisdom" able to save one's soul.[3] While Wesley leaned toward a literal reading of scripture, his real interest was soteriological. This is seen in his empha-

---

1. John Wesley, *Explanatory Notes upon the New Testament* [hereafter *ENNT*], 2 vols., 2nd ed. (London, 1757), preface §3. Though the third edition was corrected and enlarged, the notes pertaining to present and final justification remained the same.

2. Scott J. Jones, *John Wesley's Conception and Use of Scripture* (Nashville: Kingswood Books, 1995), 13, 31.

3. *ENNT*, preface §10.

sis on the wholeness of scripture and the analogy of faith. Both phrases mean the central message of the sacred text is to teach the "grand scheme of doctrine" pertaining to salvation, specifically "original sin, justification by faith, and present, inward salvation."[4] Thus, in the *Explanatory Notes* Wesley provides a full biblical exposition of his doctrine of justification.

Before we examine Wesley's *Notes*, some comments should be made about his sources. From the preface we learn that Wesley sought the insights of four contemporary commentators: the Anglican John Heylyn (d. 1759) and his first volume of *Theological Lectures at Westminster Abbey*, the Dissenting Calvinists Philip Doddridge (d. 1751) and John Guyse (d. 1761) and their multivolume paraphrastic expositions, and the Lutheran Pietist Johannes Bengel (d. 1752) and his *Gnomon Novi Testamenti*, widely respected for its critical study of the biblical text. From his sources we gather that Wesley looked beyond his own religious tradition to a broad range of sources, from scholarly analysis to popular paraphrases. His chief desire was to remain faithful to the text while communicating its message in a manner that his intended audience could understand. The *Notes* therefore do not include a scholarly description of the biblical doctrine of justification, but a faithful rendering of its message in a format the average Methodist could grasp and apply to their lives.

With these preliminary remarks we turn to Wesley's exposition of present justification before moving to final justification, his thoughts on Paul and James, and his comments on Acts 10 and Cornelius's conversion.

Present Justification

We have seen that Wesley affirmed the Anglican doctrine of double justification. The distinction between a present and final acquittal is easily discerned in his commentary on the relevant passages. Present justification is addressed primarily in the Pauline Epistles, especially Romans and Galatians, while final justification is discussed in those passages dealing with

---

4. Jones, *Wesley's Conception and Use of Scripture*, 43–47; *ENNT*, Rom. 12:6. Wesley restates the same three doctrines in his *Short History of Methodism* §10 (1765, *Works*, 9:369). Again, in his letter to John Taylor he highlights the same three doctrines as distinguishing Christianity from heathenism (Letter, July 3, 1759 [*Works*, 27:166]).

the Last Judgment, often found in the Gospels. So, we begin by turning to Romans and Galatians. The location of Wesley's comments in the *Notes* is listed by their scripture reference.

Justification by faith is the "grand doctrine" of scripture since it is rooted in the story of Abraham and reaches further back to God's eternal purposes (Rom. 8:29; Gal. 3:6). As such, its source is the "free grace of God" revealed through the "righteousness of God," a phrase that for Wesley refers to the manner God appointed for sinners to become righteous through Christ (Rom. 3:21; 5:21). But it also points to the perfections of the divine character revealed in the gospel. For in the message of the cross all the divine attributes are harmonized so that God "might evidence himself to be strictly and inviolably righteous in the administration of his government." This is accomplished by "showing justice on his own Son" while being a "merciful justifier of the sinner that believeth in Jesus" (Rom. 3:26). Consequently, in our justification the righteousness of God is exalted since "every [divine] attribute is glorified, and not one superseded, no, nor so much as clouded" (Rom. 3:26).

Justification is consistently defined according to standard Anglican terms: pardon and acceptance. These two terms appear repeatedly in Romans 3–5 to make the meaning of justification obvious to the reader.[5] Wesley further explained that God freely forgives and accepts sinners "as if [they] had been altogether righteous" (Rom. 4:3) and this entails being "accounted just or righteous before God" (Gal. 3:11; Rom. 4:11). However, in the *Explanatory Notes* this "accounting" is never interpreted as the imputation of Christ's active righteousness. Instead, the "righteousness of Christ" refers to his sinless life that qualified him to atone for sin through suffering and death, thus bringing "life" to believers that leads to eternal glory (Rom. 5:14, 21). As Wesley defined it, "forgiveness, not imputing sin, and imputing righteousness, are all one" and the same benefit (Rom. 4:9). This suggests that pardon or the non-imputation of sin is sufficient for a right standing before God. To go further and assert the imputation of Christ's active righteousness inevitably leads to antinomianism.

---

5. The texts are too numerous to list in parentheses: forgiveness/pardon/remission: Rom. 3:20, 24; 4:5, 7, 9; 5:20; acceptance: Rom. 3:20, 24, 27; 4:1, 3, 4, 9.

We need to take a closer look at Wesley's *ordo justificationis* (order of justification). He rejected outright any notion of salvation by human merit. When Paul stated that "no flesh shall be justified in his sight by works of the law," Wesley explained that "none shall be forgiven and accepted of God... on this ground, that he hath kept the law" (Rom 3:20). A corollary is that there can be no "holiness or sanctification previous to our justification" (Rom. 4:5). For a legal justification is based on personal righteousness, which is impossible for transgressors of God's law. In contrast, gospel justification is by the "righteousness of Christ," who took upon himself the "curse of the law" and suffered a "real infliction of punishment" and in this way appeased God's wrath and purchased forgiveness and acceptance for those who trust solely in his merits (Gal. 3:13; Rom. 3:24-26; 5:14). So, Wesley's *ordo justificationis* is as follows: when a sinner turns to the Lord Jesus, "Christ . . . interposes; justice is satisfied; sin is remitted, and pardon is applied to the soul, by a faith wrought by the Holy Ghost, who then begins the great work of inward sanctification" (Rom. 4:5). There is a logical priority to justification before the new birth, even though both happen in the same instant.

For Wesley justifying faith is not a work since it accrues no merit (Rom. 3:28). Instead, faith is the gift of God with the Holy Spirit as its efficient cause (Eph. 2:8; Rom. 5:5). When Paul speaks of faith being imputed for righteousness, Wesley interpreted this to mean that it is the "sole condition of our acceptance" (Rom. 4:9). For although repentance is a "necessary preparation" (Matt. 4:17), it is faith alone that justifies before God. The fruits of justifying faith are "peace, hope, love, and power over sin," which Wesley saw as the sum of chapters 5–8 in Romans (5:1). And he considered "faith which worketh by love" as the substance of "all inward and outward holiness" (Gal. 5:6). His Arminianism is evident at Galatians 2:18 when he stated that the gospel does not promise justification to anyone "continuing in sin." Consequently, pardon applies to past sin; for present sin is "continuing in sin" and reflects an unbelieving heart. Wesley argued at several places that it is possible for believers to lose their justification and be finally lost due to disobedience (Rom. 11:17-21; Heb. 6:4-6; 2 Pet. 2:20-22).

At this point, it is important to note that Wesley did not consider present justification the final word on our salvation. John Deschner was correct that Wesley's Arminianism meant that "the element of judgment, on which the finality of justification is grounded . . . is deliberately postponed until the final justification."[6] We now turn to Wesley's biblical exposition of the Last Judgment as the event when final justification takes place.

Final Justification

Up until now Wesley had written little on final justification.[7] Following his conversion in 1738, his primary concern was with present justification since it was central to the evangelical gospel of salvation by faith alone. In *Explanatory Notes* Wesley's fullest exposition of final justification is found in the teachings of Jesus.

The Lord Jesus taught that final judgment will be a public event at the end of this age when everyone will be present, including the holy angels (Matt. 25:31-32).[8] It will be a day of separation, when Christ places the righteous on his right, a position of favor, and the unrighteous on his left, to be consigned to eternal punishment (Matt. 25:33, 46.). It will be a great but solemn day, when God's people inherit the eternal kingdom while the unrighteous weep and gnash their teeth as they are cast into outer darkness (Matt. 8:11-12; Lk. 13:28-29). These statements show that the Last Judgment will be God's final word of justification for his people. Whereas present justification is private and transpires between the Lord and the believer's heart; final justification is public and involves a formal declaration of approval for God's people. In simple terms, final justification will officially ratify present justification.

---

6. Deschner, *Wesley's Christology,* 177.

7. For scholarly discussions on Wesley's doctrine of final justification, see Collins, *Theology of John Wesley,* 321–22; Deschner, *Wesley's Christology,* 177–81; Lindström, *Wesley and Sanctification,* 205–15; Oden, *John Wesley's Teachings,* 2:293–98.

8. See also Acts 17:31; Rom. 2:6-11; 2 Cor. 5:10; Rev. 20:11-13.

These teachings form the backbone of Wesley's perspective in the *Explanatory Notes*.⁹ The purpose of final judgment will be twofold: to separate true believers from false professors in the visible church (Matt. 13:28, 45), and to recompense everyone for the good or evil they did while living (2 Cor. 5:10). Therefore, our works will be the primary criterion because a court verdict requires objective evidence. "Your words," says Wesley, "as well as your actions shall be produced in evidence for or against you, to prove whether you was [*sic*] a true believer or not" (Matt. 12:37). Final judgment will be investigative in nature, in order to show who has real justifying faith (Matt. 25:1-13).¹⁰ True believers will be publicly "acquitted," and the rest "condemned" (Matt. 12:37). And the reward and punishment will be equally eternal in duration (Matt. 25:46).

As with present justification, final justification rests on the economic Trinity. As the incarnate Son, Christ will preside as judge. But since the Father and the Son share an "eternal, intimate, indissoluble unity" of the same "divine essence," his judgment will be the same as the Father's (Jn. 5:19, 23). Thus, Christ's verdict will be absolute and irreversible. There will be no court of appeals. At that time, the Son will receive equal honor with the Father (Jn. 5:23). Regarding the works that will be rewarded, Wesley consistently defined them by Paul's statement in Galatians 5:6 (NRSVUE), "faith working through love" (Matt. 25:34; Mk. 9:50; Rev. 20:12). Rejecting the Catholic notion that this verse speaks of love forming justifying faith, Wesley employs it in a Protestant sense to say that since authentic faith generates love to God and neighbor, this love serves as the motivating principle behind good works and holy living. Wesley therefore considers the "wedding garment" to signify Christ's imputed and imparted righteousness (Matt. 22:13; 2 Cor. 5:21).

One of the curiosities of Wesley theology of objective righteousness is that he seldom discussed present and final justification at the same time or in the same scripture text. In most contexts, justification simply means

---

9. Wesley's views on final judgment were also reiterated in the 1758 sermon "The Great Assize" (*Works*, 1:354–75).

10. That the Final Judgment will be investigative in nature is pointed out by Thomas Oden, *John Wesley's Teachings*, 2:293, 296.

present justification. However, there is an exception with his notes on James 2:14-26.

Reconciling Paul and James

One of the more disputed areas of exegesis in Wesley's day is the apparent discrepancy between Paul and James. Whereas Paul taught a believer is "justified by faith apart from works prescribed by the law" (Rom. 3:28 NRSVUE), James stated that believers are "justified by works" and not by faith only (Ja. 2:25). Alan Clifford summarized the historical context by saying that this "apostolic antinomy" had been a "perpetual source of embarrassment since the time of the Reformation."[11] After walking through the various ways the two apostles have been harmonized, Clifford concluded there were in Wesley's day three main interpretations. The Augustinian view was the doctrine of double justification, with the first an infusion of grace in baptism and the second by faith and works. He added that some Protestants modified this with initial justification by faith and final justification by works. The other two schools of thought were the semi-Augustinians who stressed good works as a concomitant to faith and the anti-Augustinians who saw works serving only an evidentiary role in justification.[12]

According to Clifford's three positions, Wesley belonged to the Augustinian camp. This becomes evident in his exegesis of the book of James. It also shows that Wesley felt free to depart from his sources, for neither Bengel, Doddridge, or Guyse endorsed a twofold justification. Wesley began by connecting James 2:14-16 to 1:22 and concluded that believers must be "doers of the word, not hearers only, deceiving yourselves." Wesley therefore understood James to be addressing a situation where some in the church were abusing Paul's teaching and using it to excuse their sinful living. In other words, James was opposing antinomianism; the same problem confronting Wesley in his day. In a nutshell, Wesley saw no disagreement between Paul and James; for both teach the same doctrine of justification but are confronting different errors.

---

11. Clifford, *Atonement and Justification*, 221.

12. Clifford, *Atonement and Justification*, 226.

The central issue facing Paul was the Jewish notion of justification by works of the law, whereas for James it was heretical Christian belief in salvation apart from good works. Addressing their different contexts, Wesley explained that Paul spoke of "true, living faith"; James of "dead, imaginary faith" (2:14, 24). Paul dealt with "works antecedent to faith; St. James, of works subsequent to faith" (2:24). Wesley then clarified, "Works do not give life to faith, but faith begets works, and then is perfected by them" (2:22). This is seen in the story of Abraham. Paul looked to Genesis 15 when God declared Abraham righteous for his faith and James to Genesis 22 when Abraham demonstrated his faith by obeying God's command. Wesley elaborated on the two aspects of justification:

> He [Abraham] was justified, therefore, in St. Paul's sense, (that is, *accounted* righteous,) by faith, antecedent to his works. He was justified in St. James's sense, (that is, *made* righteous,) by works, consequent to his faith. So that St. James's justification by works is the fruit of St. Paul's justification by faith.[13]

This led Wesley to conclude, "Abraham returned from the sacrifice [of Isaac] perfected in faith, and far higher in the favour of God" (Ja. 2:22).[14] For many Protestants, back then as well as today, the concept of degrees in God's favor contradicts their notion of justification as complete and finished at initial faith. Wesley, however, understood full justification to include being "made righteous" as well as being "accounted righteous." The concept of degrees is inherent in his understanding of objective righteousness as divine favor. It also follows logically from his views on salvation by faith and works.

Conversion of Cornelius

The story of Cornelius in Acts 10 played a significant role in the development of Wesley's mature doctrine of justification.[15] For some

---

13. *ENNT,* Ja. 2:21, emphasis mine.

14. In his 1765 preface to John Goodwin's *Treatise on Justification,* Wesley acknowledged "there may be as many degrees in the favour as in the image of God" (*Works,* Jackson, 10:320).

15. One of the more thorough studies on Cornelius's conversion in Wesley's soteriology is Stanley Rodes, *From Faith to Faith,* 110–32.

background, Cornelius had been referenced by Wesley on three prior occasions as an archetype of the responsive unregenerate.[16] First, during the Stillness Controversy Wesley appealed to Cornelius to show that even unbelievers who sincerely practice the means of grace receive favor from God.[17] In 1745 Cornelius serves as an example of those exceptions to the rule that justification is always associated with perceptible assurance. At the time Wesley and the Conference recognized that Cornelius was already in the favor of God before he believed in Christ.[18] Then, in 1747 Wesley distinguished between "justifying faith" and "the proper Christian faith." As we saw in the last chapter, the former category involves a deliverance from God's wrath and servile fear, but lacks the perceptible assurance associated with the new birth and "the proper Christian faith." Notably, Cornelius is listed as an example of this lower degree of "justifying faith." This background provides context for his comments on Acts 10.

In his opening remarks, Wesley argued for preparationism by rejecting the idea that all religious piety and works prior to faith in Christ are nothing more than "splendid sins" or an "abomination before God." He instead made the point that everyone who "seeks faith in Christ should seek it in prayer and doing good to all men" (Acts 10:4). Although, "in the Christian sense, Cornelius was then an unbeliever" because "he had not then faith in Christ," his religious piety and good works became a "memorial before God" and this led to an angel being sent to guide him to "full Christian salvation" (Acts 10:4; 11:14). Behind these remarks was Wesley's doctrine of prevenient grace and the principle that responsiveness to grace leads to more grace.

Wesley's Arminianism is evident at verse 34 when he states that God is "not partial in his love . . . and willeth all men should be saved." This leads to the key passage in verse 35, which is worth quoting in full:

> *But in every nation he that feareth him, and worketh righteousness*—He that first reverences God, as great, wise, good; the Cause, End, and Governor

---

16. The responsive unregenerate refers to a person who had not yet heard the gospel, and therefore is not a Christian, and yet is responsive to God and his truth as far as they know it.

17. *Journal*, June 25, 1740 (*Works*, 19:158).

18. Conference 1745 (*Works*, 10:150).

of all things; and, secondly, from this awful regard to him, not only avoids all known evil, but endeavours, according to the best light he has, to do all things well. *Is accepted of him*—Through Christ, though he knows him not. The assertion is express, and admits of no exception. He is in the favour of God, whether enjoying his written word and ordinances or not. Nevertheless, the addition of these is an unspeakable blessing to those who were before, in some measure, accepted; otherwise, God would never have sent an angel from heaven to direct Cornelius to St. Peter.

We need to unpack what Wesley says here. Prior to his evangelical conversion to "full Christian salvation" (Acts 11:14), Cornelius was already in the "favour of God" and "in some measure, accepted." Given that "favour" and "acceptance" are standard terms for justification in Wesley's theology, his comment suggests there is a degree of justification for the responsive unregenerate. Regarding the "measure" of Cornelius's acceptance, Wesley's letter to his brother Charles nine years prior gives us a clue to its meaning. As we noted before, Wesley appealed to Cornelius as an example of that "justifying faith" that delivers from God's future wrath. This was Cornelius's "measure" of acceptance, even though he was personally unaware of it. He then heard the message of gospel salvation from Peter and believed in Christ for present justification (Acts 10:44). According to Wesley, the story of Cornelius represents a temporal reversal in the order by which present and final justification are normally received. Even though present justification precedes final justification in Wesley's evangelical *ordo salutis* (baptism—present justification—sanctification—final justification—eternal glory), Peter's statement in Acts 10:35 signifies that a proleptic declaration of final justification can take place in the divine court *before* a person receives present justification and its gift of perceptible assurance.

Furthermore, Peter's declaration in Acts 10:35 became a baseline for Wesley's inclusivism. Stanley Rodes noted that Wesley appealed to Acts 10:35 to "rebuff the onslaught of antinomianism" that he saw within the Moravian and Calvinist camps. He added that Wesley perceived in Acts 10:35 a "soteriological standard found throughout Scripture," which he linked to texts like Isaiah 1:16 ("cease to do evil; learn to do good" [NRSVUE]), Deuteronomy 13:4 ("walk after the LORD your God, and fear him, and keep his commandments"), Ecclesiastes 12:13 ("Fear God, and keep his commandments"), and Job 2:3 ("feareth God, and esceweth evil").[19] Then, in December 1767 Wesley pronounced that clear conceptions of Christ's imputed righteousness and gospel justification are not necessary for final salvation. In response, he called for a "return to the plain word, 'He that feareth God, and worketh righteousness, is accepted with him.'"[20] In the next chapter we will return to Wesley's use of Acts 10:35 to examine the fate of Jews and Muslims, and his use of the servant/son metaphor, but already we see that by the 1750s his concept of degrees had developed to include the responsive unregenerate.

Treatise on Baptism

In the 1750s Wesley published three tracts on baptism.[21] The first is a short extract of three authors that he titled *Thoughts on Infant Baptism*.[22] The tract was an apology for the Church of England's practice of infant baptism. Released in 1751, Wesley followed the next year with *Serious Thoughts on Godfathers and Godmothers*, in which he appealed to the Methodists to serve as godparents. Feeling the need for a more comprehensive treatment, four years later Wesley produced an extract of his father's pamphlet on baptism published in 1700. Titled *A Treatise on Baptism*, the extract was published two years later as part of the larger work *A Preservative against Unsettled Notions of Religion* (1758) and was later included in Wesley's collected *Works* (1771–74).[23]

---

19. Rodes, *From Faith to Faith*, 121.

20. *Journal*, December 1, 1767 (*Works*, 22:114).

21. For a sample of studies on Wesley's theology of baptism, see G. Stephen Blakemore, "John Wesley's 'Evangelical Theology' of Baptism," *WTJ* 31, no. 2 (Fall 1996): 167–91; Borgen, *John Wesley on the Sacraments*; Hammond, *John Wesley in America*; Bernard Holland, *Baptism in Early Methodism* (London: Epworth Press, 1970); Knight, *The Presence of God in the Christian Life*; and David Ingersoll Naglee, *From Font to Faith: John Wesley on Infant Baptism and the Nurture of Children* (New York: Peter Lang, 1987).

22. The authors were Richard Baxter, William Wall, and Isaac Watts (*Works*, 14:252).

23. Maddox informs us that Wesley initially wrote the *Treatise on Baptism* as a manuscript and later slightly edited it for publication in *A Preservative against Unsettled Notions* (*Works*, 14:278). The manuscript version can be found in Albert Outler's *John Wesley*, 317–31, or see the footnotes in *Works*, 14:279–94.

Albert Outler reiterated that the "obvious purpose" of the extract was to "re-enforce the wavering convictions of some of the Methodist people as to the validity of infant baptism and to re-emphasize the objectivity of divine grace in this sacrament."[24] So universal was the practice of infant baptism in early Modern England that the BCP did not include a baptismal rite for adults until the Restoration of 1660. Since many people born during the Commonwealth had not been baptized, there was a need for an adult baptismal rite to be added to the 1662 edition.[25] By Wesley's day the practice of infant baptism remained practically universal in the established church, which we saw comprised around ninety percent of the population. Even so, the validity of paedo-baptism was raised by the Evangelical Revival's emphasis on adult conversion as authentic Christian faith. This explains why in the *Treatise on Baptism* Wesley dealt directly with infant and not adult baptism.[26]

Baptismal Justification

Justification is addressed in the section on benefits. Five benefits are listed by Wesley, the first being "washing away the guilt of original sin, by the application of the merits of Christ's death."[27] He then proceeded to show that this was the teaching of the Anglican Church in her Articles and BCP and that infants are proper subjects of baptism since they inherit death due to Adam's sin. Other related benefits include inclusion in the "covenant with God," admittance into the church as "mystically united to Christ," regeneration by being "born again of water and of the Spirit" (Jn. 3:5), and "title to, and an earnest of" the eternal kingdom.[28] Taken

---

24. Outler, *John Wesley*, 318.

25. Buchanan, *Historical Dictionary of Anglicanism*, 90–91.

26. Throughout the extract the discussion is solely about the baptism of infants and small children. Wesley opens section 4 by stating that this is the "grand question" (*Works*, 14:285). Another clue is found in that Wesley discusses pardon for the guilt of original sin, but not for actual sin. The latter pertains only to adult baptism. The fact he never discusses it shows where his real concern lies with the tract.

27. *Treatise on Baptism* II.1 (*Works*, 14:281).

28. *Treatise on Baptism* II.2–5 (*Works*, 14:283–84).

together, these five benefits include *pardon* for inherited guilt, *acceptance* into God's covenant people, *favor* of divine approval, and *title* to the eternal kingdom. Given the sacramental efficacy of baptism coupled with the widespread practice of infant baptism, Wesley's assertion that baptism is the "ordinary instrument of our justification" makes sense.[29] It also expressed a mainstream view in the Anglican tradition.[30]

Two questions immediately arise. First, how do we reconcile his views in the *Treatise on Baptism* with those found in the sermon "The New Birth," published around the same time? Second, how should we interpret Wesley's statements on baptismal justification in relation to his views on prevenient grace? Beginning with the first question, scholars have been divided over Wesley's views on baptismal regeneration. Some conclude from the *Treatise* that he continued to support it while others draw from the sermon that he denied it.[31] The best path forward is to note the central topic of each document. The *Treatise* deals with infant baptism, whereas the sermon focuses on adult baptism. In the sermon Wesley distinguished between baptism and regeneration by stating that "baptism is not the new birth."[32] He explained that the Church of England does not confuse or conflate the two. Baptism is the "outward and sensible sign," while the new birth is the "thing signified."[33] Wesley further noted that the new birth does not "always accompany baptism; they do not constantly go together." For a person may be "born of water" and not yet "born of the Spirit."[34]

---

29. *Treatise on Baptism* II.1 (*Works*, 14:282).

30. Olson, "The New Birth in the Early Wesley," *WTJ* 52, no. 1 (2017): 81, 83.

31. For a range of views, see Bernard Holland, *Baptism in Early Methodism*; Borgen, *John Wesley on the Sacraments*, 121–82; Collins, *Theology of John Wesley*, 262–65; Knight, *The Presence of God in the Christian Life*, 178–91; Maddox, *Responsible Grace*, 221–25; Maddox and Vickers, eds., *Cambridge Companion to John Wesley*, 239–40, 306–7; Sean McGever, *Born Again: The Evangelical Theology of Conversion in John Wesley and George Whitefield* (Bellingham: Lexham Press, 2020), 61–77.

32. *The New Birth* IV.1 (*Works*, 2:196).

33. *The New Birth* IV.1 (*Works*, 2:196).

34. *The New Birth* IV.2 (*Works*, 2:197).

Even though adult baptism and regeneration do not *always* go together, Ole Borgen was correct that "they go together *most of the time.*"[35] As for exceptions, while in the *Treatise* Wesley affirmed that "baptism doth now save us," he added the conditions "if we live answerable thereto; if we repent, believe, and obey the gospel."[36] In relation to adults, then, baptism conveys justifying and regenerating grace if the person repents and believes.[37] For infants the infusion of grace in baptism remains until lost due to "long-continued wickedness," reflecting an unrepentant attitude.[38] In chapter 2 we saw that by the early 1730s Wesley adopted the position of William Law that very few members of the established church retain their baptismal washing. Consequently, most baptized Anglicans had a nominal faith and needed spiritual rebirth. On several occasions Wesley emphasized this point. For example:

> I tell a sinner, "You must be born again." "No," say you, "He was born again in baptism. Therefore he cannot be born again now." Alas! What trifling is this? What if he was *then* a child of God? He is *now* manifestly a "child of the devil!"[39]

In the end, Wesley's views in the *Treatise on Baptism* and *The New Birth* are consistent and complementary. Taken together, they express his full thoughts on sacramental justification in relation to present evangelical justification. As for infants, sacramental justification involves pardon from original sin, but not for actual sin since they are not yet responsible moral agents.[40] Later, they will need to believe in Christ to receive evangelical justification. This is true whether they retain or lose their baptismal washing. The case with adults is more nuanced. Those adults who are

---

35. Borgen, *John Wesley on the Sacraments*, 155, emphasis his.

36. *Treatise on Baptism* II.5 (*Works*, 14:284).

37. See Wesley's remarks on the different spiritual states of five adults he baptized on January 25, 1739 (*Works*, 19:32). Their degree of repentance and faith was an essential part of his assessment of the efficacy of their baptism.

38. *Treatise on Baptism* II.4 (*Works*, 14:283–84). Wesley makes the same point in *A Farther Appeal to Men of Reason and Religion*, part I, I.5 (*Works*, 11:107).

39. *Farther Appeal*, part I, I.5 (*Works*, 11:107, emphasis his).

40. Wesley states infants are not yet guilty of actual sin, *Treatise* II.1 (*Works*, 14:282).

unconverted and remain so after their baptism, the sacrament conveys no justifying grace. To those adults who experience evangelical conversion at their baptism, they receive both sacramental and evangelical justification. For those adults who were first converted and later baptized, sacramental justification becomes a "sign and seal" of their present justification, as it was for Cornelius in Acts 10.[41] What made these latter cases exceptional to Wesley was that baptism does not actually confer justification and instead serves as a sign or witness of their acceptance received prior to their baptism. To recap, in Wesley's *ordo salutis* present justification can take place *before*, at the *same time*, or *after* baptism, depending on a person's level of moral agency and their spiritual state.

The second issue concerns how best to interpret Wesley's statements on baptismal justification in relation to his remarks on prevenient grace. Even though we will return to this subject in the next chapter, his current views are worth noting. In the *Treatise* Wesley argued from Romans 5:12-19 and Ephesians 2:3 that infants inherit the guilt of original sin and are therefore "children of wrath" and "liable to eternal damnation."[42] Following the teaching of the Anglican Church that reached back to Augustine, Wesley concluded that "in the ordinary way, they cannot be saved, unless this [guilt] be washed away by baptism."[43] So, for Wesley baptism is the "ordinary" means appointed by God to remove the stain of inherited guilt.

Wesley's other view is found in an often-quoted stanza, first published in *Hymns and Sacred Poems* in 1740:

> No dire decree obtain'd Thy seal,
> Or fix
> d the' unalterable doom,
> Consign'd my unborn soul to hell,
> Or damn'd me from my mother's womb.[44]

---

41. Wesley, *The New Birth* IV.1 (*Works*, 2:196).

42. Wesley, *Treatise on Baptism* II.1; IV.2 (*Works*, 14:282, 285–86).

43. Wesley, *Treatise on Baptism* IV.2 (*Works*, 14:286).

44. George Osborn, ed., *The Poetical Works of John and Charles Wesley*, 13 vols. (London: Wesleyan-Methodist Conference Office, 1868–72), 3:33.

The stanza expresses Wesley's opposition to the Reformed doctrine of unconditional reprobation. The last two lines are quoted with slight variation on several occasions, including *Explanatory Notes*, Matthew 20:15 (1755), his response to the Calvinists James Hervey (1756) and Richard Hill (1772), and in his sermon "The Important Question" (1775).[45] The stanza clearly represents Wesley's position that no "unborn soul" will perish due to divine decree.

The interpretive question is how to harmonize these apparently opposing statements found in the stanza and the *Tract on Baptism*. As he often did, Wesley left both statements to stand in tension without fully explaining his thoughts. And, once again, scholars have offered a range of solutions.[46] A possible way forward is with Wesley's qualification that baptism is the *ordinary* means of washing away inherited guilt. His comment bears quoting in full:

> It is true, the Second Adam has found a remedy for the disease which came upon all by the offence of the first. But the benefit of this is to be received through the means which he hath appointed; through baptism in particular, which is the ordinary means he hath appointed for that purpose; and to which God hath tied us, though he may not have tied himself. Indeed, where it cannot be had, the case is different, but extraordinary cases do not make void a standing rule.[47]

The "standing rule" is for pardon of inherited guilt to be received in baptism, since it is the means "appointed for that purpose," and for those to whom it is available "God hath tied us" to this means of grace. However, God is not "tied" to the ordinances and is free in "extraordinary cases" to show mercy. This is because of universal redemption: Christ's death provided a "remedy for the disease which came upon all [people]." As Wesley told the Baptist Gilbert Boyce, "You think the mode of baptism is 'necessary for salvation.' I deny that even baptism itself is so. If it

---

45. The last three examples are found in *Works*, 3:188; 13:342, 439.
46. On the range of scholarly opinions, see Maddox, *Responsible Grace*, 221–25.
47. Wesley, *Treatise on Baptism* IV.2 (*Works*, 14:286).

were, every Quaker must be damned, which I can in no wise believe."⁴⁸ It is therefore best to take Wesley's statements in the *Treatise* as a "standing rule" and to allow exceptions based on circumstances and a person's spiritual state. One of those exceptions is that no "unborn soul" will perish simply because of divine decree. We will return to this subject in the next chapter when we examine his mature thoughts in the *Sunday Service of the Methodists in North America*.

Degrees of Justification

At this point, it would be good to pause and digest our findings thus far on degrees of justification. The complexity of Wesley's theology of objective righteousness calls for nuance and careful exegesis. Broad brushstrokes can easily lead to misinterpretation. Yet, there is value in summarizing our findings for the sake of clarity. On several occasions Wesley acknowledged the fact of degrees, as when he responded to James Hervey's claim that justification is complete at initial faith. "Not so," replied Wesley. "There may be as many degrees in the favour of as in the image of God."⁴⁹

So far, we have seen there are *five degrees* of justification based on the above material and Wesley's 1747 letter to his brother Charles.⁵⁰ These five degrees are identified by Wesley in light of his eighteenth-century religious context that consisted of a vast majority of baptized Anglicans, a minority of Catholics and Nonconformists (except outside of England these groups were often in the majority), a smattering of Jews, and through the expanding British Empire an awareness of the Muslim and heathen worlds.⁵¹ If we plot these five degrees on a trajectory that aligns with Wesley's evangelical *ordo salutis*, they fall in the following order: (1) *measure of acceptance* for the responsive unregenerate, (2) *sacramental justification* for baptized infants (usually lost before adulthood), (3) *justifying faith* for Christians who lack the Spirit's testimony, (4) *present or evangelical justification* for

---

48. Wesley, Letter, May 22, 1750 (*Works*, 26:425).
49. Wesley, *A Letter to the Rev. Mr. James Hervey*, October 15, 1756 (*Works*, 13:326).
50. Wesley, Letter to Charles Wesley, July 31, 1747 (*Works*, 26:254–55). See chapter 3.
51. See chapter 1.

those who have "the proper Christian faith," and (5) *final justification* at the Last Judgment.

From the above discussion the reader will quickly see that the lines between these five degrees can be fuzzy and at times overlap or conflate.[52] Nor is this the end of the story, for Wesley continues to discuss the subject of degrees over the next several decades. Still, when discussing the subject, he nearly always assumed *present* justification. He rarely if ever added an adjective, like "present" or "evangelical," to identify this or any other degree of justification. The reason for this assumption is that present justification is a core element of the evangelical gospel of salvation by faith in Christ alone. There is no real Christianity without it. Even so, the concept of degrees remained crucial to how Wesley would nuance his position when discussing the spiritual condition of various people or when embroiled in controversy, like the one he had with James Hervey.

Imputed Righteousness Controversy

James Hervey (d. 1758) was eleven years Wesley's junior and was tutored by him in Hebrew at Oxford. Along with George Whitefield, Hervey joined the Oxford Methodists in 1733 and later adopted a thoroughly Calvinist creed as an evangelical. Yet, he resolved to serve as a parish priest in the established church with currencies in several locations. Even though Hervey was a Calvinist, he remained personal friends with Wesley. Kenneth Collins suggested that Hervey's attraction to Calvinism was largely due to its teaching on the imputation of Christ's active righteousness as the formal cause of justification.[53] By the eighteenth century most evangelical Arminians, like Wesley, were drawn to the views of seventeenth-century moderate Calvinists, namely Richard Baxter and John Goodwin, while evangelical Calvinists, like Hervey, were attracted to the positions of high Calvinists, such as Theodore Beza and John Owen.

---

52. An example of conflation was already pointed out. For adults who are evangelically converted at their baptism, sacramental and present justification form a single event in their Christian experience.

53. *Works*, 13:219. On formal cause, see chapter 1, footnote 22.

Historical Context[54]

Hervey was a popular writer and in 1755 released *Theron and Aspasio*, a large work that narrates in a series of dialogues and letters the conversion of Theron from a typical nominal Anglican faith to Aspasio's Calvinistic evangelical faith. In this work the imputation of Christ's active righteousness forms the heart of the evangelical gospel. Hervey sent a draft of the opening chapters to Wesley in which he offered a few corrections. Hervey responded by asking Wesley to be more direct and specific. Wesley then wrote a more thorough letter. When *Theron and Aspasio* was published, Wesley noticed that his recommendations went unheeded. So, he wrote to Hervey again freely expressing his disapproval. Not hearing back, Wesley wrote a fourth letter in which he challenged Hervey's views regarding the imputation of Christ's active righteousness. He furthermore accused Hervey of antinomianism, though Hervey himself was a devout Christian. When he did not receive a response after two years, Wesley published this fourth letter as part of a larger work, *A Preservative against Unsettled Notions in Religion* (1758).

In reaction, several of Hervey's colleagues joined the controversy. In one case, Wesley felt compelled to correct William Mason's misrepresentation of his views with the tract *Thoughts on the Imputed Righteousness of Christ* (1762). Hervey's reaction was reserved. Before he died on Christmas Day in 1758, Hervey had penned a series of letters to Wesley defending his position, but never sent them. Leaving instructions for them not to be published, an associate of Hervey issued the *Eleven Letters* in 1764 that called for a response from Wesley.[55] Over the next two years Wesley published two major works on Christ's imputed righteousness. The first was a *Treatise on Justification* by the moderate Calvinist John Goodwin. Goodwin's sole focus was to refute the high Calvinist notion of justification by the imputation of Christ's active righteousness. Second, Wesley

---

54. Wesley rehearsed the series of events in the preface to *A Treatise on Justification, Extracted from Mr. John Goodwin* 2–4 (*Works*, 13:377–80). See also Collins's remarks in *Works*, 13:219–22.

55. James Hervey, *Aspasio Vindicated*.

published the sermon "The Lord Our Righteousness" in which he spells out his settled thoughts on the subject.

Before we proceed, several areas of agreement should be noted. As Anglican ministers, both Hervey and Wesley endorsed their Church's Articles, *Homilies*, and liturgy. Both understood justification within a framework of covenant theology and affirmed the imputation of Adam's sin, including its guilt and total depravity. They both believed in salvation by grace alone and taught the penal substitution theory of the atonement. The idea of salvation by works was firmly rejected by both, as well as the notion of good works prior to present justification. And they both believed in the necessity of Christ's imputed righteousness for justification.

This last point was where their Arminian and Calvinist systems parted ways. For Hervey, justification is complete and finished at initial faith in Christ. He could assert this because he interpreted the scriptures and Anglican doctrinal statements to say that a legal standing of perfect righteousness is reckoned to a believer by the imputation of Christ's active righteousness. While Hervey believed in the imputation of Christ's passive righteousness for forgiveness of sin, he reiterated over and over in *Theron and Aspasio*, and even more forcefully in his *Eleven Letters*, that the essence of justification is the imputation of Christ's active righteousness. Apart from this there is no objective righteousness before God that secures eternal life. These ideas flow from his Calvinistic views of absolute election, limited atonement, and irresistible grace.

For Wesley this smacked of antinomianism. Instead of Hervey's eternal decrees, he understood Christ's death to have merited a general purchase of acceptance and favor for anyone who trusts in Christ. The purpose of Jesus's sinless obedience was to qualify him to serve as the Passover lamb, not to be a substitute for obedience in the life of a Christian. All of this was consonant with his doctrine of double justification. In addition, Wesley interpreted the scriptures and the church's doctrinal statements through the lens of his High Church Arminianism. This meant that Hervey and Wesley read the same scriptures and the same doctrinal statements and came to polar positions regarding Christ's imputed righteousness. With this introduction we can now look at how Wesley responded to Hervey's claims.

Wesley's Letter to Hervey

In his fourth letter Wesley works through the dialogues and letters of *Theron and Aspasio*, often commending Hervey for his "just and strong observations."[56] However, he thought his longtime friend had gone too far with his assertions about Christ's active righteousness. On this point three recurring themes stand out. First, Wesley reminded Hervey that the phrase "the imputed righteousness of Christ" is not scriptural and therefore not necessary for saving faith.[57] To clarify, Wesley acknowledged that scripture teaches the imputation of Christ's passive righteousness.[58] So, his real concern was not with the imputation doctrine, but with Hervey's preoccupation with Christ's active righteousness. When Hervey at one point agreed that Christ's death procures pardon and acceptance, Wesley's response was telling, "Why should we contend for anything more?"[59] He then pointed to the many repentant sinners who have "never heard" of the expression yet find salvation in the merits of Christ. Besides, the phrase "has done immense hurt" by encouraging converts to become "satisfied without any holiness at all" in their lives.[60] From Wesley's perspective, Hervey's gospel was antinomian for it made the law void and "thousands content to live and die 'transgressors of the law,' because Christ fulfilled it for them."[61]

A second observation is that Hervey had separated Christ's active from his passive righteousness.[62] He did this to stress the imputation of Christ's sinless obedience as the formal cause of justification. Wesley's response was

---

56. Wesley, *A Letter to the Rev. Mr. Hervey* (*Works*, 13:323, 327, 328).
57. Wesley, *Letter to Hervey* (*Works*, 13:323–24, 325, 327–28, 335).
58. Wesley, *Letter to Hervey* (*Works*, 13:324, 334).
59. Wesley, *Letter to Hervey* (*Works*, 13:324).
60. Wesley, *Letter to Hervey* (*Works*, 13:324, 326).
61. Wesley, *Letter to Hervey* (*Works*, 13:338).
62. Wesley, *Letter to Hervey* (*Works*, 13:324).

that "Christ lived and 'tasted death for every man.' And through the merits of his life and death, every believer is justified."[63] By keeping Christ's obedience linked to his passion, Wesley could maintain that they form a single work and together are the one "foundation of our justification."[64] On a related point, when Hervey asserted that Christ's sufferings did not satisfy the law, Wesley countered that they did, for the law "required only the alternative: obey or die. It required no man to obey and die too."[65] He therefore stressed Christ's death as the meritorious or procuring cause of redemption. As he told Hervey, "'Christ by his death alone' (so our Church teaches) 'fully satisfied for the sins of the whole world.'"[66]

The separation of Christ's active and passive righteousness also led Wesley to reject Hervey's definition of justifying faith. When Hervey explained that faith is a "persuasion that Christ shed his blood for me, and fulfilled all righteousness in my stead," Wesley appealed to the experience of converts, "There are hundreds, yea thousands, of true believers who never once thought one way or the other of Christ fulfilling all righteousness in their stead."[67] Again, to Hervey's point that faith in Christ's imputed righteousness is a "fundamental principle of the gospel," Wesley countered with two questions, "If so, what becomes of all those who think nothing about imputed righteousness? How many who are full of faith and love, if this be true, must perish everlastingly?"[68] As Wesley saw it, justifying faith does not require doctrinal precision, but a right disposition of the heart. In the end, he believed that Hervey required a kind of faith for salvation that went beyond scripture, the teachings of the church, and Christian experience. It therefore was contrary to reason itself.

The same year Wesley published his letter to Hervey in *Preservative against Unsettled Notions in Religion,* he addressed another stumbling block that Calvinists had with his justification doctrine. In his *Letter to*

---

63. Wesley, *Letter to Hervey* (*Works,* 13:325).
64. Wesley, *Letter to Hervey* (*Works,* 13:328).
65. Wesley, *Letter to Hervey* (*Works,* 13:330).
66. Wesley, *Letter to Hervey* (*Works,* 13:332).
67. Wesley, *Letter to Hervey* (*Works,* 13:341).
68. Wesley, *Letter to Hervey* (*Works,* 13:341).

a Gentleman at Bristol (1758), Wesley clarified to Hervey's friend William Romaine the distinction between *condition* and *merit*. In chapter 1 we saw how the Anglican doctrine of double justification rests on this distinction to avoid the pitfalls of Catholicism. Wesley explained to Romaine that a condition is "neither more or less than something *sine quâ non—without which* something else is not done."[69] By contrast, merit means to "deserve" salvation.[70] By maintaining a clear distinction between condition and merit, Wesley not only steered clear of the shoals of Catholicism but he also declared in Protestant fashion that present justification is by faith alone. Even with these clarifications many Calvinists suspected Wesley to be a closet Catholic.[71] As we will see in the next chapter, the distinction between condition and merit will play a major role in the Minutes Controversy.

Treatise on Justification

When Hervey's *Eleven Letters* appeared in 1764, Wesley knew he had to respond in kind.[72] Hervey had written a detailed biblical and theological argument that ran for nearly three hundred pages, so Wesley turned to a work by the moderate Calvinist John Goodwin. First published in 1642, Goodwin's *Imputatio Fidei, or A Treatise of Justification* was a sustained biblical and theological argument that matched Hervey's effort.[73] The monograph consists of two parts, with the first presenting arguments for the Arminian/moderate Calvinist position on Christ's imputed righteousness, and the second a point-by-point rebuttal of the high Calvinist

---

69. Wesley, *A Letter to a Gentleman at Bristol* (*Works*, 13:361).

70. Wesley, *Letter to a Gentleman at Bristol* (*Works*, 13:363).

71. On this point, see Albert Outler's introductory remarks to *The Lord Our Righteousness* (*Works*, 1:445–46).

72. James Hervey, *Aspasio Vindicated, and the Scripture-Doctrine of Imputed Righteousness Defended against the Objections and Animadversions of the Rev. Mr. John Wesley, in Eleven Letters* (Leeds: Griffin Wright, 1764).

73. John Goodwin, *Imputatio Fidei, or A Treatise of Justification wherein ye imputation of faith for righteousness is explained . . .* (London: Andrew Crooke, 1642). Quotations in this study from the *Imputatio Fidei* are from Wesley's extract.

viewpoint. In addition, throughout the entire work Goodwin claimed the support of Luther, Calvin, and other Reformed authorities, which served Wesley's purpose of showing the Calvinists that his stance on justification was consistent with the Protestant Reformation's position. Wesley's extract is titled *A Treatise on Justification* and includes for the most part only minor revisions of the original text for the sake of clarity.[74] The preface includes his letter to Mr. Hervey, plus an extended response to the personal attacks in the *Eleven Letters*. Wesley let Goodwin do the heavy lifting for the Arminian cause. The following summary is from Wesley's extract of Goodwin.

Goodwin began by showing gospel justification to be the remittance of guilt and punishment for transgressions of the divine law. It therefore cannot be justification by the law, "because the law knows no forgiveness of sin."[75] Instead, justification is free pardon through the merits of Christ's righteousness. Goodwin does not deny the doctrine of imputation, just the high Calvinist version of it. On Paul's statement that faith is imputed for righteousness (Rom. 3–4), Goodwin exegetically showed that these scriptures speak of faith as the sole condition for justification and not of the imputation of Christ's active righteousness. As the instrumental cause, faith is the "true way" for people to "attain righteousness before God."[76] Goodwin went for the jugular when he argued that justification by the imputation of Christ's personal obedience is just another form of salvation by works. "For if a man be justified by the righteousness of Christ imputed to him, he is justified by works of the law, because that righteousness of Christ consists of those works."[77] Whether Calvinists realized it or not, they were espousing a system of salvation by works, which Paul in Romans 3:20 denies as possible under the gospel.[78] As for the phrase "the righteousness of God" (Rom. 3:21), Goodwin explained that it refers

---

74. Wesley, *A Treatise on Justification* (Bristol: William Pine, 1765).
75. Wesley, *Treatise on Justification*, 2.
76. Wesley, *Treatise on Justification*, 11.
77. Wesley, *Treatise on Justification*, 27.
78. Wesley, *Treatise on Justification*, 27–32.

to God as the source and giver of that righteousness which is by faith.[79] Then in chapter 5 Goodwin showed that the high Calvinist distinction between Christ's active and passive righteousness inverts the *ordo justificationis* since Christ obeyed *before* he suffered and died. Therefore, in the Calvinist scheme the sinner should be reckoned as satisfying the law with perfect obedience before being granted forgiveness. This however makes forgiveness unnecessary since the Christian would already be legally sinless.[80] For the next several chapters Goodwin presented about two dozen arguments against the high Calvinist notion of imputation.

All these points countered Hervey's claim that the imputation of Christ's active righteousness is the formal cause of justification. But Wesley included Goodwin's discussion on causation in his extract. Regarding the different types of causation, Goodwin explained that the Holy Trinity serves as the efficient cause, the infinite love and goodness of God the moral cause, the death of Christ the meritorious cause, and the believer's faith the instrumental cause.[81] There was not much debate among the different parties about these causations, yet about formal cause Goodwin rejected the Calvinist view that stressed the imputation of Christ's sinless obedience. For this suggested the justified believer "may lawfully be reputed never to have sinned." This was so "notorious an untruth" that Goodwin proposed forgiveness and pardon as the formal cause.[82]

He then gave six arguments in support. First, remission of sin is the first and immediate act of God whereby he justifies a sinner, therefore it is pardon that makes a person righteous before God. Second, since those forgiven are known as justified, consequently pardon must be the formal cause. Third, absolution from sin's punishment alters a sinner's standing before God. Fourth, forgiveness is what makes a justified person completely righteous before God. Fifth, if remission of sin is a complete righteousness before God, then it is what justifies a sinner. Lastly, since forgiveness and the non-imputation of sin signify the same privilege and standing as

---

79. Wesley, *Treatise on Justification*, 33–34.
80. Wesley, *Treatise on Justification*, 36–37.
81. Wesley, *Treatise on Justification*, 136–42.
82. Wesley, *Treatise on Justification*, 142–43.

a justified person, then the forgiveness of sin serves as the formal cause.[83] In the end, these six arguments ground justification directly on the passive righteousness of Christ. By this Goodwin did not mean that Christ's sinless obedience was not necessary for redemption, for it qualified him to atone for human sin. But it was Christ's passion and death that directly satisfied God's justice and procured divine favor by removing the barrier caused by sin and its punishment.

By publishing Goodwin's work Wesley let it be known where he stood on the question of formal cause. This should have been evident to an observant reader of his many statements over the years. Nevertheless, the controversy with Hervey compelled Wesley to be more explicit on this vital question. Still, we would not want to assume that Wesley agreed with every expression or argument Goodwin made. Wesley was not inclined to use causation language in his descriptions of justification. A possible reason was that it was too philosophical for his liking. He preferred more standard terms—foundation, merit, purchase, and procure—to describe the redemptive work of the cross. There were other small differences between Goodwin and Wesley, and these become evident in Wesley's sermon "The Lord Our Righteousness."

The Lord Our Righteousness

Even though Wesley hoped the publication of Goodwin's *Imputatio Fidei* would "stop the mouths of gainsayers," the controversy did not die down.[84] So, in early 1766 Wesley published his settled thoughts on the subject in the sermon "The Lord Our Righteousness," preached the prior November in Seven-Dials.[85] The preamble opens with Wesley lamenting the divisions among God's people over matters of doctrine, experience, and opinion. He was especially troubled about controversies due to misunderstandings between the parties and felt that people of goodwill should attempt to heal such breaches. In many ways, Wesley felt this described his

---

83. Wesley, *Treatise on Justification*, 145–47.
84. Letter, November 2, 1764 (*Works*, 27:399).
85. "The Lord Our Righteousness" (*Works*, 1:447–65).

recent break with Hervey, who had been a longtime colleague and friend. In good faith Wesley decided to present his views on the controverted subject of Christ's imputed righteousness in hope for better goodwill between the parties.

The sermon contains three sections, though Wesley outlined only two. First, he explained what the righteousness of Christ is. Next, he described when and how Christ's righteousness is imputed. And, lastly, Wesley answered objections to clear up any misunderstandings. In the first section, Christ's divine and human righteousness are distinguished to clarify that it is his human righteousness that is imputed to believers. Regarding Christ's human righteousness, Wesley elaborated on Jesus's internal and external fulfillment of God's law, noting that his obedience includes his willingness to suffer and die as an atonement for sin.[86] Together, these constitute his active and passive righteousness. Here, Wesley departed in expression from Goodwin by stating that since these were "never in fact separated from each other, so we never need separate them at all, either in speaking or even in thinking."[87] This became Wesley's bedrock principle concerning Christ's active and passive righteousness: they must never be separated or treated independent of each other. The doctrine of imputation must keep them bound together as a single work, representing the one righteousness of Christ. A principal objection Wesley had to Hervey's position was that he separated them and thus opened the door to antinomianism.

On the question when Christ's righteousness is imputed, Wesley answered, "It is imputed to everyone that believes, as soon as he believes: faith and the righteousness of Christ are inseparable."[88] This cut against the views of certain hyper-Calvinists who affirmed an eternal justification with their doctrine of decrees. Wesley then counseled that saving faith does not require correct theology on the subject. Believers often disagree regarding language and sentiment over doctrine. His catholic spirit allowed people to have opinions and expressions that are "confused and inaccurate" and still have a heart that cleaves to God "through the Son of

---

86. *The Lord Our Righteousness* I.2–4 (*Works*, 1:452–53).
87. *The Lord Our Righteousness* I.4 (*Works*, 1:453).
88. *The Lord Our Righteousness* II.1 (*Works*, 1:454).

his love."[89] As long as one trusts in the merits of Christ for salvation, they share in his righteousness.[90] When he explained in what sense Christ's righteousness is imputed, Wesley's Arminian convictions stood out:

> "But in what sense is this righteousness imputed to believers?" In this: all believers are forgiven and accepted, not for the sake of anything in them, or of anything that ever was, that is, or even can be done by them, but wholly and solely for the sake of what Christ hath done and suffered for them.[91]

As the meritorious cause of justification, Christ's active and passive righteousness work together to procure forgiveness and acceptance. How this is accomplished is by the sinless Son of God dying to satisfy God's justice, thereby paying the ransom for sinners to be restored to divine favor. Thus, the "*merit* and *deserving* of our justification [belongs] to Christ only."[92] This put Wesley in agreement with Goodwin and in opposition to Hervey regarding formal cause. It also allowed Wesley to maintain his Arminian convictions and proclaim the Reformation doctrine of justification by faith alone.

After this Wesley quoted several of his prior publications to show that this had been his doctrine since 1738. On this point he was not forthright. After all, Wesley did teach an imputation doctrine like Hervey's in the period immediately following his evangelical conversion. In the first quotation, taken from his extract of the Anglican *Homilies*, Wesley removed the phrase stating that Christ fulfilled the law for believers.[93] Likewise, he did not mention that in other places of the extract the imputation of Christ's active righteousness is clearly taught.[94] So, on the matter of imputation

---

89. *The Lord Our Righteousness* II.3 (*Works*, 1:454).

90. *The Lord Our Righteousness* II.4 (*Works*, 1:455).

91. *The Lord Our Righteousness* II.5 (*Works*, 1:455).

92. *The Lord Our Righteousness* II.6, 8 (*Works*, 1:456, 457, italics his).

93. Compare *The Lord Our Righteousness* II.6 to *Doctrine of Salvation, Faith, and Good Works* I.5 (*Works*, 1:456; 13:34).

94. *Doctrine of Salvation, Faith, and Good Works* I.7 (*Works*, 13:34–35).

Wesley's views had changed since 1738 and he ignored this fact in the sermon.

Wesley's response to objections repeats these same points but adds an important qualification. He reaffirmed that "God *implants* righteousness in everyone to who he has *imputed* it."[95] Just as Christ's active and passive righteousness cannot be separated, neither can imputed and implanted righteousness. Those whom God *accounts* as righteous, are then *made* righteous. For everyone who believes in Christ, "God sanctifies, as well as justifies."[96] There is one gospel, one salvation, and one righteousness for which Christ's righteousness is the "whole and sole foundation."[97]

On this point John Deschner offered several insights into Wesley's theology of Christ's active righteousness. Just as Christ's passive righteousness purchased our redemption, so Christ's active righteousness serves as the "proto-type for the progressive conformity to God's righteousness in man."[98] Wesley often described holiness as "having 'the mind which was in Christ' and 'walking as Christ also walked.'"[99] Deschner pointed out that these statements refer to Christ's active righteousness and suggest a connection with the internal work of sanctification. Three points follow. First, Christ's human nature and obedience serve as the pattern for holy living and therefore as the eschatological *imago* that believers are being conformed to.[100] This means that Christ's active righteousness is the alpha and omega of the sanctification process. Second, the "mind which was in Christ" is a phrase that denotes the inward work of regeneration and sanctification.[101] Third, and most important, Wesley understood the renewal process to take place by

---

95. *The Lord Our Righteousness* II.12 (*Works*, 1:458, italics his).

96. *The Lord Our Righteousness* II.12 (*Works*, 1:459).

97. *The Lord Our Righteousness* II.13 (*Works*, 1:459).

98. Deschner, *Wesley's Christology*, 159.

99. Wesley, *A Plain Account of Christian Perfection, as Believed and Taught by the Rev. Mr. John Wesley, from the Year 1725 to 1765* §5 (*Works*, 13:137). Wesley is quoting Phil. 2:5 and 1 Jn. 2:6.

100. *Plain Account of Christian Perfection* §5 (*Works*, 13:137); *ENNT*, Phil. 3:21.

101. *The Scripture Way of Salvation* I.4; III.5 (*Works*, 2:158, 164); *The New Birth* II.5 (*Works*, 2:194); *The Repentance of Believers* III.2 (*Works*, 1:351).

the Spirit implanting in believers the "mind which was in Christ."[102] Thus, sanctification involves Christ's active righteousness becoming the believer's subjective righteousness, thereby preparing them for final justification.

If these insights are valid, there is more to be said about Wesley's understanding of Christ's active and passive righteousness in relation to formal cause. Although Wesley was not fond of the phrase since he never used it in his own writings, the subject is important to plumb the inner workings of his justification doctrine. We saw above that Wesley supported Goodwin's position regarding the forgiveness of sin as the formal cause of present justification. This could be restated that the imputation of Christ's passive righteousness is what makes believers to stand righteous before God in this life. But what about final justification? If Deschner's argument is valid, the implantation of Christ's active righteousness is what serves as its formal cause. For it is by the "mind which was in Christ" being formed in believers that produces the holy life upon which they receive final acquittal at the Last Judgment. All of this suggests that the doctrine of double justification enabled Wesley to avoid the antinomian pitfall of the Calvinists and to underscore both Christ's active and passive righteousness as essential to the Christian's present and final justification.

Justification and Assurance, Part Two

We saw in the last chapter that by 1747 Wesley was distinguishing between two levels of justifying faith. Evangelical faith includes a perceptible assurance of present justification while a lower degree of justifying faith does not. In the 1750s and 1760s Wesley continued to refine his views on degrees of justifying faith.

In an exchange of letters with Richard Tompson, Wesley explained once more his thoughts on these two degrees of saving faith. Evangelical "Christian faith" is equated to "the proper Christian faith" and being a "real Christian."[103] From his remarks it is evident this is the standard

---

102. Wesley at times spoke of feeling the mind of Christ within and being filled with the mind that Christ had while on earth. See *The Witness of Our Own Spirit* §16; *Upon Our Lord's Sermon on the Mount* VIII §4; *Original Sin* III.5 (*Works*, 1:310, 614; 2:185).

103. Letter, July 25, 1756 (*Works*, 26:575).

definition for saving, justifying faith. However, not every believer in Christ feels this assurance of pardon. For these believers, their faith is in-between evangelical faith and the faith of a "devil" (nominal Christian faith) or that of a "heathen" (general belief in God).[104] But Wesley conceded that these believers do have sufficient faith to be admitted to the Lord's Supper. This indicates that he considered this lower degree of justifying faith to be a "kind or degree" of Christian faith, or else admission to the sacrament would have been denied.[105] A decade later, the same point was made when he told Ann Foard that she could marry a person with this lower degree of faith because "such an one is not an unbeliever in the sense wherein that word is taken in 2 Corinthians 6:14."[106]

Wesley's thoughts on this lower degree of justifying faith turned personal in a letter to his brother Charles in June 1766. In a private moment Wesley shared his innermost thoughts about his own spiritual state:

> I do not feel the wrath of God abiding on me; nor can I believe it does. And yet (this is the mystery), I do not love God. I never did. Therefore I never believed, in the Christian sense of the word. Therefore I am only an honest heathen, a proselyte of the Temple, one of the God-fearers; (Acts 13:16) . . . I have no direct witness (I do not say that I am a child of God) but of anything invisible or eternal.[107]

Wesley's heirs have offered a variety of interpretations for what Richard Heitzenrater called an "unusual bearing of his soul."[108] For our purposes this confession opens a window into what he possibly meant

---

104. Letter, July 25, 1755 (*Works*, 26:575). On the categories of the faith of a devil and a heathen, see *Salvation by Faith* I.1–2. The first category refers to a nominal Christian faith and the last to a general, vague knowledge of God. In *Salvation by faith* the next category is the faith of the disciples during Christ's earthly ministry. Wesley's comments to Tompson suggest a link between the disciples' faith and those who have this lower degree of Christian faith.

105. Letter, July 25, 1756 (*Works*, 26:575). See Collins's discussion on these points in *Theology of John Wesley*, 133–34.

106. Letter, April 20, 1767 (*Telford*, 5:45).

107. Letter, June 27, 1766 (*Telford*, 5:16).

108. Heitzenrater, *Wesley and the People Called Methodists*, 251. On interpretations of this letter, see Olson, *John Wesley's Theology of Christian Perfection*, 195–96; Rack, *Reasonable Enthusiast*, 546–50.

by this lower degree of justifying faith. To begin with, Wesley stated he was not under God's wrath, which is one of the marks of this lower degree of justifying faith.[109] He moreover acknowledged the witness of his own spirit by addressing his feelings ("I do not feel . . .").[110] So, Wesley appeared confident about his final justification. But he also claimed to lack a perceptible assurance ("direct witness") associated with evangelical faith. He therefore denied having Christian faith and did not consider himself a child of God. Taken at face value, these statements indicate that Wesley lacked the new birth and present justification. He instead belonged to a category similar to the responsive unregenerate, like Cornelius in Acts 10.[111]

As for the root causes behind sincere Christians (like himself) not enjoying the direct testimony of the Spirit, he suggested to Thomas Rutherford it is "usually owing to either disorder of body, or ignorance of the Gospel promises."[112] Wesley agreed with Tompson (and Rutherford) there is a full assurance of faith that "excludes all doubt." However, there are "lower degrees of faith" that "do not exclude doubt." He then pointed to the frailty of human nature as a general cause, by referring to himself: "*I believe feebly.*"[113] This suggests there was something in Wesley's personality and temperament that led him to have occasional bouts with doubt.[114] The same could be said about many early Methodists who struggled to maintain their assurance of salvation.[115]

Returning to Wesley's letter to his brother, besides the question of how to interpret this confession considering his spiritual journey, the theological implications are revealing as to how he understood this lower degree of

---

109. Letter, July 31, 1747 (*Works,* 26:254–55).

110. *The Witness of the Spirit* I I.1–6 (*Works,* 1:270–73).

111. For more discussion on Wesley's confession, see Olson, *John Wesley's Theology of Christian Perfection,* 194–202.

112. Letter, March 28, 1768 (*Telford,* 5:358, emphasis his).

113. Letter, February 5, 1757 (*Works,* 27:9–10, emphasis his).

114. On Wesley's continuing struggles with doubt over his life, see Olson, *Wesley and Aldersgate,* 12–14, 16–17, 76–81, 94–98.

115. Olson, *Wesley and Aldersgate,* 124–31.

justifying faith. For in two years Wesley will begin to counsel those who have the *faith of a servant* to seek after the *faith of a son*. "He has already given you the faith of a servant," he told Ann Bolton. "You want only the faith of a child."[116] In the next chapter we will see how the servant/son metaphor becomes an important development in Wesley's mature doctrine of justification.

---

116.   Letter, April 7, 1768 (*Telford*, 5:86).

CHAPTER FIVE
THE MINUTES CONTROVERSY AND DEGREES OF JUSTIFICATION: 1770–91

The last twenty years of Wesley's life saw several developments that would define his mature doctrine of justification. The first concerned the role of works in relation to evangelical salvation. From the time of Wesley's spiritual awakening in 1725, he believed "no [one] shall see the Lord" without holiness.[1] Anglican holy living divines had so impressed this truth on the early Wesley that he believed there would be no final justification without good works as the fruit of inward holiness. Even after his evangelical conversion in 1738, Wesley continued to stress the necessity of good works and personal holiness for authentic faith and final justification. To many Calvinists this was Catholicism dressed up in Protestant garb. The issue exploded into a major controversy in the 1770s that led Wesley to refine his position once more.

A second development concerned degrees of justification. In the 1770s Wesley began to employ the concept of dispensations to outline his distinction between two degrees of saving faith: the *faith of a servant* and the *faith of a son*. The concept of dispensations was based on Wesley's federal theology that reached back to his Oxford period and earlier, but

---

1. Heb. 12:14.

now became more explicit through the influence of John Fletcher. In the same manner, Wesley's dispensationalism led him to address the question of final salvation for the responsive unregenerate. And, once again, his reflections on the subject were influenced by Fletcher. The result was a form of inclusivism that grounded final salvation on divine grace made available through the redemptive work of the cross, but experientially defined by the degree of revelation found in the different dispensations of grace.

Another area of development involved Wesley's sacramental theology. Some scholars argue that in his later years Wesley abandoned his High Church views on baptismal justification while maintaining his High Church perspective of the Lord's Supper. The position presented below is that Wesley's sacramentalism remained substantially unchanged and continued to inform his mature understanding of justification. Lastly, a word must be said about the primacy of present, evangelical justification. In 1780 Wesley published a new hymnal for general use in the Methodist societies. The collection of hymns represented a "little body of experimental and practical divinity," and therefore offers insights into how present justification was appropriated into early Methodist spirituality.[2] The chapter closes with a brief look at how present justification informed early Methodist identity and continued to do so over the past two centuries.

1770 Conference Minutes

The doctrinal section at the end of the 1770 Conference Minutes probably represents the most significant statement made by Wesley on justification in the last two decades of his life. First published in the 1770 Annual Minutes, the section was immediately incorporated into the 1770 "Large" or Disciplinary Minutes and reissued another three times during Wesley's lifetime (1772, 1780, and 1789).[3] The same doctrinal section was then included at the head of John Fletcher's *Vindication of the Rev. Mr. Wesley's Minutes*, which was edited and published by Wesley in Au-

---

2. Preface §4, *A Collection of Hymns for the Use of the People Called Methodists* (*Works*, 7:74).

3. *Works* 10:392–94, 908–9, 935. On publication dates for "Large" Minutes, see p. 843.

gust 1771.[4] The *Vindication* would be released another four times during Wesley's life.[5] This makes a total of ten times that these minutes were published, suggesting that Wesley wanted to make these minutes as widely distributed as possible among the Methodists and general public. The importance of the minutes is further seen in that they represent a shift in emphasis on the salvific role of good works. The doctrinal minutes, therefore, require a closer look to ascertain how the mature Wesley understood the relationship between works and justification.

Methodist historians list several precursors to the Minutes Controversy with the Calvinist Evangelicals.[6] Although the dispute with James Hervey appeared to settle down, Hervey's supporters never accepted Wesley's posture toward imputed righteousness. By 1769 a pamphlet war was brewing once more. Augustus Toplady published a work claiming that Calvinism was the true faith of the established church, which prompted a response from Wesley's colleague, Walter Sellon. Attacks on Wesley in the press came from several Calvinist quarters, including supporters of Hervey. By this time Wesley had given up any hope of forming a union with the Calvinists to advance the gospel. He had soured even more on their antinomian piety.[7] The Countess of Huntingdon, a longtime acquaintance of Wesley and a committed Calvinist, recently founded a college at Trevecca to train evangelical ministers. The Methodists John Fletcher and Joseph Benson (d. 1821) served as president and principal, and soon became dissatisfied with Trevecca, prompting Wesley to caution Benson against muttering a word about Christian perfection in the hearing of the

---

4. Jeffrey Wallace, ed., *The Works of John Fletcher*, 4 vols. (Brookfield: Apprehending Truth Publishers, 2011–17), 1:13–70. Wesley made the decision to publish the *Vindication*.

5. Baker, Union Catalog #278B, 140.

6. One of the most thorough discussions of the build-up to the controversy is found in Luke Tyerman, *The Life and Times of the Rev. John Wesley, M.A.*, 3 vols., 6th ed. (Stoke-on-Trent: Tentmaker Publications, 2003), 3:33–100. See also Collins, *John Wesley*, 216–27; Gunter, *Love Divine*, 248–49; Heitzenrater, *Wesley and the People Called Methodists*, 268–69; Rack, *Responsible Enthusiast*, 453–57. Robert Southey spends an entire chapter on the controversy in *The Life of Wesley; and the Rise and Progress of Methodism*, 2 vols., 2nd ed. (London: Longman, Hurst, Rees, Orme, and Brown, 1820), 2:349–94.

7. Heitzenrater, *Wesley and the People Called Methodists*, 268–69; Rack, *Responsible Enthusiast*, 303–4.

Countess.[8] The annual conference in 1770 gave Wesley the perfect platform upon which to engage what he perceived were inherent dangers in the Calvinist gospel.

Leaned Too Much Toward Calvinism

The question that set up Wesley's doctrinal remarks was "What can be done to revive the work of God where it is decayed?"[9] Practical matters were discussed first, like visitation, preaching, corporate fasting, and ministry to children, before turning to the burning issue at hand—"Take heed to your doctrine." Reaching back to the 1744 Conference, Wesley once more claimed the Methodists had "leaned too much toward Calvinism."[10] He then specified three areas where this was happening:

> I. With regard to *man's faithfulness*. Our Lord himself taught us to use the expression. And we ought never to be ashamed of it. We ought steadily to assert it, on his authority, that if a man is not "faithful in the unrighteous mammon," God will not "give him the true riches."
>
> II. With regard to working for life. This also our Lord has expressly commanded us. "Labor"—erazesthe—literally, "work for the meat that endureth to everlasting life." And in fact every believer, till he comes to glory, works for as well as from life.
>
> III. We have received it as a maxim that "a man is to do nothing *in order to* justification." Nothing can be more false. Whoever desire to find favour with God should "cease from evil and learn to do well." Whoever repents should "do works meet for repentance." And if this is not in *order* to find favor, what does he do them for?[11]

---

8. Letter, December 26, 1769 (*Telford*, 5:166).

9. This question is found in the Annual Conference Minutes, 1770, and in the "Large" Minutes for 1770–72. The "Large" Minutes, 1780–89, replace this question with "What is the direct antidote to Methodism, the doctrine of heart-holiness?" The answer is Calvinism (*Works*, 10:934; *Works*, Jackson, 8:336). This change reflects that the Minutes Controversy led Wesley to harden his views on Calvinism.

10. For the 1744 Conference reference, see *Works*, 10:130.

11. Conference Minutes, 1770 Q.28 (*Works*, 10:392–93).

Each proposition countered the antinomian gospel of the Calvinists by appealing to scriptures that stress human response or works as a *condition* for salvation, both present and final. Central to these comments was the High Church distinction between merit and condition. That Wesley was thinking of works as *conditions* of salvation, and not as *meriting* divine favor, becomes evident in the series of eight theses in which he briefly reviewed the entire matter. From Theses #1 and #2 Wesley developed his thought on works as condition and merit over the next several theses:

1. Who of us is *now* accepted of God?

He that now believes in Christ with a loving and obedient heart.

2. But who among those that never heard of Christ?

He that feareth God and worketh righteousness according to the light he has.

3. Is this the same with "he that is sincere"?

Nearly, if not quite.

4. Is not this salvation by works?

Not by the *merit* of works, but by works as a *condition*.

5. What have we, then, been disputing about these thirty years?

I am afraid about words.

6. As to *merit* itself, of which we have been so dreadfully afraid: we are rewarded according to our works, yea, because of our works. How does this differ from *for the sake of our works*? And how differs this from *secundum merita operum*? As our works *deserve*? Can you split this hair?

I doubt I cannot.

7. The grand objection to one of the preceding propositions is drawn from matter of fact. God does in fact justify those who, by their own

confession, neither feared God nor wrought righteousness. Is not this an exception to the general rule?

It is a doubt, God makes any exception at all. But how are we sure that the person in question never did fear God and work righteousness? His own saying so is not proof: for we know how all that are convinced of sin so undervalue themselves in every respect.

8. Does not talking of a justified or a sanctified state tend to mislead men? Almost naturally leading them to trust in what was done in one moment?

Whereas we are every hour and every moment pleasing or displeasing to God, *according to our works*—according to the whole of our inward tempers, and our outward behavior.[12]

The Calvinists were shocked by these minutes and considered them as nothing short of popery and advocating a merit-based salvation.[13] Lady Huntingdon demanded everyone at Trevecca to renounce the minutes and for students to state their position in writing. In a lengthy letter to the Countess, Fletcher acknowledged the minutes were too brief for a subject "so exceedingly delicate," but he defended them at length for expressing necessary biblical truths.[14] Stephen Gunter noted that Fletcher's response "essentially defined the lines along which the next six years of theological battle would be fought."[15] Fletcher closed his letter by resigning his post as president. He would become one of Wesley's most ardent supporters and is considered by many as Methodism's first theologian.

On Wesley's part, he considered revising the minutes but the more he reflected on them he could see "they contain truths of the deepest importance" that should be "continually inculcated" in every believer.[16] Leading up to the 1771 Conference, Wesley wrote to several of his preachers that

---

12. Conference Minutes, 1770 Q.28 (*Works*, 10:393–94, emphasis his).

13. *Works*, 10:394n340; Gunter, *Love Divine*, 252; Wallace, *Works of John Fletcher*, 1:33.

14. Peter S. Forsaith, ed., *Unexampled Labors: Letters of the Revd John Fletcher to Leaders in the Evangelical Revival* (Peterborough: Epworth, 2008), 260–70. The quote is from p. 269.

15. Gunter, *Love Divine*, 252.

16. Letter, May 27, 1771 (*Telford*, 5:252).

his central concern was about believers *retaining* the favor of God rather than sinners "*gaining* the favour of God."[17] A month later he reiterated to the Countess that the "principles established in the Minutes" are in "no way contrary" to that "great truth justification by faith" which he had "preached for above thirty years."[18] He then pointed Lady Huntingdon to calmly consider Fletcher's explanation in the *Vindication*. With these preliminary remarks we can now examine the "principles" of the doctrinal minutes regarding the salvific role of good works.

Necessity of Works

The minutes clearly express the necessity of works for salvation, both present and final. Only once, in response to the first thesis, did Wesley reference salvation by faith. But even there the accent falls on those works that confirm justifying faith ("with a loving and obedient heart"). On the surface, the absence of a clear statement concerning salvation by faith alone led many to conclude that Wesley was propagating the "dreadful heresy" of salvation by works.[19] However, as Wesley and Fletcher noted, when one considers each proposition and thesis it becomes evident they express vital biblical truths.[20] And, Wesley's belief in the necessity of good works had been stressed throughout his ministry, reaching back to his Oxford days, so his Calvinist opponents should have been well aware of his long-standing position on the subject.[21]

---

17. Letter, July 10, 1771 (*Telford*, 5:262–65, emphasis his). In fact, Wesley made this point three times in the letter (see propositions 1, 5, and 7 on pp. 263–65).

18. Letters, June 19 and August 14, 1771 (*Telford*, 5:259, 274, emphasis his).

19. A charge the Calvinist Walter Shirley made, which Fletcher quoted in his letter, June 24, 1771 (Forsaith, *Unexampled Labors*, 278) and in his *Vindication* (Wallace, *Works of John Fletcher*, 1:15).

20. Fletcher made this point to Lady Huntingdon on March 7, 1771 (Forsaith, *Unexampled Labours*, 260–70) and Wesley to Mary Bishop on May 21, 1771 (*Telford*, 5:251–52).

21. On Wesley's early views on the necessity of good works and holy living, see chapter 2. After Aldersgate, see *Salvation by Faith* III.1 (*Works*, 1:125); *Doctrine of Salvation, Faith, and Good Works* II.4–6 (*Works*, 12:40–41); Conference Minutes, 1744 Q. 11–14 (*Works*, 10:128–29); *Scripture Way of Salvation* III.4–5 (*Works*, 2:164).

A second characteristic of the minutes is that the propositions reference different *kinds* of works. Proposition III addresses works that *precede* present justification, whereas propositions I and II speak of works that *follow* present justification and *precede* final justification ("works *for* as well as *from* life"). Besides the temporal distinction, Wesley referenced works as the necessary *fruit* and *evidence* of justifying faith. In Thesis #1 he concisely restated standard Protestant doctrine that was codified in the English Articles of Religion, "Good works, which are the fruits of faith, and follow after justification . . . do spring out necessarily of a true and lively faith; inasmuch that by them a lively faith may be as evidently known as a tree discerned by the fruit" (Art. XII). The same evidentiary role of works is applied to the responsive unregenerate in Thesis #2. Earlier, we saw that Wesley considered Acts 10:35 to express a "fundamental soteriological standard revealed throughout Holy Writ."[22] Essential to this standard was the expectation that the responsive unregenerate work righteousness "according to the light he has"—an allusion to the concept of dispensations (more on this below). Finally, in Thesis #8 a similar evidentiary role for works is applied, but this time more broadly to include sanctification as well as justification. Once again, it is works, not faith, that determines whether a believer is "every hour and every moment pleasing or displeasing to God." Four years later Wesley would make the same point and add that those who deny this "important truth . . . sap the very foundation of both inward and outward holiness."[23]

A third feature of the works mentioned concerns their *nature*. By works Wesley meant both external actions and internal dispositions. External works include faithfulness regarding material things like money (P.I), amending one's lifestyle (P.III), living righteously (Th.2), and "outward behavior" (Th.8). Internal works consist of having teachable attitudes (P.III), a "loving, obedient heart" (Th.1), and holy "tempers" and dispositions (Th.8). Behind these various descriptions is Wesley's firm belief in the necessity of *intentional response* to divine grace for salvation to be received and appropriated. Randy Maddox expressed this orienting

---

22. Rodes, *From Faith to Faith*, 122.
23. *Journal*, March 22, 1774 (*Works*, 22:400).

concern with his well-known phrase "responsible grace."[24] This orienting concern had come to Wesley from his upbringing in the Arminian tradition that he refined into a mature soteriology.[25] Similarly, from his High Church roots Wesley developed a deep appreciation for the means of grace that nurture the spiritual life through faithful participation and practice. Human response was therefore understood as a gift of grace, not a human achievement. This meant Wesley had a different perspective toward works than did his Calvinist opponents, whose viewpoint was informed by their doctrines of unconditional election and absolute predestination. By contrast, Wesley's soteriology included a strong element of synergism, which enabled him to make a distinction between *merit* and *condition* when addressing works in relation to justification and salvation.

Merit and Condition

So, how did Wesley thread the needle to affirm the necessity of works as a condition without falling into a merit-based salvation? It was on this specific point that the Methodist Conference of 1771 agreed that the 1770 Minutes were not "sufficiently guarded."[26] In Thesis #4 Wesley made a clear distinction by disavowing any "merit of works." Yet the distinction was blurred in the eyes of many by his remarks on the necessity of "works meet for repentance" to attain present justification (P.III) and by his statement concerning the merit of rewards at the Final Judgment (Th.6). It was easy to see that the doctrinal minutes called for further clarification.

---

24. Maddox, *Responsible Grace*, 18–19, 254–56.

25. Gregory Crofford traces the development of prevenient grace in Wesley's theology from his early period up to his later years. By the mid-1760s the doctrine became part of Wesley's explication of the gospel (*Streams of Mercy: Prevenient Grace in the Theology of John and Charles Wesley* (Lexington, KY: Emeth Press, 2010), 67–94. See *The Scripture Way of Salvation* I.2 (*Works*, 2:156).

26. Conference Minutes, 1771 (*Works*, 10:403). Charles Wesley called the minutes "soundly unguarded" (Letter, June 22, 1771 [Kenneth G. C. Newport and Gareth Lloyd, eds., *The Letter of Charles Wesley: A Critical Edition with Introduction and Notes*, 2 vols. (Oxford: Oxford University Press, 2013, 2021), 2:248]).

What becomes evident is that Wesley's position was more nuanced now than before. About earning salvation, his views had not changed.[27] But in terms of heavenly rewards, he had inched closer to the position of Rome. At the close of the 1771 Conference Wesley included a statement to satisfy the Calvinists by denouncing the "doctrine of justification by works" and of works "meriting or purchasing our justification."[28] He also reaffirmed that Christ is the sole meritorious cause of justification. A couple months later Wesley repudiated the notion of works meriting salvation to Philothea Briggs and did so again three years later to Mrs. Bennis.[29] So, his position on this point was settled. Nevertheless, just days before the 1771 Conference Wesley told his brother Charles that he "never did, neither do now, contend for the use" of the word *merit*, yet added that in regard to heavenly rewards the word appropriately applies since it is impossible to distinguish between "merit" and "deserving."[30] As he previously told his Methodist preachers, at the Last Judgment believers will be rewarded "according to their works," which is just another way of saying "because of their works" or "as our works deserve."[31] To Charles he explained that the word *merit* has two shades of meaning. In its "proper sense" it denotes that no goodness in us can earn salvation. But, in a more "loose sense" the word means "no more than rewardable."[32]

Since Wesley edited and published Fletcher's *Vindication*, the latter's remarks are relevant here. Fletcher argued that God will reward only those works that proceed from the grace given in Christ. He goes on to explain that since Christ alone did works that are meritorious, and his Spirit produces these same works in believers, the good works done by believers are

---

27. As early as 1745 Wesley supported the standard Anglican position: (1) good works cannot go before justification, (2) no degree of sanctification can be prior to justification, (3) the meritorious cause of justification is the life and death of Christ and the condition is faith alone, (4) outward and inward holiness is the condition of final justification (*Farther Appeal, Pt. I*, II.8 [*Works*, 11:115]).

28. Conference Minutes, 1771 (*Works*, 10:403).

29. Letter, October 6, 1771; March 1, 1774 (*Telford*, 5:280; 6:76).

30. Letter, August 3, 1771 (*Telford*, 5:269).

31. Letter, July 10, 1771 (*Telford*, 5:264).

32. Letter, August 3, 1771 (*Telford*, 5:270).

therefore meritorious or deserving of rewards. He then praised Wesley for "restoring works of righteousness to their deserved glory, without detracting from the glory of 'the Lord our righteousness.'"[33] So, good works cannot merit salvation, but deserve to be rewarded at the Final Judgment, which will include the pronounced blessing to enter the eternal kingdom (Matt. 25:34).[34] Wesley, no doubt, agreed with Fletcher on these points.

If Wesley's theology of merit involved subtle distinctions, his stance on works as condition was equally nuanced. Even though the 1771 Conference had rejected the notion of works earning salvation, "either in whole or in part," Wesley added toward the end of the statement that no one can have saving faith or be finally saved unless they do good works "where there is time and opportunity."[35] This qualification was integral to Wesley's position on repentance and faith as conditions for both justification and sanctification. The same point is made in the *Farther Appeal, Part I* (1745) and *The Scripture Way of Salvation* (1765).[36] Whereas faith is strictly speaking the "only condition" for justification and full salvation, since the "moment" a person believes they are justified or sanctified, repentance is "remotely" necessary if "there be time and opportunity. Otherwise, a man may be justified [or] sanctified without them."[37] In this way Wesley attempted to proclaim a message of *sola fide* while maintaining the necessity of "works meet for repentance" for initial and full salvation. Kenneth Collins responded that "once again, grace-assisted cooperation, and not human merit or works righteousness, is the chord struck" by Wesley.[38]

Following the 1770 Conference Wesley made it clear that his real concern in the doctrinal minutes was how to *retain* God's favor for final

---

33. Wallace, *Works of John Fletcher*, 55, 57.

34. In *Explanatory Notes* Wesley commented on Matt. 25:34, "Purchased by my blood, for all who have believed in me, with the faith which wrought by love."

35. Conference Minutes, 1771 (*Works*, 10:403).

36. *Farther Appeal, Pt. I*, II.11 (*Works*, 11:117); *Scripture Way of Salvation* III.2–13 (*Works*, 2:162–67).

37. *Scripture Way of Salvation* III.2, 13 (*Works*, 2:163, 167). In both locations the sentence has the exact same wording except for the exchange of "justified" and "sanctified."

38. Collins, *Theology of John Wesley*, 223.

justification.³⁹ As he told Mrs. Bennis, "Works are a condition of final salvation."⁴⁰ This is certainly true in regard to good works, for Anglican doctrine taught that they follow and not precede present justification.⁴¹ However, by the 1770s Wesley had adopted a more positive view of works *before* present justification since salvation as it pertains to the "entire work of God" begins with preventing grace.⁴² This point was restated by Fletcher in his *Vindication*. Drawing on the same definition as did Wesley, Fletcher defines a "condition" to be "*sine quibus non*, without which salvation and glory neither can nor will follow."⁴³ He then applies this definition to repentance and faith for present salvation and to holiness of heart and life for final salvation. Once again, as the editor of the *Vindication* Wesley concurred with Fletcher on these points.

On one occasion Wesley clarified that works are the "appointed way wherein we wait for free salvation."⁴⁴ By listing works as the "appointed way," Wesley identified them with the means of grace, which are the "ordinary channels" whereby God confers "preventing, justifying, or sanctifying grace."⁴⁵ Seen in this light, Wesley's insistence on works in the 1770 Minutes simply reflected his Anglican understanding of the *via salutis*, or as Wesley's aptly called the "scripture way of salvation."⁴⁶ That is, salvation

---

39. Letter, July 10, 1771, Theses #1, 4, 5, 7 (*Telford*, 5:263–65).

40. Letter, March 1, 1774 (*Telford*, 6:76). For a discussion on works as a condition for final salvation in Wesley's thought, see Harold Lindström, *Wesley and Sanctification*, 205–15.

41. Articles XII, XIII, Articles of Religion. Wesley affirmed the same position in *Farther Appeal, Pt. I*, II.5 *(Works,* 11:112–13). On works, the means of grace, and salvation, see discussions by Chang, *The Theologies of the Law in Martin Luther and John Wesley*, 161–87; Collins, *Theology of John Wesley*, 257–70; Cunningham, *John Wesley's Pneumatology*, 109–34; Knight, *The Presence of God in the Christian Life*; Maddox, *Responsible Grace*, 192–229; Rodes, *From Faith to Faith*, 99–108.

42. *The Scripture Way of Salvation* I.2 (*Works*, 2:156–57). See also, *On Working Out Our Own Salvation* II.1 (*Works*, 3:203–4). The Late Wesley's more positive view of works preceding justification is also suggested by the fact that he removed Article XIII (Of Works before Justification) from *The Sunday Service of the Methodists in North America* (1784).

43. Wallace, *Works of John Fletcher*, 1:52.

44. Letter, October 6, 1771 (*Telford*, 5:280).

45. "The Means of Grace," II.1 (*Works*, 1:381, emphasis his).

46. The title of Wesley's landmark sermon (*Works*, 2:152–69).

is worked out as preventing, justifying, and sanctifying grace is conveyed through faithful participation in "works of piety" and "works of mercy."[47] As the "appointed way," Wesley reminded his followers that while the death of Christ is the meritorious cause of their salvation, Spirit-inspired works done in faith are the instrumental means of salvation since they are the conduit of grace.[48] Or, as Wesley told James Creighton, "No man can be saved without his own endeavors."[49]

Working Out Our Own Salvation

The role of works in Wesley's mature soteriology finds its most extensive treatment in the landmark sermon "On Working Out Our Own Salvation" (1785).[50] Published several years after the close of the Minutes Controversy, the sermon sums up Wesley's theology of salvific works. As does the 1770 Minutes, the sermon barely mentions salvation by faith and instead focuses the reader's attention on the necessity of works for present and final salvation.[51] The sermon therefore serves as a fitting bookend to the Minutes Controversy from Wesley's perspective.

The text is Philippians 2:12-13, an Anglican favorite on the believer's active participation in salvation. The synergism of Wesley's soteriology is evident with his two main points: "First, God works; therefore you *can* work. Second, God works; therefore you *must* work" (III.2). The necessity of works for salvation could not be more magnified while still holding to a soteriology of free grace. The discourse begins by reminding readers that salvation is the work of the economic Trinity. The Father is the gracious

---

47. *Scripture Way of Salvation* III.8–10 (*Works,* 2:166). Wesley made this point in his disputes with the Moravians over stillness, "The way to attain faith is to wait for Christ and be still, in using 'all the means of grace'" (Journal, December 31, 1739; *Works,* 19:132–33).

48. Letter, May 2, 1774 (*Telford,* 6:80).

49. Letter, May 24, 1773 (*Telford,* 628).

50. *Works,* 3:199–209. For other sermons about works and salvation, see *The Good Steward* (1768 [*Works,* 2:281–99]); *The Reward of Righteousness* (1777 [*Works,* 3:400–414]); and *The Wedding Garment* (1790 [*Works,* 4:139–48]).

51. Salvation by faith is mentioned, but not elaborated on at I.1 and II.4. The words *believe* and *believer* are mentioned in the introduction (§4, John 3:16) and at III.6. The "good fight of faith" (1 Tim. 6:12) appears at III.7.

cause of salvation, the Son is the meritorious cause, and the Spirit is the transforming cause. God's salvific work is to breathe into his people "every good desire" and "every right disposition" to equip them for "every good word and work" (I.1–3). Since the economic Trinity is the efficient cause of salvation, it "removes all imagination of [human] merit" and gives "God the whole glory" (I.1).

Wesley proceeded to break down the "gracious dispensations" (III.7) of the *via salutis*. Employing a broader usage of the term "salvation," Wesley explained that it begins with "preventing grace" ("some degree of salvation") and is carried forward by "convincing grace" till a person "experiences the proper Christian salvation . . . justification and sanctification." Justification involves deliverance from sin's guilt and reinstatement to divine favor, while sanctification is liberation from the "power and root of sin" and restoration to the divine image. The path of salvation includes both instantaneous moments (justification and entire sanctification) and continual growth in the love of God and neighbor, until the believer attains in the eschatological future the "measure of the stature of the fullness of Christ" (II.1).

With the "scripture way of salvation" delineated, the next question becomes, "How are we to 'work out' this salvation?" (II.2). Recalling themes that reached back to his Oxford days, Wesley pressed the reader to have a "single eye" and to obey with the "utmost diligence, speed, punctuality, and exactness" (II.2–3). Regarding the "steps" of salvation, Wesley repeated themes and phrases found in the 1770 Minutes. Seekers are to "cease to do evil; learn to do well." They must avoid "every evil word and work" and learn to be "zealous of good works," including "works of piety, as well as works of mercy." Examples are taken from the means of grace: private and family prayer, fasting, searching the scriptures, partaking of the Lord's Supper, doing good to all people, and practicing self-denial (II.4).

Wesley then explained *why* his readers must "work" in order to be saved. He began by pointing out that a person *can* work since divine grace is active in them. And once more he reminded his readers that this is "without any merit" on their part (III.4–5). A common pitfall, though, is to have a "mock humility" and exclaim as the Calvinists do, "Oh, I can do nothing" (III.6). For Wesley, nothing could be further from the truth. Works are God's appointed way for grace to be appropriated for present and final salvation. Consequently, the reader *must* work or else God "will cease working" in them. To Augustine's, "He that made us without ourselves, will not save us without ourselves" (III.7), Wesley added John 6:27, "Labour, then, not for the meat that perisheth, but for that which endureth to everlasting life" (III.8).

In Wesley's mature soteriology everyone "works *for* as well as *from* life."[52] The synergism of the *via salutis* begins with the unmerited gift of preventing grace, "There is no man, unless he has quenched the Spirit, that is wholly void of the grace of God." For "everyone has some measure of that light . . . which sooner or later . . . enlightens every man that cometh into the world" (III.4). The same principle holds true for the Christian. They too "work *for* as well as *from* life," having been justified by faith through the righteousness of Christ, and put on the "wedding garment" of "personal holiness" to receive final justification when Christ returns.[53] In one of his last sermons Wesley explained that "without the righteousness of Christ" the believer has "no *claim* to glory," and "without holiness" they have "no *fitness* for it."[54] *Claim* and *fitness* now encapsulate the central purpose of present and final justification, which is to legally and to transformationally prepare a believer for life in the eternal kingdom. Salvation in all its stages and degrees necessarily requires free human response to divine grace. Grace is the originating source and efficient cause of kingdom life, while works are the appointed means by which faith appropriates saving grace into one's heart and life. Wesley could even say that if works "spring from a right principle, they are the perfection of religion."[55] In the end, Wesley believed there is a direct connection between grace and works regarding justification and salvation. Harold

---

52. Conference Minutes, 1770 (*Works*, 10:392, emphasis his).

53. *On the Wedding Garment* §10 (*Works*, 4:144).

54. *On the Wedding Garment* §10 (*Works*, 4:144, emphasis his).

55. *The Reward of Righteousness* I.6 (*Works*, 3:405).

Lindström captured this point well when he stated that "man's relation to God is seen by Wesley in terms of works as well as grace."[56]

Justification in the Ordo Salutis

There is more to be said about the place of present and final justification in Wesley's mature soteriology. At the height of the Minutes Controversy in 1773, Wesley took the time to delineate his views on the "whole work of God in the salvation of man" from its beginning in eternity past until it "terminates in glory."[57] Later titled *On Predestination*, Wesley expounded on Romans 8:29-30, a favorite text of the Calvinists on the *ordo salutis*. Wesley's aversion to Reformed notions of absolute predestination was (and is) well known and stems from his upbringing in the Epworth parsonage where he was nurtured in the Arminian point of view. In the past Wesley disclosed his views in such works as *Predestination Calmly Considered* (1752), but now he spelled them out succinctly and in their salvific order.[58]

The Apostle Paul lists God's purpose under five headings, which Wesley referred to as "steps" in the eternal purpose of salvation: foreknowledge, predestination, calling, justification, and glorification. Wesley believed the Apostle was not describing a "chain of causes and effects" as much as showing the "order" in which God accomplishes the different "branches of salvation" (§4). He opened by affirming God's *foreknowledge* of everyone in human history who will believe unto salvation (§5). While we are creatures of time, God dwells in "one eternal now" (§15). He "sees at once whatever was, is, or will be to the end of time." Thus, Wesley considered foreknowledge to be an anthropomorphism.[59] It expresses from a finite human perspective God's

---

56. Lindström, *Wesley and Sanctification*, 208.

57. *On Predestination* §5 (*Works*, 2:416–17).

58. Other prior works by Wesley on Calvinistic predestination include *Free Grace* (1739), *A Dialogue between a Predestinarian and His Friend* (1741), and *Serious Thoughts upon the Perseverance of the Saints* (1751).

59. For discussion of Wesley's concept of "eternal now," see Thomas C. Oden, *John Wesley's Teachings*, 4 vols. (Grand Rapids: Zondervan, 2012–14), 1:35–39.

exhaustive knowledge of the past, present, and future. But he added that God's infinite knowledge does not cause things to be. Instead, "he knows them because they are."[60] People are free to believe or not to believe, for such freedom is a gift of preventing grace (§6).

With God's exhaustive knowledge of who will be finally saved, his decree of *predestination* to conform believers into the likeness of Christ logically follows (§7). In typical Arminian fashion, Wesley argued that God's eternal decree is conditional and inclusive, in contrast to the Calvinist position. Drawing on Mark 16:16, he asserted that the "unchangeable, irreversible, irresistible decree of God" is "He that believeth shall be saved; he that believeth not shall be damned." So, God's eternal decree is fixed and cannot change, but what is decreed is the plan of salvation that is available to "everyone who believes," for God's love encompasses the entire human race (Jn. 3:16). Wesley further suggested that predestination pertains not so much to initial faith (who will believe) but to the future destiny of God's people (conformed to the image of Christ). After expounding on God's redemptive work that spans from eternity past to eternity future, he then addressed how this plan is accomplished in the next three "steps."

Under *calling* and *justification* Wesley presented his doctrine of double justification. On the aspect of calling, he interpreted Paul to mean "effectual calling" (§8). That is, the call to salvation begins "outwardly" with the "word of grace" proclaimed, then works "inwardly" by the "application of [God's] word to the heart," enabling a person to freely trust in Christ for present justification, with the Spirit bearing witness to their adoption (§12). Those who are effectually called, meaning evangelical believers, are then justified in the broader sense of being "made just or righteous," or as he added, "sanctified" (§9). The last "step" is *glorification* (§10). Having been made "meet" or fit for the "inheritance of the saints of light," the Lord gives his people the "kingdom which was prepared for them before the world began" (Matt. 25:34; Col. 1:12).

---

60. Wesley's teachings on God's eternity and foreknowledge are discussed elsewhere in *On Eternity* (*Works*, 358–72); *God's Love to Fallen Man* §3 (*Works*, 2:424); *The Imperfection of Human Knowledge* I.3 (*Works*, 2:570); *What is Man?* II.1–4 (*Works*, 3:458–59); and *The Unity of the Divine Being* §§2, 6 (*Works*, 4:61, 62).

From this sermon we learn that justification has a pivotal place in Wesley's *ordo salutis*, which he defined as the "plan [God] laid down from eternity" (§10). This "plan" flows from God's eternal decree to save everyone who trusts in Christ and perseveres for final salvation. Full justification encompasses the entire journey of faith from effectual calling to glorification. It not only includes a declaration of righteousness that gives *claim* to eternal life but comprises the renewal in righteousness that *fits* for kingdom life. Stated another way, present justification deals with the legal aspect of inheriting eternal life whereas final justification addresses issues of health and fitness for kingdom life. Both acts of justification are indispensable to the "whole work of God in the salvation of man" (§5), yet each is distinct in that they take place at different stages in the "scripture way of salvation." This explains why Wesley stressed faith as the primary condition for present justification and works for final justification. For Christ's *passive* righteousness has purchased a legal standing before God and faith is the empty hand that receives what Christ acquired. In a similar way, Christ's *active* righteousness has achieved the goal that believers are predestined to be conformed to and is attained by Spirit-inspired works and holy living. Once more, the economic Trinity served as the foundation of Wesley's theology of objective and subjective righteousness. For in each phase of the *via salutis* the members of the Trinity serve a vital salvific role in the believer's justification, sanctification, and redemption (1 Cor. 1:30).[61]

Degrees of Acceptance

In the 1770s and 1780s Wesley continued to refine his position on degrees of justification. The servant/son metaphor played a central role, but so did the soteriological standing of the responsive unregenerate. Both cases reflect the complexity and depth of Wesley's full doctrine of justification. Yet behind these developments stood his covenant theology that was influenced by John Fletcher's dispensationalism. Besides these degrees, Wesley also addressed the subject of sacramental justification. As we will

---

61. On this topic, see Colyer, *The Trinitarian Dimension of John Wesley's Theology*.

see, his High Church sacramentalism continued to inform his mature doctrine of justification.

Faith of a Servant

Whereas the *ordo salutis* centers primarily on the logical sequence of Christian salvation, Wesley was equally drawn to ponder the soteriological standing of those with a lower degree of faith than evangelical belief. One of the more important developments in Wesley's mature doctrine of justification was the *servant/son* metaphor. Stanley Rodes showed that the metaphor stems from Wesley's covenant theology that includes several dispensations within the covenant of grace.[62] Although the metaphor is suggested in his sermon "Christian Perfection," it first appears in the 1746 Conference Minutes and later that year in the sermon "The Spirit of Bondage and of Adoption."[63] After this it is found in his *Explanatory Notes* but drops out of use until Wesley's letter to Ann Bolton in 1768, mentioned at the end of chapter 4.[64] After this the metaphor was employed on numerous occasions to describe a degree of justifying faith lower than evangelical belief.

As for the roots of the metaphor, in chapter 2 we saw that Wesley learned the basics of covenant theology from his parents and Anglican education. The covenant of works belonged to prelapsarian Adam and the covenant of grace to postlapsarian Adam and his posterity. The covenant of grace contains a series of dispensations, including the Mosaic (Jewish) and Christian (evangelical), and these dispensations pertain to specific spiritual states in the *via salutis*. The concept of spiritual states was further developed from Wesley's reading of Anglicans John Norris, Richard Lucas, and William Law, as well as from the Roman Catholic Blaise Pascal.[65] So, by 1734 Wesley and the Oxford Methodists were discussing three

---

62. Rodes, *From Faith to Faith*, 14–36.

63. *Christian Perfection* II.10 (*Works*, 2:109–10); Conference Minutes, 1746 (*Works*, 10:171); and *Spirit of Bondage and of Adoption* §2, IV.2 (*Works*, 1:250, 265).

64. The metaphor appears in *Explanatory Notes* at Jn. 17:24; Rom. 1:7; Gal.4:1-7; Heb. 3:1-7; and Jude 1.

65. Olson, *Wesley and Aldersgate*, 60.

spiritual states: natural, legal (Jewish), and evangelical.[66] Among the Oxford Methodists it was further agreed that the legal state is defined by having a fear of the Lord and that eternal salvation applies to both the legal and evangelical states. Both elements would become a staple in the servant/son metaphor.[67]

From the metaphor's increased use after 1770, Rodes rightfully concluded that it began to "resonate" more with the founder of Methodism.[68] In the mid-1770s Wesley reissued his first and second journal extracts that tell the story of his evangelical conversion in May 1738. This time he included a series of corrective comments that identified his pre-evangelical faith with the *faith of a servant*.[69] Whereas he previously believed he had been in a state of damnation before his evangelical conversion, Wesley now denied this.[70] He concluded that before his Aldersgate conversion he had faith, even the *faith of a servant*, but not evangelical Christian faith, the *faith of a son*.[71] Wesley deduced that even though he was not in a state of damnation prior to Aldersgate, he had not yet attained "the full, Christian salvation" of a child of God.[72] This was experienced when his heart was "strangely warmed" on May 24 and he received an assurance of present justification ("taken away *my* sins") and the new birth ("saved *me* from the law of sin and death").[73]

Wesley's journal notations on the metaphor imply there are degrees of justification for those who sincerely profess the Christian religion. These

---

66. Heitzenrater, *Diary of Benjamin Ingham*, 134n66.

67. Rodes includes a helpful study of Wesley's interaction with Reformed covenant theology in the 1740s, but he is mistaken that Wesley developed his covenant theology from the Reformed tradition. He did not examine Wesley's earlier exposure to Anglican covenant theology from his parents and education.

68. Rodes, *From Faith to Faith*, 33.

69. For a full study of the journal errata and footnotes, see Olson, *Wesley and Aldersgate*, 99–103.

70. *Journal*, February 1, 1738 (*Works*, 18:215 notes i, j). See also his confession in *The Almost Christian*.

71. *Journal*, February 1, 1738 (*Works*, 18:215 note k).

72. *Journal*, March 5, 1738 (*Works*, 18:228).

73. *Journal*, May 24, 1738 (*Works*, 18:250, emphasis his). That these two phrases referred to present justification and new birth, see Olson, *Wesley and Aldersgate*, 48–50.

degrees align with his doctrine of double justification. Before his evangelical conversion, Wesley had the *faith of a servant*, but he was not in a state of damnation. This level of faith pertained to his future salvation or final justification. At Aldersgate he received a perceptible assurance of present, evangelical justification. This was the *faith of a son* and confirmed he had received "the proper Christian faith."[74] What is evident from Wesley's inclusion of the servant/son metaphor in his Aldersgate testimony in the 1770s is that the metaphor identified two different degrees of justifying faith in his spiritual journey. Back in 1747 Wesley had listed "justifying faith" and "the proper Christian faith" as two degrees of Christian faith.[75] By appealing to his own experience, he now employed the servant/son metaphor to make the same point. Before Aldersgate Wesley was a Christian with "justifying faith," but afterward he was a *real* Christian with "the proper Christian faith." The point is the metaphor delineated two levels of Christian faith in his religious experience (more on this below).

In 1788 Wesley wrote two sermons in which he explained the servant/son metaphor in more detail. The first sermon, "On Faith, Hebrews 11:6," opens with John Fletcher's account of four dispensations within the covenant of grace: heathen, Jewish, John the Baptist, and Christian.[76] Fletcher proposed that each successive dispensation includes a greater degree of spiritual light or salvific knowledge, and that each dispensation offers final salvation to those who believe according to its degree of revealed truth. Fundamental to this soteriology was an Arminian concept of free grace that is "inclusive not exclusive."[77] Using Fletcher's dispensations as a springboard, Wesley walked through "several sorts of faith," from the

---

74. *Journal*, May 24, 1738 (*Works*, 18:242 note b).

75. His letter to Charles on July 31, 1747.

76. Fletcher proposed four dispensations in the fourth letter of his *Vindication* (Wallace, *Works of John Fletcher*, 1:48–49), in his *Third Check* (Wallace, *Works of John Fletcher*, 1:160–61), and again in *Doctrines of Grace and Justice* (Wallace, *Works of Fletcher*, 4:4–5). In his *Essay on Truth* (section V) Fletcher argued that salvation is available in each dispensation according to its degree of truth (Wallace, *Works of John Fletcher*, 2:138). For a study of Fletcher's dispensations, see Frazier, *True Christianity*.

77. Kenneth Collins, "John Wesley's Engagement with Islam: Exploring the Soteriological Possibilities in Light of a Diversity of Graces and Theological Frameworks," *WTJ* 56–52 (Fall 2021): 11.

lowest to the highest, until he reached the two degrees of faith that are "properly saving" and bring "eternal salvation" to all who keep them—the *faith of a servant* and the *faith of a son* (I.10). The servant is an "infant" in the faith among those who "fear God and work righteousness" (Acts 10:35). Such a person is "at that very moment in a state of acceptance" since "'the wrath of God' no longer 'abideth on him'" (I.10). By contrast, those born of God have received the Spirit of adoption and can testify of receiving the indwelling Christ (Gal. 2:20). They have the "faith of a child" and the inner testimony of the Spirit assuring them of present salvation (I.12).

Even though the servant and the son have justifying faith, Wesley drew a clear line between their degrees of justification. First, he quoted 1 John 5:10 to make the point that a "child of God 'hath the witness in himself.'" But then adds, "This the servant hath not" (I.12). The dissimilarity over assurance of present forgiveness was for Wesley a mark of deeper significance. Two months later in the sermon "On the Discoveries of Faith," he noted that the servant belongs to the legal state (Jewish dispensation) and the son to the evangelical state (Christian dispensation). The servant is motivated by a reverent fear and a lack of assurance whereas the son is drawn by "childlike love." With "Christ revealed in his heart," the born-again believer cries out, "Abba Father" (§14). Six months later Wesley was again explicit: the servant remains a "Jewish" believer while the son is a "real Christian."[78] The difference in experience could not be put in more stark terms. Another way Wesley distinguished between the two degrees of saving faith is easily missed. In the sermon "On Faith," he employed the language of justification ("state of acceptance") to describe the servant's faith and the terminology of assurance and regeneration to identify the son's faith (§§10–12). In this way Wesley could stress the servant's faith as justifying and yet falling short of evangelical salvation and its assurance of present justification.[79]

---

78. *Walking by Sight and Walking by Faith* §1 (*Works*, 4:49).

79. There has been debate among scholars over whether the servant is justified or not. Those who deny the servant is justified, see Collins, *Theology of John Wesley*, 134–35; Rodes, *From Faith to Faith*, 204–5. For the other position, see Laura Bartels Fellman, "John Wesley and the 'Servant of God,'" *WTJ* 41–42 (Fall 2006): 72–86; Maddox, *Responsible Grace*, 161; Olson, *Wesley and Aldersgate*, 108–10.

Even with the sharp disjunction between the two degrees of justifying faith, Wesley was addressing two levels of *Christian* justification. This is evident from his own testimony in the journal and is confirmed in the sermon *On Faith*. For in the sermon Wesley recounted that at the beginning of the Evangelical Revival he and other Methodist preachers would tell seekers of evangelical salvation in Christ, who could not give a clear testimony of assurance, that their faith was not yet saving (I.11). The point here is that Wesley was addressing people who already had a degree of Christian faith.[80] They were not adherents of another religion, nor were they just nominal professors of the faith. The same point is seen in Wesley's letters. When he told Ann Bolton and Alexander Knox that they had the *faith of a servant*, Wesley understood they were sincere believers in Christ and therefore Christians, as the term was commonly employed. What they lacked was the Spirit of adoption associated with evangelical conversion and new birth.[81] Thus, we see from Wesley's journal, letters, and sermons that the metaphor served to delineate two degrees of *Christian* justification in his mature soteriology.

General Justification

The *faith of a servant* was not the only area where Wesley's theology was fertile in his later years. Fletcher's teachings on the four dispensations within the covenant of grace led Wesley to reflect more deeply on the soteriological standing of the responsive unregenerate. On several occasions he commended Fletcher's works to his followers, telling Elizabeth Richie, "Mr. Fletcher has given us a wonderful view of the different dispensations

---

80. This point is also made in *On Friendship with the World* §§7, 12, which places the servant and son in the same category when it comes to belonging to the world or to God (*Works*, 3:130, 132).

81. While Wesley consistently referred to regenerate believers as "real Christians," the use of the adjective ("real") signified that the term "Christian" had a broader meaning than evangelical faith. Wesley told Ann Bolton that the *faith of a servant* can include one who "trusts not in his own righteousness but in the atoning blood" (August 12, 1770; *Telford*, 5:197). He expressed to Ellen Gretton that a person who fears God and waits for salvation is not an "unbeliever" (December 31, 1782; *Telford*, 7:157). In the same way, Wesley's comments to Knox on August 29, 1777, make it clear Alexander was already a Christian according to common usage of the term (*Telford*, 6:272–73).

which we are under. I believe that difficult subject was never placed in so clear a light before."[82]

As we learned in chapter 1, Fletcher taught there are several degrees of justification. Like Wesley, he understood Peter's declaration in Acts 10:35—"in every nation anyone who fears [God] and does what is right is acceptable to him"—to be the fundamental standard for final salvation in Holy Writ. He therefore pronounced in his *Vindication* of the 1770 Minutes that the acceptance Peter referred to in Acts 10 constitutes a "general justification" for those in the heathen and Jewish dispensations that meet this basic soteriological standard.[83] Fletcher explained, "Whenever a heathen is accepted, it is merely through the merits of Christ. . . . All is therefore of grace; the light [Jn. 1:9], the works of righteousness done by that light, and acceptance in consequence of them." Again, "All the heathen who are saved, attain salvation through the name, that is, through the merits and Spirit of Christ; by framing their life . . . according to the supernatural light which Christ graciously affords them in the dispensations they are under."[84] Fletcher's arguments presented a solid rationale for Wesley's own position that there is a degree of justification for the responsive unregenerate.[85]

In a recent article, Kenneth Collins catalogued several of Wesley's negative assessments of the heathen and Muslim worlds from the 1750s to the 1780s.[86] Widespread ignorance of the true God combined with religious and moral fanaticism form the bulk of these remarks. But Wesley remained optimistic there are individuals in the heathen, Muslim, and Jewish worlds that do have a faith that sincerely "feareth God and worketh righteousness, according to the degree of light they have."[87] These

---

82. Letter, January 17, 1775 (*Telford*, 6:137). For other examples of Wesley recommending Fletcher's works, see *Telford*, 6:123, 134, 239, 272.

83. Wallace, *Works of John Fletcher*, 48.

84. Wallace, *Works of John Fletcher*, 47–48.

85. *ENNT*, Acts 10:35. We already saw above that Wesley edited and published the *Vindication* without Fletcher's direct approval. This demonstrates his strong agreement with Fletcher's apology of the Minutes.

86. Collins, "John Wesley's Engagement with Islam," 26–27.

87. Conference Minutes, 1770, Thesis #2 (*Works*, 10:393). On the salvation of the responsive unregenerate, see J. Robert Ewbank, *John Wesley, Natural Man, and the "Isms"* (Eugene, OR: Resource Publications, 2009), 28–34.

individuals represent "another spirit." They are "taught of God, by the inward voice" of prevenient grace of "all the essentials of true religion," which Wesley summarized as "right tempers towards God and man."[88] To those who were quick to condemn the entire non-Christian world, Wesley cautioned that no one has a "right to sentence all the heathen and Mahometan world to damnation." He counseled it is "far better to leave them to the 'Father of spirits of all flesh'; who is the God of the heathens as well as the Christians."[89]

A closer look at the servant and the responsive unregenerate categories reveals both similarities and differences in their degrees of acceptance. As for similarities, the soteriological standard of their justification is found in Acts 10:35 and concerns their final justification. For neither group enjoys an assurance of present pardon found in evangelical justification. However, the fundamental difference is that the servant has a knowledge of the gospel and a degree of faith in Jesus Christ while the responsive unregenerate have only a general knowledge of the supreme God and his attributes. The servant also has access to the church, the body of the living Christ, and to its sacramental life. The responsive unregenerate have none of these benefits. Even so, the doctrine of universal redemption promises that grace freely received leads to more grace and to higher degrees of salvific knowledge.[90] For the servant this means transitioning to the *faith of a son* and for the responsive unregenerate it means greater knowledge of the one true God and possible providential access to the gospel. To summarize, then, Wesley's inclusive view of free grace meant that justification in some degree is available in every dispensation of the covenant of grace—and therefore to every person.[91] For support he appealed to the Apostle

---

88. *On Faith*, Heb. 11:6 I.4; *The Unity of the Divine Being* §16 (*Works*, 3:494; 4:66).

89. *On Living without God* §14 (*Works*, 4:174). See also *On Charity* II.3 (*Works*, 3:295–96).

90. Wesley makes this point in *On Faith* I.13; II.4 (*Works*, 3:498, 500).

91. On Wesley's inclusivism, see Mark K. Olson, "Opening Salvation's Door: Acts 10:35 and John Wesley's Inclusivism," WesleyScholar.com, http://www.wesleyscholar.com/opening-salvations-door-acts-1035--and-john-wesleys-inclusivism (accessed December 17, 2021).

Paul's universal statement that by Jesus Christ the "free gift came upon all men to justification of life" (Rom. 5:18).[92]

Sacramental Justification: Baptism

The appeal to Romans 5:18 was not limited to the servant and the responsive unregenerate but was equally applied to infants. To John Mason in late 1776, Wesley commended Fletcher's description of preventing grace at work in every person, to which he added "every degree of grace is a degree of life."[93] This summarized Wesley's mature perspective expressed in the landmark sermons "The Scripture Way of Salvation" (1765) and "On Working Out Our Own Salvation" (1785).

In his *Third Check*, Fletcher detailed the different degrees of spiritual death and spiritual life before elaborating on the "four degrees that make up a glorified saint's eternal justification."[94] While the latter three degrees address the Christian's present and final justification, it is the first degree that now requires our attention. Fletcher stated there is a universal justification of all infants from the guilt of original sin so that none suffer eternal death on account of Adam's sin. Like Wesley, Fletcher appealed to the universal motif of Romans 5:18 for support. In his letter to Mason, Wesley agreed with Fletcher's use of Paul to conclude that "no infant ever was or ever will be 'sent to hell for the guilt of Adam's sin,' seeing it is cancelled by the righteousness of Christ as soon as they are sent into the world."[95]

There is nothing new in this statement since it had been Wesley's position since 1740, and probably earlier. Wesley's Arminianism compelled him to reject the Calvinist notion of eternal reprobation for the non-elect, while at the same time affirm the Church of England's teaching that baptism cancels the guilt of original sin. In his tract on baptism Wesley even

---

92. *ENNT*, Rom. 5:18. This was Wesley's interpretation of the text since the early 1740s, if not earlier. See Conference Minutes, 1744 Q. 16 (*Works*, 10:129, 781). Fletcher also appealed to Rom. 5:18 in his *Vindication* (Wallace, *Works of John Fletcher*, 48).

93. Letter, November 21, 1776 (*Telford*, 6:239).

94. Wallace, *Works of John Fletcher*, 1:159–62. In this section Fletcher also includes his four dispensations.

95. Letter, November 21, 1776 (*Telford*, 6:239–40).

appealed to Romans 5:18 to support the position of the Church.[96] The question before us now is whether Wesley modified his views on paedo-baptism in his *Sunday Service of the Methodists in North America* (1784). The *Sunday Service* was adapted from the Anglican Book of Common Prayer and in so doing Wesley made editorial changes to the baptismal liturgy. Sean McGever recently outlined the revisions Wesley made to the text. He observed that Wesley "retained the language of regeneration before actual baptism but omitted the language of regeneration after the actual baptism."[97] This led McGever to conclude that Wesley adjusted his views on paedo-baptism to fit his evangelical teachings on adult conversion.[98]

A closer look at the *Sunday Service* suggests other possibilities. In the liturgy Wesley did retain after the actual baptism the statements affirming the baptized child is "grafted into the body of Christ's church" and is God's "own child by adoption."[99] On their face these declarations suppose regeneration. Even so, the plot thickens when we realize that at these two locations in the liturgy Wesley removed the word *regenerate* from the BCP text. Since Wesley never explained why he deleted the word, we can only surmise why he did so. To unravel this knot, we first need to restate what we have established so far. First, over the course of his life Wesley rejected the Calvinist notion of eternal reprobation for infants. So, his views on prevenient grace regarding this matter did not change over time. What he stated to John Mason in 1776 was what he had always believed. Second, Wesley taught that baptism cancels the guilt of original sin for infants. This was reaffirmed in the *Sunday Service* with the prayer for God to "sanctify this water to the mystical washing away of sin."[100] This language is similar to that found in the *Tract on Baptism* ("washing away the guilt of original sin") and conveys the same meaning since infants do not have

---

96. *Treatise on Baptism* II.1 (*Works*, Jackson, 10:190).

97. McGever, *Born Again,* 70. James F. White made the same point in his notes on Wesley's *The Sunday Service of the Methodists of North America* (Akron: OSL Publications, 1991), 22.

98. Frank Baker concluded Wesley had softened his position on baptismal justification in the *Sunday Service (John Wesley and the Church of England,* 246–47).

99. White, *Sunday Service,* 142–43.

100. White, *Sunday Service,* 141. See also the prayer for remission of sins on p. 140.

actual sin. Moreover, Christopher McAlilly observed that Wesley did retain in the *Sunday Service* the church's teaching on baptismal regeneration in his revision of the Anglican Articles of Religion.[101]

What was proposed in the last chapter is that baptism serves as the "ordinary means" of washing away Adamic guilt while God remains free in "extraordinary cases" to pardon those who either have no access to the sacrament or have a different theology on the matter.[102] This proposal remains valid with the *Sunday Service*. When the entire baptismal liturgy in the *Sunday Service* is weighed, considering everything Wesley retained and redacted, there is no need to alter this proposal. As Karen Westerfield Tucker explained:

> On the matter of infant baptismal regeneration, Wesley never wavered. Infant baptism was effectual and efficacious. But Wesley observed that persons baptized in infancy often appeared later to be children of the devil than children of God. . . . Hence, those who had lost the "principle of grace," who lacked the inward witness of the Spirit or had not manifested the Spirit's fruits, needed to be regenerated or "born anew" a second time, not through baptism if they had been validly baptized previously, but by the "circumcision of the heart."[103]

Regarding the removal of the word *regenerate*, a possible solution is found in the religious context of the Methodist movement in the 1780s. Methodism held a robust doctrine of adult conversion that redefined what it meant to be a "real Christian." In Wesley's sermons, as McAlilly noted, we see a "growing concern . . . for the need for 'new birth' beyond the sacramental benefits of baptism."[104] Even though Wesley published three tracts on baptism in the 1750s, the evangelical view of regeneration was standard doctrine in the Methodist movement. A possibility is that Wesley removed the word *regenerate* from these two locations in the *Sunday Ser-*

---

101. Christopher T. McAlilly, "Wesley's Removal of the Rite of Confirmation and Its Consequences for American Methodism," *WTJ* 56–52 (Fall 2021): 84.

102. See chapter 4; *Tract on Baptism*, IV.2 (*Works*, Jackson, 10:193).

103. Karen Westerfield Tucker, "The Rites of Christian Initiation," quoted in Christopher T. McAlilly, "Wesley's Removal of the Rite of Confirmation," 85–86.

104. McAlilly, "Wesley's Removal of the Rite of Confirmation," 85.

vice to not confuse or to conflate baptismal regeneration with evangelical new birth. As written, the text of the liturgy clearly supports baptismal regeneration and sacramental justification that is in keeping with the *Tract on Baptism* and Wesley's High Churchmanship, without demoting his evangelical emphasis on present justification and the new birth through adult conversion found in his various writings. If this makes sense, by softening the liturgy on baptismal justification Wesley was able to prioritize evangelical justification over the other degrees, including sacramental justification. He simply did not want any adult to rely solely on their baptism for their Christian hope of salvation. For Wesley, present justification was the sole standard for "the proper Christian faith," as we will see below.

Sacramental Justification: Lord's Supper

In 1787 Wesley published *The Duty of Constant Communion* in the spring edition of the *Arminian Magazine*. The sermon was a revision of an extract he wrote fifty-five years prior from a work by the famed Anglican liturgist Robert Nelson (d. 1715). Albert Outler remarked that *Constant Communion* represents "Wesley's fullest and most explicit statement of his eucharistic doctrine and praxis."[105] The sermon confirms that Wesley's views on the Lord's Supper did not materially change over his life and that his sacramentalism continued to inform his mature doctrine of justification.

To recap, throughout his ministry Wesley considered Holy Communion to be a confirming and converting ordinance.[106] John Bowmer explained that for the Church of England the sacrament serves as a confirming ordinance.[107] As we saw in chapter 3, after his Aldersgate conversion Wesley witnessed many communicants receiving evangelical conversion while partaking. This convinced him that the sacrament is also a converting ordinance. A major influence here was Wesley's Arminian convictions. Bowmer described how Wesley's belief in God's universal love led him to

---

105. Albert Outler, introduction to *The Duty of Constant Communion* (*Works*, 3:427–28).
106. See above, pp. 89–90.
107. Bowmer, *Sacrament of the Lord's Supper*, 108.

see the sacrament as a channel of free grace for seekers as well as for born-again believers.[108]

In *Constant Communion* Wesley reminded his followers why it is their duty to "receive the Lord's Supper as often as they can."[109] The first reason is that it is a command of Christ (I.1). The exhortation to "do this in remembrance of me" (1 Cor. 11:24 NRSVUE) "obliged" the apostles to "bless, break, and give the bread to all that joined with them," and in this way are "all Christians obliged to receive those signs of Christ's body and blood." A second argument is that the "benefits of doing it are so great" (I.2). Two benefits are the "forgiveness of our past sins and the present strengthening and refreshing of our souls." For there is no "surer way" for "procuring pardon" than by partaking of these "tokens of the body and blood of Christ." Likewise, the sacrament confers enabling grace to leave our sins by imparting "strength to perform our duty" and to "lead us on to perfection" (I.3). Thus, the ordinance served two vital purposes in Wesley's doctrine of justification: first, to maintain a state of present justification by granting fresh pardon; and second, to prepare for final justification by imparting sanctifying strength.[110] As we have seen, this was Wesley's consistent position regarding the purpose of the sacrament.[111]

For a restatement, the *Sunday Service* and the sermon "Constant Communion" demonstrate that Wesley maintained a sacramental element in his doctrine of justification throughout his entire life, even after becoming an evangelical in 1738. While much changed and developed in his soteriology over the decades, his beliefs about baptism and the Lord's Supper remained consistent. Their general purpose can be summarized as follows: baptism initiates spiritual life; Holy Communion maintains that life for the eternal kingdom. The exception was evangelical conversion. Having lost their baptismal washing, most early Methodists experienced evangelical conversion in the years following their baptism, and many

---

108. Bowmer, *Sacrament of the Lord's Supper*, 108–11.

109. Albert Outler, preface to *The Duty of Constant Communion* (*Works*, 3:428).

110. These same two benefits are found in Wesley's communion liturgy in the *Sunday Service*. See White, *Sunday Service*, 131–33.

111. See above, pp. 36–37, 89–90

while partaking of the Holy Meal. In these cases, the Lord's Table served as a converting ordinance. So, Wesley adjusted his sacramental theology to make room for evangelical conversion. In the same way, with evangelical faith serving as the mark of real Christianity, the mature Wesley somewhat softened his stance on paedo-baptism to not confuse or to conflate sacramental justification with present justification. Wesley firmly believed in the primacy of present justification over the other degrees of acceptance.

Primacy of Present Justification

1780 Hymnal

Throughout our study we have seen that after 1738, evangelical justification served as the default setting whenever Wesley spoke of or referenced justification in his sermons and writings. This priority is clearly evident in the *Collection of Hymns for the Use of the People Called Methodists*, first published in 1780.[112] The theological importance of the hymns was noted by Franz Hildebrandt when he listed the *Hymns* along with the *Sermons* and *Explanatory Notes* as the "standard books on Wesleyan doctrine."[113] Although Wesley served primarily as an editor and translator, he did author a handful of the hymns, and his theological priorities are evident in how he arranged the materials according to his *via salutis*.[114] As he stated in the preface, "The hymns are not carelessly jumbled together, but carefully arranged under proper heads, according to the experience of *real* Christians."[115]

---

112. For studies on Wesley and early Methodist hymnody and worship, see Swee Hong Lim, "Music and Hymnody," in *The Oxford Handbook of Methodist Studies*, ed. William Abraham and James E. Kirby (Oxford: Oxford University Press, 2009), 332–43; Rack, *Reasonable Enthusiast*, 409–19; Karen B. Westerfield Tucker, "Wesley's Emphases on Worship and the Means of Grace," in Maddox and Vickers, *The Cambridge Companion to John Wesley*, 225–41. On this hymnal, see Franz Hildebrandt and Oliver A. Beckerlegge, eds., *A Collection of Hymns for the Use of the People Called Methodists* (*Works*, 7:1–69).

113. Hildebrandt and Beckerlegge, *Collection of Hymns* (*Works*, 7:1).

114. See Introduction, section three (*Works*, 7:31–38).

115. Preface §4, *Collection of Hymns* (*Works*, 7:74, emphasis mine).

The format of the hymnal demonstrates the primacy of evangelical justification. We have seen that Wesley held five degrees of justification (responsive unregenerate, baptized infants, faith of a servant, evangelical justification, and final justification). Of these five degrees it is present justification that fills the pages of the *Collection of Hymns* from beginning to end. There is no mention of the *faith of a servant*, apart from a single reference in the section on "Mourners Convinced of Sin."[116] But even there it is present justification that absorbs the attention, since that is what the servant yearns to attain. Nor is much attention given to final justification in the hymns. Instead, the reader's attention is persistently drawn to the joys of evangelical justification and its perceptible assurance of God's pardoning love.

From the table of contents, we see how Wesley structured the hymnal to mirror the "scripture way of salvation." Of the five parts, the first four experientially address the three spiritual states of the *via salutis*: natural, legal, and evangelical. Part 1 deals with themes of ultimate concern, like the happiness of religion, the goodness of God, death and final judgment, and the eternal states of heaven and hell. The aim here is to arouse sleepy sinners in the *natural state* out of their false security. Part 2 is short but of utmost importance, since it contrasts nominal with real, inward Christianity. After this, the third section appeals to those spiritually awakened in the *legal state*. The themes of repentance, conviction of sin, seeking salvation, and the restoration of backsliders are the focus of these hymns. The next section (part 4) addresses the Christian's pilgrimage in the *evangelical state*, while the final section (part 5) includes hymns for when a Methodist society gathers.

What is most striking about this *Collection of Hymns* is the experiential element. Justification is described as more than a belief or a doctrine; it was an *experience* that Wesley and the early Methodists celebrated when they gathered for worship. The opening section of part 4 ("Rejoicing") contains many hymns commemorating the release and freedom that the early Methodists felt when they sang about their new life in Christ. The

---

116. Hymn 119.5 (*Works*, 7:230).

hymns breathe with cheerful awareness of sins forgiven and felt assurance of salvation in Christ. It is here that Christ's imputed righteousness is proclaimed and extoled,[117] as in this famous hymn written by Charles Wesley soon after his conversion in May 1738:

> And can it be, that I should gain
>> An interest in the Saviour's blood?
> Died he for me, who caused him pain?
>> For me? Who him to death pursued?
> Amazing love! How can it be
>> That thou, my God, shouldst die for me?
>
> No condemnation now I dread,
>> Jesus, and all in him, is mine.
> Alive in him, my living head,
>> And clothed in righteousness divine,
> Bold I approach th'eternal throne,
>> And claim the crown, through Christ my own.[118]

Even though the word *justification* and its cognates seldom appear in the *Collection of Hymns*,[119] its synonyms and poetic expressions abound everywhere, so that its meaning was easily grasped by the average lay Methodist.[120] Justification is proclaimed in relation to the cross, as would be expected. Throughout the hymns Christ is presented as the meritorious cause of salvation by providing a penal satisfaction for sin, thereby purchasing pardon and acceptance for all who believe.[121] The central idea is the great exchange. Christ died in our place so that through his righteousness we can be forgiven and restored to God's favor.[122] Absent

---

117. Hymns 183.1, 11; 189.3; 419.4 (*Works*, 7:309, 311, 318, 595).

118. Hymn 193.1, 5 (*Works*, 3:222–23).

119. For an exception, see Hymn 1.6 (*Works*, 7:80).

120. Examples abound, like pardon, forgiveness, approval, acceptance, favor, reconciled, no condemnation, chains fell off, and peace.

121. Meritorious cause, hymns 139.4–5; 183.4–5; 423.4 (*Works*, 7:256, 310, 599); penal satisfaction and salvation purchased, hymns 119.6; 125.2; 139.5; 181.1 (*Works*, 7:230, 236, 256, 306).

122. E.g., hymns 1.7; 30.2; 111.2; 123.6; 139.4 (*Works*, 7:81, 118, 221, 234, 256).

is the Calvinist notion of an imputation of Christ's active righteousness. Instead, it is the Son's passion and death that directly redeems and saves.

The source of salvation is God's free unmerited grace, flowing from his infinite love and mercy. Even the idea of sovereign grace appears at times, which speaks of those salvific moments in the *via salutis* when God alone acts—for "who can forgive sins but God alone?"[123] The inclusion of sovereign grace reminds us that Wesley's doctrine of justification does include an element of monergism. The analogy of healing is another recurring theme of God's redemptive grace, as it is found elsewhere in Wesley's writings.[124] On the question of merit, faith is defined as trust and not a human work. A recurring theme is that saving faith is a gift of sheer grace, the work of the Triune God in the human heart.[125] Any inkling of merit or of earning salvation is utterly foreign to the expressions and spirit of the hymns. This pertains to all phases of the *via salutis*, beginning with prevenient grace in the early hymns to full salvation in the later hymns. As a result, assurance of salvation is the fruit of inward religion, with the indwelling Spirit witnessing directly to the "blood applied" and indirectly by "his fruits we show."[126]

The concept of believers working out their salvation is another prevalent theme, taking up nearly half of the hymnal, and reflects the synergism of Wesley's soteriology. Part 4 opens with a celebration of experiential salvation in Christ, and then proceeds to several sections devoted to the disciplines of warfare, prayer, alertness, working, suffering, perfecting, and intercession. Once again, the idea of merit is absent from these hymns of aspiration and testimony. In its place are the fervent appeals of total dependence on the Triune God to live a holy life. For example, in Hymn 346:

---

123. Hymns 195.1; 207.3; 271.8 (*Works*, 7:325, 338, 419); Mark 2:7.

124. Hymns 127.4; 131.1 (*Works*, 7:238, 242). On the therapeutic motif in Wesley's theology and writings, see Maddox, *Responsible Grace*, 144–45.

125. Hymns 114.3; 135.3 (*Works*, 7:225, 249).

126. Hymn 93.2, 4 (*Works*, 7:196–97).

> Lord, I believe thy every word,
> > Thy every promise true;
> And lo! I wait on thee, my Lord,
> > Till I my strength renew.
>
> I shall, a weak and helpless worm,
> > Through Jesus strengthening me,
> Impossibilities perform,
> > And live from sinning free.[127]

This attitude of filial trust and childlike reliance pervades the section "For Believers Working."[128] The eight hymns of this small section do not boast about human ability to live for God. To the contrary, they are filled with prayers for grace and inner strength to imitate the example of Christ and express a heartfelt desire to give one's all to God in holy love.

Another pervading theme is the economic Trinity as the originating source, procuring cause, transformative power, and final goal behind every aspect of redemption, including justification.[129] Elmer Colyer described the *Collection of Hymns* as having an "evangelical, doxological, and participatory Trinitarian dimension."[130] This means that present justification involves the "forgiveness of our sins and our guilt because of the love of God the Father that comes to us through Christ's life, death, and resurrection and is made real in our lives by the Holy Spirit."[131] Wesley made this same point in his sermon "On the Trinity":

> I know not how anyone can be a Christian believer till "he hath" (as St. John speaks) "the witness in himself" . . . till God the Holy Ghost witnesses that God the Father has accepted him through the merits of God the Son—and having this witness he honours the Son and the blessed Spirit "even as he honours the Father."[132]

---

127. Hymn 346.1, 9 (*Works*, 7:509–10).
128. Hymns 312–319 (*Works*, 7:466–75).
129. E.g., hymns 225–227, 234 (*Works*, 7:363–66, 375–77).
130. Colyer, *Trinitarian Dimension of John Wesley's Theology*, 302.
131. Colyer, *Trinitarian Dimension of John Wesley's Theology*, 167.
132. *On the Trinity* §17 (*Works*, 2:385).

The evangelical experience of justification includes both monergistic and synergistic elements and is Trinitarian at its core. The Father grants pardon through the mediatorship of the Son, with the Spirit's gift of assurance including a believer's free response and participation.

Methodist Identity

We close this chapter and our story with a brief word on Wesley's doctrine of present justification as a core element of early Methodist identity. Later in life Wesley would often rehearse the rise of the Methodist movement to explain to his followers their identity as Methodists.[133] In 1788 Wesley recounted in the sermon "On God's Vineyard" the Methodists' unique calling within the Christian world as the "vineyard of the Lord."[134] He claimed this special status for several reasons, one being its doctrinal position on justification and sanctification as the heart of the gospel *via salutis*.

Wesley opened by retelling the history of the Methodist movement. Since its origins in the 1720s the Methodists had been a people of one book, the word of God, and a central aim of restoring the primitive faith of the apostolic church (I.1).[135] Besides the primitive faith, there were three other sources that shaped the movement's doctrinal identity. The first was the holy living divine, William Law (I.2). As we saw in chapter 2, Law was largely responsible for Methodism's adoption of adult conversion for holy living. Law convinced the young Wesley that the majority of Anglicans had sinned away their baptismal washing and must be reconverted by devoting themselves to God. The next source was the Lutheran Pietist Count Zinzendorf and the Moravians (I.3), who mentored Wesley in the evangelical experience of instantaneous conversion as a present assurance

---

133. For a similar survey of Wesley rehearsing Methodist identity, see Olson, *Wesley and Aldersgate*, 148–49.

134. Preface to *On God's Vineyard* (*Works*, 3:503).

135. To explore more of Wesley's interest in primitive Christianity, see Hammond, *John Wesley in America: Restoring Primitive Christianity*; Olson, *Wesley and Aldersgate*, 150–51.

of salvation. However, on the "grand point of justification by faith" Wesley and his fellow Methodists were "never clearly convinced that we are justified by faith alone" until they consulted the Anglican *Book of Homilies* and Articles of Religion (I.4). As we have seen in this study, each one of these sources contributed important elements to Wesley's doctrine of present, evangelical justification.

In the end the Wesleyan *via salutis* accents the twin moments of "free, full, present justification" and "entire sanctification both of heart and life" within a lifelong progression of spiritual growth and maturation (I.6–8).[136] Wesley noted the trend in Christian traditions was to focus either on justification or sanctification and to ignore the other (I.5). He concluded the Methodists' chief contribution was that "they do not think or speak of justification so as to supersede sanctification, so neither do they think or speak of sanctification so as to supersede justification" (I.8). As Wesley saw it, present, evangelical justification and Christian perfection form the essence of Methodism's message and identity.

His reasoning makes sense. Of the different degrees of acceptance, it is present justification that represents the "experience of real Christians," who being "justified by faith, have peace with God through our Lord Jesus Christ; and at the same time are 'born again'" and in "whom is that whole mind, all those tempers, which were also in Christ Jesus."[137] This is the "experience" of "the proper Christian salvation" that is summarized in Ephesians 2:8 ("By grace ye are saved through faith") and Hebrews 12:14 ("Without [holiness] no man shall see the Lord").[138] Both scripture texts capture the motifs of present justification and Christian perfection that

---

136. Besides the recap of the *via salutis* in "On God's Vineyard" I.6–7, Wesley rehearsed it elsewhere in *The Scripture Way of Salvation* I.2–4; *On Friendship with the World* §7; *In What Sense We Are to Leave the World* §§23–24; *On Working Out Our Own Salvation* II.1; *On Faith, Heb. 11:6*, II.4–5; *On the Discoveries of Faith* §§12–17 (*Works*, 2:156–58; 3:130, 152–54, 203–4, 500–501; 4:34–38).

137. Preface §4, *Collection of Hymns* (*Works*, 7:74); *On God's Vineyard* I.9 (*Works*, 3:507–8).

138. *On Working Out Our Own Salvation* II.1 and *On the Wedding Garment* §18 (*Works*, 3:204; 4:148).

defined Wesley's gospel since his *annus mirabilis* in 1738. These same two motifs helped fuel the Methodist revival that over the past two centuries has spawned countless Wesleyan associations and denominations that today number upward of seventy-five million.[139]

---

139. *Annus mirabilis* is Latin for miraculous year. See Albert Outler, "The Place of Wesley in the Christian Tradition," in *The Wesleyan Theological Heritage: Essays of Albert C. Outler*, ed. Thomas C. Oden and Leicester R. Longden (Grand Rapids: Zondervan, 1991), 84. On the numerical growth of Methodism today, see Abraham and Kirby, *The Oxford Handbook of Methodist Studies*, ix.

CONCLUSION
ENDURING THEMES

Now that the story of John Wesley's doctrine of justification has been told we can retrace its central features. We begin with the multifaceted and evolving nature of its development. This was largely due to Wesley's wide range of religious experiences combined with theological controversies in which he formed firm convictions about what it means to be in right standing before God. Although he interacted with numerous people, writings, and traditions on the subject, Wesley's doctrine can be characterized as Anglican, Evangelical, and Arminian. Having been reared and educated in the Anglican sacramental view of the Christian life and its doctrine of double justification, Wesley adopted in 1738 an evangelical view of gospel justification by faith alone. The fusing of these two traditions, plus other influences, led him to form an eclectic understanding of justification in which his Arminianism framed and nuanced every facet of his thought.

Wesley's eclecticism included a series of conjunctives that function as dialectical tensions: present and final, sacramental and non-sacramental, relation and real, free and cooperant, condition and merit, imputed and imparted, faith and works. The list is not exhaustive but shows that Wesley's full perspective on the subject cannot be reduced to a single, unitary definition or concept. Even though Wesley was an evangelical, High Church Anglican with strong Arminian convictions, he drank from other theological streams that made important contributions to his perspective. Examples include those with whom he agreed (like Baxter and Goodwin) and disagreed (James Hervey). The cultural and religious context therefore become critical for us to fully appreciate the particulars of his doctrine and their explanatory power of our salvation in Christ.

Our narrative study also demarcates Wesley as a doctrinal theologian. Randy Maddox noted that Wesley was a "serious student of theology" at Oxford and considered theology essential to the cultivation of a "worldview that frames the temperament and practice of believers' lives in the world."[1] Kenneth Collins added that Wesley had a "decidedly scriptural orientation" in which the "truth of Scripture must be actualized, operationalized in increasing Christlikeness in both the personal life and in the broader community."[2] Soteriological interests were therefore primary to Wesley as a doctrinal theologian. He wanted to know "one thing," the "way to heaven" and "how to land safe on that happy shore."[3] Practical divinity—explicating the *ordo salutis* in the "scripture way of salvation"—became a specialty for Wesley as a doctrinal theologian. And it stands out in our story.

Throughout the narrative we saw the attention to detail that Wesley devoted to the doctrine of justification. He returned to the subject time and again throughout his long career to work through the particulars. He understood that our participation in the salvific blessings of the gospel hinge upon a proper understanding of this vital truth. One way to capture the breadth of Wesley's viewpoint is to survey its enduring themes and to flesh out its internal logic and coherence. We begin with the Trinitarian foundation of his justification doctrine.

Economic Trinity

John Wesley was a Trinitarian Christian. Throughout our study we have seen that his doctrine of justification was Trinitarian at its core. It was how Wesley conceived, spoke, and wrote about our pardon and acceptance by God. Following the pattern found in scripture, the ancient ecumenical creeds, and his own Anglican tradition, Wesley recognized

---

1. Maddox, *Responsible Grace*, 15, 17.
2. Collins, *Theology of John Wesley*, 2.
3. Preface §5, *Sermons on Several Occasions* (*Works*, 1:105).

specific roles for the Father, Son, and Holy Spirit in our justification before God. Known as the law of appropriation, Wesley defined the roles to be the Father *loves* and *declares*, the Son *procures* and *intercedes*, the Spirit *testifies* and *imparts*.[4] Below we will address these roles in some detail.

Behind the salvific activity of the Triune persons is the gracious disposition to save. Since Wesley taught there are several degrees of acceptance, his Anglican theology of grace was multifaceted. Scholars accent his view of *prevenient grace* that is universally present and elicits free response to divine truth according to one's degree of salvific knowledge. From his High Church Anglicanism Wesley inherited an Augustinian concept of *infused grace* conveyed through the sacraments.[5] A Protestant definition of grace as *favor* was passed down to him from the Magisterial Reformers through his Anglican heritage. Most important, Wesley came to an evangelical understanding of *free grace* as perceptible assurance of pardon through his interactions with Pietism. In all these forms of grace the "Triune God is active on our behalf in the gospel."[6]

Lastly, the economic Trinity informed Wesley's Arminian understanding of the divine decrees. On more than one occasion he stated that from eternity God made an "unchangeable, irreversible, irresistible decree" that "He that believeth shall be saved; he that believeth not shall be damned."[7] What is notable about this statement is that it pertains to the "scripture

---

4. See above, pp. 45–52. Kenneth Collins made a similar summary in terms of revelation, "The name 'Father' designates the origin of the revelation, the Son, the historic Mediator, and the Holy Spirit, the present reality of this revelation" (*Theology of John Wesley*, 145).

5. Scholars suggest that Wesley had a Catholic notion of infused grace as a metaphysical force or substance. On this point, see Thomas A. Noble, *Holy Trinity: Holy People, The Theology of Christian Perfecting* (Eugene, OR: Cascade Books, 2013), 100; Hammond, *John Wesley in America*, 51–52, 62–64; Theodore Runyon, *The New Creation: John Wesley's Theology Today* (Nashville: Abingdon Press, 1998), 150. Coyler disagrees (*Trinitarian Dimension of John Wesley's Theology*, 143). On the subject of infused grace, see also James R. Ginther, *The Westminster Handbook to Medieval Theology* (Louisville: Westminster John Knox Press, 2009), 76, 161–62.

6. Coyler, *Trinitarian Dimension of John Wesley's Theology*, 143.

7. *On Predestination* §7 (*Works*, 2:418). Wesley quotes Mk 16:16. In *Predestination Calmly Considered* §59 Wesley grounds this unchangeable decree on God's immutable nature (*Works*, 13:296). Thus, his doctrine of decrees follows from his doctrine of God.

way of salvation" and not to a determination of who will believe. He therefore understood election and predestination to pertain to the plan of redemption worked out in salvation history. In this plan divine pardon and acceptance are available to every child of Adam. As he famously stated, grace is "free in all, and free for all."[8] The universal availability of justifying grace finds expression in his covenant theology.

Covenant Theology

Federal theology served as the framework for Wesley's soteriology and doctrine of justification. It is through the covenant structure that the Father, Son, and Holy Spirit accomplish their saving activities. Derived from his Anglican heritage and refined through his reading of Puritan authors, Wesley taught that God instituted a covenant of works with prelapsarian Adam who was fully capable of fulfilling its conditions for eternal life. But Adam sinned and the covenant of works was replaced with a covenant of grace under the headship of Christ. Wesley followed standard Anglican theology by not conflating the covenant of works with the Mosaic Law, as was commonly done in Puritan theology. This meant the entire period of salvation history from the protoevangelium in Genesis 3:15 to the Christian era that began at Pentecost was under the covenant of grace.

For our purposes the important aspect of Wesley's covenant theology was his concept of dispensations. Following the lead of John Fletcher, Wesley listed several dispensations in the covenant of grace, namely heathen/patriarchal, Jewish, John the Baptist (which included Christ's human ministry), and Christian.[9] Although historically progressive, Wesley believed a degree of salvation was available in each dispensation according to an increasing revelation of divine truth. Only at Pentecost did "full, Christian salvation" become attainable through the redemptive work of Christ and the gift of the eschatological Spirit. At this point, Wesley's doctrine of dispensations takes an interesting turn by linking specific historical dis-

---

8. *Free Grace* §2 (*Works*, 3:544).

9. Wesley followed Fletcher's lead on this point. *On Faith* §2 (*Works*, 3:492). On the three spiritual states, see *The Spirit of Bondage and of Adoption* (*Works*, 1:248–66).

pensations to different levels of spiritual experience today. This became the theological basis for degrees of acceptance in his doctrine of justification.

Degrees of Acceptance

Our study showed there are five basic degrees of justification in Wesley's soteriology, even though he argued at times there are as "many degrees in the favour of" God as in our renewal of the "image of God."[10] The five degrees are (1) *measure of acceptance* for the responsive unregenerate; (2) *sacramental justification* for baptized infants (usually lost before adulthood) and believing adults converted before or at their baptism; (3) *justifying faith* for those Christians who have the *faith of a servant* but lack the Spirit's testimony; (4) *present, evangelical justification* for believers who are born again and have "the proper Christian faith"; and (5) *final justification* at the Last Judgment.[11]

As God's administrations of saving grace progressed by degrees through salvation history, in terms of revelation and soteriological benefits, progression characterizes the different degrees of acceptance in the favor of God today. It begins with a "measure of acceptance" for the *responsive unregenerate* who have a general knowledge of the one true God and practice righteousness as far as they know it. This degree aligns to the heathen or patriarchal dispensation. The favor of God increases with the *faith of a servant* that includes a sincere devotion to God and participation in the sacramental life of the church but lacks the Spirit's testimony of assurance. This characterizes the Jewish and Baptist dispensations (and Wesley's pre-Aldersgate spiritual state). Both degrees of acceptance are grounded on the soteriological standard found in Acts 10:35, "He that feareth [God] and worketh righteousness is accepted."[12] A significantly larger measure of divine favor is experienced with

---

10. Wesley, *A Letter to the Rev. Mr. James Hervey,* October 15, 1756 (*Works,* 13:326).

11. On the five degrees, see chapter 3, section "Justification and Assurance, Part One"; chapter 4, sections "Explanatory Notes upon the New Testament" (Conversion of Cornelius) and *Treatise on Baptism;* chapter 5, section "Degrees of Acceptance."

12. See above, pp. 103–6.

present, evangelical justification and its perceptible assurance of pardon. This degree enjoys the poured-out Spirit of Pentecost and the soteriological benefits of the Christian dispensation.

Then, there is *final justification* in the eschatological future when the Lord will grant official access to the eternal kingdom. While the other three degrees are conditioned on faith, final justification will be according to works, as the scriptures declare. Lastly, there is *sacramental justification* that overlaps the servant and evangelical degrees of acceptance. The sacraments signify and convey preventing, justifying, and sanctifying grace according to the spiritual need and faith of the recipient.[13] To look more closely at the differences in soteriological standing among the five degrees we turn next to the Trinitarian roles of the Father, Son, and Holy Spirit.

Trinitarian Roles

As a doctrinal theologian John Wesley demonstrated great care in how he sequenced the doctrines of salvation in his descriptions of the "scripture way of salvation." For instance, Wesley ordered present justification before the new birth even though both happen at the same time. Other examples include his distinctions between real and relative change, and between repentance and faith as remote and immediate conditions. In the same way, our study uncovered an internal order or structure to Wesley's doctrine of justification that offers important insights into how our justification takes place. These insights also pertain directly to his concept of degrees. To flesh out his perspective on the matter, we return to the Trinitarian roles of the Father who *loves* and *declares*, the Son who *procures* and *intercedes*, and the Spirit who *testifies* and *imparts*.

Father Loves and Declares

In Wesley's soteriology love is the "reigning attribute" of the divine character, the font from which the Triune activity of justifying and sav-

---

13. See above, pp. 30–37, 87–94, 106–13.

ing grace flows.[14] Divine love is what moved the Father to send his Son, for the Son to sacrifice his life, and for the Spirit to testify of the Father's pardoning love.[15] At this point in the economy of salvation, divine justice takes a back seat to the Father's love. It must be satisfied for pardon to be granted, but Wesley's Arminian convictions would not accept justice as the motivating reason behind God's plan to justify sinners. As we saw above, by anchoring justifying grace in the love of God, the eternal decrees are reinterpreted to ordain the "scripture way of salvation" in the dispensations of grace, with the predestined goal of full conformity to the glorified Christ in the new creation.[16]

As a Protestant Wesley held that justification means to be *declared righteous*. And he employed the terms "pardon," "acceptance," "favor," and "title" to explain what this declaration entails.[17] His use of these terms proved critical to his doctrine of degrees. *Pardon* was considered by Wesley to be the "plain scriptural notion of justification." He defined it as "that act of God the Father whereby, for the sake of the propitiation made by the blood of his Son," past sins are remitted, forgiven, and covered.[18] At other times he communicated the idea in more visual terms. Past sins are "blotted out," "canceled," and "vanish away as the morning dew." They are "driven away as chaff, are gone, are lost, swallowed up, remembered no more" so there remains "no condemnation."[19] To avoid the pitfalls of antinomianism Wesley consistently applied our pardon to only past sins.

Another widely used term was "acceptance." The term refers to divine approval, approbation, and inclusion. When paired with "pardon"

---

14. *ENNT,* 1 Jn. 4:8.

15. *God's Love to Fallen Man* I.5 (*Works,* 2:428).

16. Rom. 8:29. In Wesley's federal theology salvation history runs from the Creation to the end of this present age when the new creation arrives (Olson, *John Wesley Reader on Eschatology,* 41–42, 47–50).

17. These terms are found throughout chapters 2 through 5. For "title," see above, pp. 45–52, 106–13.

18. *Justification by Faith* II.5 (*Works,* 1:189).

19. *The First-fruits of the Spirit* III.1–2; *The Repentance of Believers* III.3 (*Works,* 1:243–44, 351).

Wesley nearly always listed it after "pardon."[20] When evangelical assurance is included, the order became pardon—acceptance—assurance, as when Wesley shared his testimony in 1767:

> First I heard,
> "Thy sins are forgiven! Accepted thou art!"
> I listened, and heaven sprung up in my heart.[21]

There is an inherent logic to this order. Divine pardon removes the barrier that enables divine acceptance, which in turn generates divine assurance. For Wesley, each link in the chain is essential to present justification. If any link is broken, the evangelical experience evaporates.

When we turn to the soteriological standing of the responsive unregenerate and the servant, an interesting insight emerges: Wesley never used the language of pardon to describe their degrees of justification. Instead, he wrote about their "measure of acceptance."[22] The language of pardon is reserved for present, evangelical justification. This makes sense since pardon, strictly speaking, allows no degrees. By denying that the responsive unregenerate and servant are presently pardoned, Wesley suggested that their present justification awaits the *final justification* at the Last Judgment.[23] To state it another way, their present "measure of acceptance" represents a "justifying faith" in anticipation of the perceptible assurance of pardon they will receive on the final day.

The next synonym for justification was "favor," which often connotes God's gracious disposition to give salvation as a "free, undeserved gift."[24] Along with acceptance, Wesley consistently ordered favor after pardon

---

20. Examples include *Justification by Faith* II.5; *The Righteousness of Faith* §§2, 4; *The Lord Our Righteousness* II.5; *The Scripture Way of Salvation* I.3 (*Works*, 1:189–90, 203–4, 455; 2:157). For an exception, see *Farther Appeal, Pt. I*, II.10 (*Works*, 11.116).

21. *The Witness of the Spirit II* III.6 (*Works*, 1:290).

22. *ENNT*, Acts 10:35; *On Faith* I.10; *On the Discoveries of Faith* §13 (*Works*, 3:497; 4:35).

23. On the responsive unregenerate and servant being now in the favor of God, see *ENNT*, Acts 10:35. Concerning general justification, see above, pp. 151–154.

24. *Salvation by Faith* §1, III.3; *Justification by Faith* IV.9 (*Works*, 1:117–18, 126, 198).

in his descriptions of evangelical salvation.[25] These two terms were practically synonymous in Wesley's descriptions of degrees of acceptance because both refer to a divine attitude that can vary in strength. The fourth term was "title" and pertains to our final justification and end-time rewards.[26] We saw earlier that Wesley understood "merit" to refer either to earning salvation by personal goodness or to deserving a reward. It was in this latter sense that he employed the term in the sermon "The Wedding Garment":

> The former is necessary to *entitle* us to heaven; the latter, to *qualify* us for it. Without the righteousness of Christ we could have no *claim* to glory; without holiness we could have no *fitness* for it. By the former we become members of Christ, children of God, and heirs of the kingdom of heaven. By the latter we are "made meet to be partakers of the inheritance of the saints of light."[27]

To summarize, the terms "pardon," "acceptance," "favor," and "title" help to clarify Wesley's point that justification is a *relational* change in contrast to the *real* change of the new birth. In our justification God "does something for us" by changing our "outward relation to God" and "taking away our guilt" so that he "restores us to his favour."[28] In other words, *pardon* removes our guilt, *acceptance* and *favor* provide us with inclusion and approval, and *title* gives us rightful claim to the eternal "enjoyment of the Three-One God, and of all the creatures in him."[29] All these terms add up to a right standing before God.

---

25. *The Almost Christian*, II.5; *Justification by Faith* IV.3; *On the Discoveries of Faith* §15 (*Works*, 1:139, 195; 4:37). Wesley also spoke of degrees of favor. See *On Charity* II.2; *Letter to James Hervey*, 1.159 (*Works*, 3:299; 13:326).

26. On Wesley's uses of the term "title," see *Extract of Baxter's Aphorisms* IV.8; IV.8.9 (*Works*, 12:57–58); *Sermons on the Mount V* IV.11; *VIII* §1, *X* §15 (*Works*, 1:568, 612, 656).

27. *The Wedding Garment* §10 (*Works*, 4:144, emphasis his).

28. *The Great Privilege of Those That Are Born of God* §2 (*Works*, 1:431–32). See also *Justification by Faith*, II.1; *The Scripture Way of Salvation*, I.4 (*Works*, 1:187; 2:158).

29. *The New Creation* §18 (*Works*, 2:510).

Son Procures and Intercedes

With justification defined as the Father's declaration of righteousness, the next question becomes what procures or merits a right standing before God, given his just and holy character. Wesley's answer was the Son's sufferings and death, also known as his passive righteousness. The atonement was one of the more stable elements in Wesley's doctrine of justification, for he never strayed far from the language of his church, with terms like "oblation (offering)," "sacrifice," "propitiation," "ransom," "redemption," and "satisfaction."[30] Although Wesley never produced a sermon or tract on the atonement, his many remarks confirm that he adopted an Arminian version of the penal substitution theory to explain how the blood of Christ procures our justification before God.

Central to Wesley's notion of justification is that sinners have objective guilt that deserves God's righteous condemnation. To remove this guilt and its condemnation the Son offered himself (*oblation*) as a *sacrifice* for sin to *propitiate* the Father's aggrieved anger and thereby *satisfy* his justice by bearing the *punishment* for sin, so that justifying grace could be freely extended to every sinner without compromising God's holy character.[31] In this scheme Christ's death serves as the meritorious cause of our justification and the imputation of his passive righteousness the formal cause.[32] While Wesley taught a penal substitution theory of redemption, he understood the cross also serves as a moral influence to draw people to Christ through the preventing and convicting work of the Spirit.

Just as the Son's death merits our justification before the Father, so his heavenly intercession before the Father procures the dispensing of justifying grace, according to a person's faith and degree of salvific knowl-

---

30. BCP, Liturgy of Communion, 260; Art. XXXI (BCP, 562); Wesley, *Doctrine of Salvation, Faith, and Good Works* I.7 (*Works*, 12:34).

31. Wesley's use of these terms and language is found in many places, *Collection of Forms of Prayer* (*Works*, Jackson, 11:210, 218, 222); *ENNT*, Rom. 3:23–26; 1 Jn. 2:2; *Salvation by Faith* II.3; *Justification by Faith* I.7–8; IV.5; *The Lord Our Righteousness* II.6–9 (*Works*, 1:122, 185–86, 196, 456–57).

32. Wesley never stated directly what he considered the formal cause to be. But his extract of Goodwin's tract on justification (1765) did explicitly list pardon, which is the imputation of Christ's passive righteousness, as the formal cause. See above, pp. 118–121.

edge.³³ In this way Wesley linked our justification to Christ's resurrection and ascension. His High Church beliefs also connected the Son's glorified presence to the sacraments. Christ's advocacy before the Father therefore secures the impartation of justifying (as well as preventing and sanctifying) grace in the sacraments of baptism and Holy Communion.³⁴ More on the means of grace below.

To summarize, the Son procured our justification in his suffering and death and in his resurrection perpetually intercedes before the Father for the dispensing of justifying grace into our lives. Wesley, however, believed that our justification in this life remains incomplete, just a "measure of acceptance," until the Spirit testifies and imparts the righteousness of Christ.

Spirit Testifies and Imparts

When Wesley adopted his "new gospel" in 1738 he redefined present justification as a perceptible assurance of forgiveness and acceptance.³⁵ This meant, as Joseph Cunningham noted, that evangelical justification is a "thoroughly pneumatological event."³⁶ It involves the twofold activity of the Spirit's testimony of present forgiveness and impartation of righteousness as its fruit. As Wesley stated, the Spirit "implants righteousness in everyone" to whom the Father has "imputed it."³⁷ This pneumatological element became the defining mark of the Christian dispensation in Wesley's covenant theology and is what differentiates evangelical justification from the servant's "measure of acceptance." Wesley, moreover, taught that these two works of the Spirit—testimony and impartation—are organically connected:

---

33. References to Christ's heavenly session by Wesley include *Scriptural Christianity* II.4 (*Works*, 1:166).

34. See above, pp. 30–53, 87–94, 106–13.

35. On Wesley's "new gospel," see chapter 3.

36. Cunningham, *John Wesley's Pneumatology*, 52. See above, pp. 91–94, 125–128.

37. *The New Birth* II.5 (*Works*, 2:194); *The Lord Our Righteousness* II.12 (*Works*, 1:458, emphasis his).

We must be holy of heart and holy in life before we can be conscious that we are so. . . . But we must love God before we can be holy at all; this being the root of all holiness. Now we cannot love God till we know he loves us: "We love him, because he first loved us." And we cannot know his pardoning love to us till his Spirit witnesses it to our spirit.[38]

Wesley here described the *experience* of present, evangelical justification, illustrated so amply in the Methodist *hymnals*.[39] The Spirit's perceptible testimony of God's pardoning love naturally generates in the born-again Christian a response of holy love. The spiritual senses come alive to *see, hear, taste*, and *feel* the Triune God, who is now reconciled to the justified believer.[40] The sequence was important to Wesley: *pardon* illumines *perception* that births *participation* in the life of the Triune God. All three works involve the salvific activity of the Spirit in present justification. The same point was made when Wesley described evangelical faith, "Faith, according to the scriptural account, is the eye of the new-born soul . . . the ear of the soul . . . the palate of the soul . . . the feeling of the soul," by which we perceive and "experience" God in this life.[41] This is "the proper, Christian faith" that composes "the proper, Christian salvation." Wesley had no other standard for gospel justification.

Repentance, Faith, and Good Works

The Anglican distinction between condition and merit proved critical to how Wesley related repentance, faith, and good works to justification in all its degrees. For instance, it allowed him to stress repentance and holy living as necessary for present and final salvation and still proclaim a gospel of free grace. And it possibly contributed to his distinction between

---

38. *The Witness of the Spirit I* I.8 (*Works*, 1:274).

39. See above, pp. 159–66.

40. Wesley often spoke of God being reconciled to the world through the penal satisfaction of the Son. The reason is the separation caused by sin affected not only the world of sinners but also the Creator. In his holiness God stepped back in the relationship and felt the separation due to sin. By removing the barrier of sin, it can be said that both parties, including God, are reconciled in the relationship.

41. *Earnest Appeal* §§7, 10 (*Works*, 11:46–48).

repentance and faith as *remotely* and *immediately* necessary. Whereas repentance and its fruit are "remotely necessary" if there be "time and opportunity for them," faith is "immediately and directly necessary."[42] For as soon as a person believes, they receive justifying grace. Still, repentance remains a condition since a change of mind and heart toward sin is essential for saving faith in any of the degrees of justification.[43]

Wesley's understanding of faith developed over time, and this contributed to his doctrine of degrees. Initially, he understood faith to be an assent to Christian truth. But this changed in 1725 when he came to see faith as a vital, life-changing devotion to God. Then, in 1738 his views changed once more when he adopted the Pietist view of faith as trust in Christ for a perceptible assurance of present justification. Then in the mid-1740s Wesley expanded this evangelical definition to include a "demonstrative evidence of things unseen, the supernatural evidence of things invisible," based on Hebrews 11:1.[44] Saving faith now became a divinely inspired conviction in the heart according to a person's degree of salvific knowledge. After this it did not take long for degrees of justification to appear in his writings.

The salvific role of good works was even more nuanced by Wesley than repentance and faith. Like other Protestants, Wesley stood firm that good works can neither merit nor precede our present justification before God, but they do necessarily follow as evidence and fruit of justifying faith. But these lines became somewhat blurred when he associated good works with the means of grace. This redefined good works as a means to receive preventing, justifying, and sanctifying grace. His later descriptions of the "scripture way of salvation" that include a description of prevenient grace led to a more positive evaluation of good works before present justification. Such works were no longer deemed void of grace but as evidence of a degree of spiritual life and a "measure of acceptance" for the responsive unregenerate and the servant.

---

42. *The Scripture Way of Salvation* III.2 (*Works*, 2:163). See above, pp. 78–87, 96–103.

43. Kenneth J. Collins, "The Doctrine of Justification: Historic Wesleyan and Contemporary Understandings," in *Justification: What's at Stake in the Current Debates,* ed. Mark Husbands and Daniel J. Treier (Downers Grove, IL: InterVarsity Press, 2004), 193.

44. *Earnest Appeal* §6 (*Works,* 11:46).

Good works also serve as a condition for final justification. Wesley followed a literal reading of scripture that the Last Judgment will be according to works.[45] He therefore considered holy living and good works to be prerequisites for final justification, since they serve as evidence in the court's verdict and fit a person for life in the eternal kingdom. This sanctifying work is the product of Christ's active righteousness being implanted in believers by the Spirit of Christ. In this way Christ's active righteousness becomes the formal cause of final justification by *making* us righteous in God's sight. Consequently, Wesley's Arminianism rejected any notion of an eternal justification in this life, as Calvinism taught. Only at the Last Judgment will the declaration be public and irreversible. On that day our justification will be final and *title* to the new creation officially granted. Only then will the eschatological fulfillment of our justification in the Three-One God attain its *terminus ad quem*—the restored *imago Dei*.

We have now finished the story of Wesley's doctrine of justification and recapped its central themes. Our study began with Wesley's statement that justification is the "foundation of all our hope" and the "pillar and ground of that faith" from which "alone cometh salvation."[46] Hopefully the journey of learning about Wesley's doctrine of justification has enriched your knowledge and faith and will lead you to think more deeply about what it means to be in right relationship with God.

---

45. Matt. 24:31-46; Jn. 5:29; Rom. 2:6-11; 2 Cor. 5:10.

46. "Justification by Faith" §1, *The Lord Our Righteousness* §4 (*Works*, 1:106, 182, 451).

BIBLIOGRAPHY

Primary Sources

Baker, Frank, Richard Heitzenrater, and Randy L. Maddox, gen. eds. *The Works of John Wesley*, Bicentennial Edition. 35 vols. Oxford: Clarendon Press, 1975–83. Nashville: Abingdon Press, 1984–Present.

Jackson, Thomas, ed. *The Works of John Wesley*. 14 vols. 3rd ed. Grand Rapids: Baker Book House, 1984.

Osborn, George, ed. *The Poetical Works of John and Charles Wesley*. 13 vols. London: Wesleyan-Methodist Conference Office, 1868–72.

Telford, John, ed. *The Letters of the Rev. John Wesley, A.M.* 8 vols. London: Epworth Press, 1931.

Wesley, John. *Complete English Dictionary*, 2nd ed. Bristol: William Pine, 1764.

———. *Explanatory Notes Upon the New Testament*. 2 vols. Grand Rapids: Baker Book House, 1980.

Secondary Sources

Abraham, William, and James E. Kirby, eds. *The Oxford Handbook of Methodist Studies*. Oxford: Oxford University Press, 2009.

Allison, C. FitzSimons. *The Rise of Moralism: The Proclamation of the Gospel from Hooker to Baxter*. Wilton: Morehouse Barlow, 1966.

Althaus, Paul. *Theology of Martin Luther*. Minneapolis: Fortress Press, 1966.

Arnold, Brian J. *Justification in the Second Century*. Waco, TX: Baylor University Press, 2018.

Avis, Paul. *Anglicanism and the Christian Church*. Edinburgh: T & T Clark, 1989.

———. *In Search of Authority: Anglican Theological Method from the Reformation to the Enlightenment*. London: Bloomsbury, 2014.

Baker, Frank. *John Wesley and the Church of England*. London: Epworth Press, 1970.

———. *A Union Catalogue of the Publications of John and Charles Wesley*. 2nd ed. Stone Mountain, GA: George Zimmermann, 1991.

Baker, Frank, and Fredrick Hunter. *Proceedings of the Wesley Historical Society*, vol. 37 (Oct. 1969, June 1970, Oct. 1970).

Barclay, Robert. *An Apology for the True Christian Divinity*. 11th ed. London: Edward Marsh, 1849.

Bebbington, D. W. *Evangelicalism in Modern Britain: A History from the 1730s to the 1980s*. New York: Routledge, 1989.

Beeke, Joel R., ed. *Memoirs of the Rev. Thomas Halyburton*. Grand Rapids: Reformation Heritage Books, 1996.

Benham, Daniel, ed. *Memoirs of James Hutton: Comprising the Annals of His Life and Connection with the United Brethren*. London: Hamilton, Adams, and Co., 1856.

The Book of Common Prayer, 1662 Version. London: Everyman's Library, 1999.

Borgen, Ole E. *John Wesley on the Sacraments: A Definitive Study of John Wesley's Theology of Worship*. Grand Rapids: Francis Asbury Press, 1972.

Bounds, Christopher T. "How Are People Saved? The Major Views of Salvation with a Focus on Wesleyan Perspectives and Their Implications." *Wesley and Methodist Studies* 3 (2011): 31–54.

Bowmer, John C. *The Sacrament of the Lord's Supper in Early Methodism*. London: Dacre Press, 1951.

Brevint, Daniel. *The Christian Sacrament and Sacrifice; by Way of Discourse, Meditation, and Prayer upon the Nature, Parts, and Blessings of the Holy Communion*. Oxford: Sheldonian Theatre, 1673.

Buchanan, Colin. *Historical Dictionary of Anglicanism*. 2nd ed. New York: Rowman & Littlefield, 2015.

Buchanan, James. *The Doctrine of Justification: An Outline of Its History in the Church and of Its Exposition from Scripture.* Edinburgh: T & T Clark, 1867.

Buckley, Theodore Alois, trans. *Canons and Decrees of the Council of Trent.* London: George Routledge, 1851.

Calvin, John. *Institutes of the Christian Religion.* 2 vols. Louisville: Westminster John Knox Press, 1960.

Campbell, Ted A. *John Wesley and Christian Antiquity: Religious Vision and Cultural Change.* Nashville: Kingswood Books, 1991.

———. *The Religion of the Heart: A Study of European Religious Life in the Seventeenth and Eighteenth Centuries.* Columbia: University of South Carolina Press, 1991.

Cannon, William Ragsdale. *The Theology of John Wesley, with Special Reference to the Doctrine of Justification.* London: University Press of America, 1974.

Cell, George Croft. *The Rediscovery of John Wesley.* New York: Henry Holt & Co., 1935.

Chamberlain, Jeffrey S. "Moralism, Justification, and the Controversy over Methodism." *Journal of Ecclesiastical History* 44, no. 4 (October 1993): 652–78.

Chang, Kiyeong. *The Theologies of the Law in Martin Luther and John Wesley.* Lexington, KY: Emeth Press, 2014.

Chapman, Mark. *Anglican Theology.* New York: T & T Clark, 2012.

Clifford, Alan C. *Atonement and Justification: English Evangelical Theology 1640–1790, An Evaluation.* Oxford: Clarendon Press, 1990.

Coffey, John, and Paul C. H. Lim, eds. *The Cambridge Companion to Puritanism.* Cambridge: Cambridge University Press, 2008.

Collins, Kenneth J. *John Wesley: A Theological Journey.* Nashville: Abingdon Press, 2003.

———. "John Wesley's Engagement with Islam: Exploring the Soteriological Possibilities in Light of a Diversity of Graces and Theological Frameworks." *Wesleyan Theological Journal* 56, no. 2 (Fall 2021): 9–36.

———. *The Theology of John Wesley: Holy Love and the Shape of Grace.* Nashville: Abingdon Press, 2007.

Collins, Kenneth J., and Ryan N. Danker, eds. *The Next Methodism: Theological, Social, and Missional Foundations for Global Methodism*. Franklin, TN: Seedbed Publishing, 2022.

Collins, Kenneth J., and John H. Tyson, eds. *Conversion in the Wesleyan Tradition*. Nashville: Abingdon Press, 2001.

Colyer, Elmer M. *The Trinitarian Dimension of John Wesley's Theology*. Nashville: New Room Books, 2019.

Cooper, Tim. *John Owen, Richard Baxter and the Formation of Nonconformity*. New York: Routledge, 2016.

Coppedge, Allen. *John Wesley in Theological Debate*. Wilmore: Wesley Heritage Press, 1987.

Cragg, G. R. *From Puritanism to the Age of Reason*. Cambridge: Cambridge University Press, 1966.

Crofford, J. Gregory. *Streams of Mercy: Prevenient Grace in the Theology of John and Charles Wesley*. Lexington, KY: Emeth Press, 2010.

Cunningham, Joseph W. *John Wesley's Pneumatology: Perceptible Inspiration*. Burlington: Ashgate, 2014.

Danker, Ryan Nicholas. *Wesley and the Anglican: Political Division in Early Evangelicalism*. Downers Grove: InterVarsity Press, 2016.

Dreyer, Frederick. *The Genesis of Methodism*. Bethlehem, PA: Lehigh University Press, 1999.

Dulles, Avery. *The Assurance of Things Hoped For: A Theology of Faith*. Oxford: Oxford University Press, 1994.

Ewbank, J. Robert. *John Wesley, Natural Man, and the "Isms."* Eugene, OR: Resource Publications, 2009.

Fellman, Laura Bartels. "John Wesley and the 'Servant of God.'" *Wesleyan Theological Journal* 41, no. 2 (Fall 2006): 72–86.

Fitzgerald, Allan D., gen ed. *Augustine through the Ages: An Encyclopedia*. Grand Rapids: William B. Eerdmans, 1999.

Forsaith, Peter S., ed. *Unexampled Labors: Letters of the Revd John Fletcher to Leaders in the Evangelical Revival*. Peterborough: Epworth, 2008.

Franke, August Hermann. *Nicodemis: Or, A Treatise against the Fear of Man*. London: Joseph Downing, 1706.

Freeman, Arthur J. *An Ecumenical Theology of the Heart: The Theology of Count Nicholas Ludwig von Zinzendorf.* Bethlehem: The Moravian Church in America, 1998.

Garden, Alexander. *The Doctrine of Justification . . . in a Letter to A. Croswell.* Charles-Town: Peter Timothy, 1742.

Gibson, William. *The Church of England 1688–1832: Unity and Accord.* London: Routledge, 2012.

Ginther, James R. *The Westminster Handbook to Medieval Theology.* Louisville: Westminster John Knox Press, 2009.

Goen, C. C., ed. *The Works of Jonathan Edwards: The Great Awakening*, vol. 4. New Haven, CT: Yale University Press, 1972.

Goodwin, John. *Imputatio Fidei, or A Treatise of Justification wherein Ye Imputation of Faith for Righteousness Is Explained.* London: Andrew Crooke, 1642.

Goold, William H., ed. *The Works of John Owen.* 16 vols. Carlisle: The Banner of Truth Trust, 1965.

Green, Richard. *The Works of John and Charles Wesley: A Bibliography.* 2nd ed. London: Methodist Publishing House, 1906.

Green, V. H. H. *The Young Mr. Wesley.* London: Edward Arnold, 1961.

Grey, Gerald, ed. *The Books of Homilies: A Critical Edition.* Cambridge: James Clarke & Co, 2015.

Hammond, Geordan. *John Wesley in America: Restoring Primitive Christianity.* Oxford: Oxford University Press, 2014.

Harper, Steve, "The Devotional Life of John Wesley, 1703–1738." PhD diss. Duke University, 1981.

Heitzenrater, Richard P. *Dairy of an Oxford Methodist: Benjamin Ingham, 1733–1734.* Durham, NC: Duke University Press, 1985.

———. *Mirror and Memory: Reflections on Early Methodism.* Nashville: Kingswood Books, 1989.

———. *Wesley and the People Called Methodists.* 2nd ed. Nashville: Abingdon Press, 2013.

Hervey, James. *Aspasio Vindicated, and the Scripture-Doctrine of Imputed Righteousness Defended against the Objections and Animadversions of the Rev. Mr. John Wesley, in Eleven Letters.* Leeds: Griffin Wright, 1764.

———. *Theron and Aspasio: or, a Series of Dialogues and Letters, upon the Most Interesting and Important Subjects*. 2 vols. Dublin: Robert Main, 1755.

Hindmarsh, D. Bruce. *The Evangelical Conversion Narrative: Spiritual Autobiography in the Early Modern Period*. Oxford: Oxford University Press, 2005.

Holden, Harrington W. *John Wesley in Company with High Churchmen*. London: Church Press Company, 1870.

Holland, Bernard. *Baptism in Early Methodism*. London: Epworth Press, 1970.

Horton, Michael. *Justification*. 2 vols. Grand Rapids: Zondervan, 2018.

Husbands, Mark, and Daniel J. Treier, eds. *Justification: What's at Stake in the Current Debates*. Downers Grove, IL: InterVarsity Press, 2004.

Johnson, John. *The Unbloody Sacrifice, and Altar, Unvail'd and Supported*. London: Robert Knaplock, 1714, 1718.

Keble, John, ed. *The Works of That Learned and Judicious Divine, Mr. Richard Hooker*. 3 vols. 5th ed. Oxford: Clarendon Press, 1865.

Kimborough, S. T., Jr., and Kenneth G. C. Newport. *The Manuscript Journal of the Reverend Charles Wesley, M. A*. 2 vols. Nashville: Kingswood Books, 2008.

Kirkpatrick, Daniel. *Monergism or Synergism: Is Salvation Cooperative or the Work of God Alone?* Eugene, OR: Pickwick Publications, 2018.

Kisker, Scott Thomas. *Foundation for Revival: Anthony Horneck, the Religious Societies, and the Construction of Anglican Pietism*. Lanham, MD: Scarecrow Press, 2008.

Knight, Henry H., III. *The Presence of God in the Christian Life: John Wesley and the Means of Grace*. London: Scarecrow Press, 1992.

Langham, Mark. *The Caroline Divines and the Church of Rome: A Contribution to Current Ecumenical Dialogue*. London: Routledge, 2018.

Laud, William. *A Summarie of Devotions of William Laud*. Oxford: William Hall, 1667.

Law, William. *Of Justification by Faith and Works: A Dialogue between a Methodist and a Churchman*. London: J. Richardson, 1760.

———. *A Practical Treatise upon Christian Perfection*. Eugene, OR: Wipf and Stock, 2001 (orig. 1726).

———. *A Serious Call to a Devout and Holy Life*. Alachua: Bridge-Logos, 2008 (orig. 1729).

Lecky, William E. H. *A History of England in the Eighteenth Century*. 8 vols. New York: Appleton & Company, 1888.

Lindberg, Carter, ed. *The Pietist Theologians*. Malden: Blackwell, 2005.

Lindström, Harald. *Wesley and Sanctification*. Nappanee: Francis Asbury, 1980.

Lockwood, John P., ed. *Memorials of the Life of Peter Bohler, Bishop of the Church of the United Brethren*. London: Wesleyan Conference Room, 1868.

Lohse, Bernhard. *Martin Luther's Theology: Its Historical and Systematic Development*. Minneapolis: Fortress Press, 2006.

Long, D. Stephen. *John Wesley's Moral Theology: The Quest for God and Goodness*. Nashville: Kingswood Books, 2005.

Lull, Timothy F., and William R. Russell, eds. *Martin Luther's Basic Theological Writings*. 3rd ed. Minneapolis: Fortress Press, 2012.

Lutheran World Federation and Roman Catholic Church. *Joint Declaration on the Doctrine of Justification*. English edition. Grand Rapids: Eerdmanns, 2000.

Madan, Spencer. *Justification by Works, and Not by Faith Only, Stated, Explained, and Reconciled with Justification by Faith, Without Works*. London, 1761.

Maddox, Randy L., ed. *Aldersgate Reconsidered*. Nashville: Kingswood Books, 1990.

———, ed. "John Wesley's Manuscript Prayer Manual" (c.1730–1734). The Wesley Works Editorial Project-Online Resources, 2018.

———. *Responsible Grace: John Wesley's Practical Theology*. Nashville: Kingswood Books, 1994.

Maddox, Randy L., and Jason E. Vickers, gen. eds. *The Cambridge Companion to John Wesley*. Cambridge: Cambridge University Press, 2010.

Mannermaa, Tuomo. *Christ Present in Faith: Luther's View of Justification*. Minneapolis: Fortress Press, 2005.

McAlilly, Christopher T. "Wesley's Removal of the Rite of Confirmation and Its Consequences for American Methodism." *Wesleyan Theological Journal* 56, no. 2 (Fall 2021).

McCormick, K. Steve. *Triune Love: John Wesley's Theology*. Nashville: Abingdon Press, 2019.

McGever, Sean. *Born Again: The Evangelical Theology of Conversion in John Wesley and George Whitefield.* Bellingham: Lexham Press, 2020.

McGrath, Alister E. *Iustitia Dei: A History of the Christian Doctrine of Justification.* 3rd ed. Cambridge: Cambridge University Press, 2005.

McNight, Scot, and B. J. Oropeza, eds. *Perspectives on Paul.* Grand Rapids: Baker Academic, 2020.

Monk, Robert C. *John Wesley: His Puritan Heritage.* Nashville: Abingdon Press, 1966.

Moorman, J. R. H. *A History of the Church in England.* 3rd ed. Harrisburg: Morehouse Publishing, 1980.

Muller, Richard A. *Dictionary of Latin and Greek Theological Terms: Drawn Principally from Protestant Scholastic Theology.* Grand Rapids: Baker Book House, 1985.

Naglee, David Ingersoll. *From Font to Faith: John Wesley on Infant Baptism and the Nurture of Children.* New York: Peter Lang, 1987.

Nelson, Robert. *The Great Duty of Frequenting the Christian Sacrifice.* London: W. Boyer, 1706.

Newport, Kenneth G. C., and Gareth Lloyd, eds. *The Letter of Charles Wesley: A Critical Edition with Introduction and Notes.* 2 vols. Oxford: Oxford University Press, 2013, 2021.

Noble, Thomas A. *Holy Trinity: Holy People, The Theology of Christian Perfecting.* Eugene: Cascade Books, 2013.

Noll, Mark A. *The Rise of Evangelicalism: The Age of Edwards, Whitefield and the Wesleys.* Downers Grove: InterVarsity Press, 2003.

———. *Turning Points: Decisive Moments in the History of Christianity.* 2nd ed. Grand Rapids: Baker Academic, 2007.

Oden, Thomas C. *Classic Christianity: A Systematic Theology.* New York: HarperOne, 2009.

———. *John Wesley's Teachings.* 4 vols. Grand Rapids: Zondervan, 2012–14.

Oden, Thomas C., and Leicester R. Longden, eds. *The Wesleyan Theological Heritage: Essays of Albert C. Outler.* Grand Rapids: Zondervan, 1991.

Oh, Gwang Seok. *John Wesley's Ecclesiology: A Study in Its Sources and Development.* Lanham, MD: Scarecrow Press, 2007.

Olson, Mark. K. "The Holy Spirit in the Preaching of John Wesley." In *Holy Spirit: Unfinished Agenda*. Edited by Johnson T. K. Lim. Singapore: Word N Works, 2015.

———, ed. *A John Wesley Reader on Eschatology.* Hayden: Truth in Heart, 2011.

———. *John Wesley's Theology of Christian Perfection: Developments in Doctrine and Theological System.* Fenwick: Truth in Heart, 2007.

———. "Martin Luther's Contribution to John Wesley's Doctrine of Justification." *Wesley and Methodist Studies* 13, no. 2 (2021): 130–53.

———. "The New Birth in the Early Wesley." *Wesleyan Theological Journal* 52, no. 1 (2017).

———. "Opening Salvation's Door: Acts 10:35 and John Wesley's Inclusivism." WesleyScholar.com. http://www.wesleyscholar.com/opening-salvations-door-acts-1035--and-john-wesleys-inclusivism (2019).

———. *Wesley and Aldersgate: Interpreting Conversion Narratives.* New York: Routledge, 2019.

Olson, Roger E. *The Story of Christian Theology: Twenty Centuries of Tradition and Reform.* Downers Grove: InterVarsity Press, 1999.

Osborn, George, ed. *The Poetical Works of John and Charles Wesley.* 13 vols. London: Wesleyan-Methodist Conference Office, 1868–72.

Parker, T. H. L., ed. *The Library of Christian Classics: English Reformers.* Louisville: Westminster John Knox Press, 2006.

Pelikan, Jaroslav. *Reformation of Church and Dogma (1300–1700).* Chicago: University of Chicago Press, 1984.

Piette, Maximin. *John Wesley in the Evolution of Protestantism.* New York: Sheed & Ward, 1937.

Rack, Henry D. *Reasonable Enthusiast: John Wesley and the Rise of Methodism.* 3rd ed. London: Epworth Press, 2002.

Ramsey, Boniface, ed. *On Christian Belief.* New York: New City Press, 2005.

Rigg, James H. *The Churchmanship of John Wesley, and the Relations of Wesleyan Methodism to the Church of England.* London: Wesleyan-Methodist Book-Room, 1886.

Rodes, Stanley J. *From Faith to Faith: John Wesley's Covenant Theology and the Way of Salvation.* Eugene: Pickwick Publications, 2013.

Runyon, Theodore. *The New Creation: John Wesley's Theology Today*. Nashville: Abingdon Press, 1998.

Rusch, William G., ed. *Justification and the Future of the Ecumenical Movement: The Joint Declaration on the Doctrine of Justification*. Collegeville, MN: Liturgical Press, 2003.

Sander, Fred. *Wesley on the Christian Life: The Heart Renewed in Love*. Wheaton: Crossway, 2013.

Sanders, E. P. *Paul and Palestinian Judaism*. Minneapolis: SCM, 1977.

Schaff, Philip. *The Creeds of Christendom*. 3 vols. Grand Rapids: Baker Book House, 1990.

Schmidt, Martin. *John Wesley: A Theological Biography*. 3 vols. Translated by Norman Goldhawk. Nashville: Abingdon Press, 1962, 1972, 1973.

Sirota, Brent S. *The Christian Monitors: The Church of England and the Age of Benevolence, 1680–1730*. New Haven, CT: Yale University Press, 2014.

Southey, Robert. *The Life of Wesley; and the Rise and Progress of Methodism*. 2nd ed. 2 vols. London: Longman, Hurst, Rees, Orme, and Brown, 1820.

Stephen, Leslie. *History of English Thought in the Eighteenth Century*. 2 vols. 3rd ed. London: Smith, Elder & Co., 1902.

Stone, Howard W., and James O. Duke. *How to Think Theologically*. 2nd ed. Minneapolis: Fortress Press, 2006.

Taylor, Jeremy. *Holy Living and Holy Dying: With Prayers Containing the Whole Duty of a Christian*. New York: Cosmo Classics, 2007

Thomas, Keith. *The Ends of Life: Roads to Fulfillment in Early Modern England*. Oxford: Oxford University Press, 2009.

Thorsen, Don. *Calvin vs Wesley: Bringing Belief in Line with Practice*. Nashville: Abingdon Press, 2013.

Torpy, Arthur Alan. *The Prevenient Piety of Samuel Wesley, Sr.* Lanham, MD: Scarecrow Press, 2009.

Towlson, Clifford W. *Moravian and Methodist: Relationships and Influences in the Eighteenth Century*. London: Epworth Press, 1957.

Trinklein, John. "Holiness unto Whom? John Wesley's Doctrine of Entire Sanctification in Light of the Two Kinds of Righteousness." PhD diss., Concordia University, 2016.

Tucker, Josiah. "A Short and Familiar Way of Explaining the Doctrine of Justification." *Methodist History* 44, no. 3 (April 2006).

Tyerman, Luke. *The Life and Times of the Rev. John Wesley, M.A.* 6th ed. 3 vols. Stoke-on-Trent: Tentmaker Publications, 2003.

Wallace, Charles, Jr. *Susanna Wesley: The Complete Writings*. Oxford: Oxford University Press, 1997.

Wallace, Jeffrey, ed. *The Works of John Fletcher*. 4 vols. Brookfield: Apprehending Truth Publishers, 2011–17.

Ward, W. R. *Early Evangelicalism: A Global Intellectual History, 1670–1789*. Cambridge: Cambridge University Press, 2006.

———. *The Protestant Evangelical Awakening*. Cambridge: Cambridge University Press, 1992.

Webster, Robert, ed. *Perfecting Perfection: Essays in Honour of Henry D. Rack*. Cambridge: James Clark & Co, 2016.

Wesley, Samuel. *The Pious Communicant Rightly Prepar'd; Or, A Discourse concerning the Blessed Sacrament*. London: Charles Harper, 1700.

White, James F., ed. *The Sunday Service of the Methodists of North America*. Akron: OSL Publications, 1991.

Whiting, Michael S. *Luther in English: The Influence of His Theology of Law and Gospel on Early English Evangelicals, 1525–35*. Eugene, OR: Pickwick Publications, 2010.

Williams, Colin W. *John Wesley's Theology Today: A Study of the Wesleyan Tradition in Light of Current Theological Dialogue*. Nashville: Abingdon Press, 1960.

SCRIPTURE INDEX

References are to main text.

Genesis
   3:15 . . . . 31, 34, 170
   15, 22. 103

Deuteronomy
   13:4 105

Job
   2:3 106

Ecclesiastes
   12:13 105

Isaiah
   1:16 105

Matthew
   4:17 99
   8:11-12 100
   12:37 101
   13:28, 45 101
   20:15 111
   22:13 101
   25:1-13 101
   25:23 45
   25:31-46 . . . . 83, 100,
                          101, 139, 145

Mark
   9:50 101

Luke
   10:42 43
   13:28-29 100

John
   1:9 152
   1:29 69
   3:5 107
   3:16 145
   3:20 . . . . 99, 119
   5:19, 23 . . . . 101, 132
   6:27 . . . . 132, 143

Acts
   10:1–11:18. . . . . 103–6, 127
   10:35 . . . . .104, 134, 136, 150,
                                152, 171

Romans
   3–5 98–100
   3:20 . . . . 70, 99, 119
   4:3 98
   4:25 35
   5:12-19 110
   5:18 . . . . 154, 155
   5:19 79
   5:21 98
   8:2 69
   8:29-30 . . . . 98, 144–46

1 Corinthians
    11:24 . . . . 89, 158

2 Corinthians
    5:10 . . . . 84, 101
    5:21 101
    6:14 126

Galatians
    2:20 . . . . 49, 150
    3:6, 11, 13 98
    5:6 . . . . 11, 99, 101

Ephesians
    2:3 110
    2:8 165

Philippians
    2:12-13 141

Colossians
    1:12 145

Hebrews
    6:4-6 99
    11:1 . . . . 54–55, 56, 79, 80
    12:14 . . . . 129, 165

James
    2:14-26 102–3

1 Peter
    1:2 23
    1:17 84

2 Peter
    2:20-22 99

1 John
    5:10 150

Revelation
    20:12 101

AUTHOR INDEX

References are to introduction and main text.

Baker, Frank, 37
Borgen, Ole, 109
Bowmer, John, 157

Cannon, William, viii
Chamberlain, Jeffrey, 7
Clifford, Alan, 102
Collins, Kenneth, ix, 91, 93, 113, 139, 152
Colyer, Elmer, 77, 163
Coppedge, Allen, 26
Croft Cell, George, viii
Cunningham, Joseph, 177

Deschner, John, 100, 124

Green, Vivian, 6
Gunter, Steven, 134

Hammond, Geordan, 6, 88
Heitzenrater, Richard, 38, 49, 126
Hildebrandt, Frank, 159

Jones, Scott, 96

Lindström, Harald, 71
Lohse, Berhard, 10

Maddox, Randy, ix, 86, 136
McAlilly, Christopher, 156
McGever, Sean, 155
McGrath, Alister, 13, 22
Muller, Richard, 14

Noll, Mark, 3

Oden, Thomas, x
Olson, Roger, 11
Outler, Albert, 107, 157

Rack, Henry, 3, 6
Rodes, Stan, 105, 148

Sanders, Fred, 75
Sirota, Brent, 3

Tuttle, Robert, 9

Westerfield Tucker, Karen, 156
Whiting, Michael, 73
Williams, Colin, viii–ix

Yates, Arthur, 91

SUBJECT INDEX

References are to main text.

Abraham, 31, 80, 98, 103
Adam, 28, 31, 34, 43, 55, 66, 67, 79, 83, 84, 107, 115, 147, 17
Adam's fall, 31, 34, 43, 67, 107
Analogy of faith, 97
Anglican/Anglicanism
    Anglican evangelicals, 4, 26, 27, 113, 137
    Articles of Religion, 14–15, 19, 73, 75, 80, 93, 115, 136, 165
    Book of Common Prayer (BCP), 15, 45, 107, 115, 155
    Classical Anglicanism, 17–19
    High Church tradition, 5–9, 22, 30–37, 39, 44, 51, 56, 88, 95, 133, 137, 167, 169, 177
    Holy living tradition, 9, 22, 37, 51
    Homilies, 9, 15, 16, 32, 72, 80, 81, 115, 123, 165
    Laudism, 18
    Anglican *Ordo salutis*, 7, 23, 38, 40, 50, 78
    Anglican *Via media*, 6, 16, 22, 26
Antinomianism, 8, 21, 22, 27, 75, 79, 80, 81–84, 98, 105, 115, 116, 125, 133
Apostasy, 25, 30, 41, 42, 99, 109

Arminian/Arminianism, 9, 16, 19, 22, 25–28, 30, 69, 78, 89, 96, 99, 104, 113, 115, 118, 123, 137, 144–45, 167, 169, 176, 180
Arminius, Jacob, 25
Arndt, Johann, 23, 55
Assurance
    Anglican view, 9, 18, 23, 33, 35, 56, 57
    Pietist view, 53, 54, 56, 64–65
    Puritan view, 21, 59
    Wesley's view, 44, 62, 69, 71, 75, 88, 90, 91–94, 104, 125–28, 145, 149–51, 160, 177–78
Atonement, 14, 19, 20, 21, 24, 25, 32, 35, 36, 40, 47, 48, 50, 60, 70, 74, 76, 77, 98, 115, 122, 161, 176
    Penal substitution, 14, 15, 35, 36, 74, 76, 86, 115, 161, 176
    Wesley's view, 47–48, 76, 86, 176
Augustine/Augustinianism, 10, 18, 44, 49, 102, 110, 143, 169

Baptism, 7, 11, 16, 30, 33, 34, 35, 36, 39, 41–42, 43, 44, 78, 81, 88, 102, 106–12, 154–57, 171–72
Barclay, Robert, 24
Barnes, Robert, 72

Subject Index

Baxter, Richard, 20–21, 26, 81–84, 86, 95, 113
Benson, Joseph, 131
Beveridge, William, 23, 74, 85, 86
Beza, Theodore, 19, 20, 25, 27, 113
Bohler, Peter, 61, 64, 68
Brevint, Daniel, 50, 88
Bull, George, 23, 44, 80
Busskampf, 65

Calvin, John, 13, 14, 119
Calvinist/Calvinism, 13, 25, 80, 81–84, 95, 105, 113–19, 131–37, 143, 162, 180
  Hyper, 20, 26, 27, 122
  High, 20, 21, 25, 26, 27, 118, 120
  Moderate, 17, 20, 21, 22, 26, 81, 113, 114, 118
Caroline divines, 6, 22–23, 44
Catholicism/Roman Catholic, 3, 4, 8, 9, 10–12, 14, 16, 17, 18, 19, 22, 101, 118, 129, 133, 147
Conjunctive/dialectic, 167
Cornelius (Acts 10), 103–6, 127
Covenant theology, 20, 27, 31, 33, 34, 83, 85–86, 115, 129, 146, 147, 149, 170, 177
  Baptismal covenant, 32, 41, 107
  Covenant of grace, 27, 31, 34, 49, 147, 149, 151, 153, 170
  Covenant of works, 31, 34, 83, 86, 147, 170
  Dispensations, 136, 142, 147, 149, 151, 152, 153, 170–72, 177
  Gospel covenant, 27, 28, 30
  New covenant, 31, 32, 34, 40, 51, 83, 107
  Spiritual states, 147–48, 150, 160
Cox, Lady, 76
Cranmer, Thomas, 15, 72–75
Creeds (Apostles, Nicene), 34–35, 47, 51, 77, 168

Dissent/Non-conformity, 4, 26, 31

Election/Predestination, 13, 19, 20, 25, 110–11, 115, 137, 144–45, 154, 169, 173
Embedded theology, 29
Evangelical conversion, 54, 59, 62, 63–64, 66, 76, 90, 151, 156–57 158–59, 177–78

Faith, 11, 12, 14, 15, 17, 28, 44, 45, 56, 60, 66, 68, 70–71, 75, 91–94, 119, 125, 139, 140, 149–50, 159, 162, 179
  Degrees of, 57, 91–94, 126–28
  Faith imputed, 99
  Justifying faith, 60, 70, 75, 80, 91–94, 99, 117, 122, 125–26, 161, 179
  "The proper Christian faith," 92, 93, 104, 113, 125, 149, 157, 171, 178
  Unbelief, 66, 68, 54, 66, 67
Fletcher, John, 27–28, 130, 131, 134, 135, 138, 139, 149, 151–52, 154
  Vindication of Rev. Mr. Wesley's Minutes, 130, 131, 135, 138, 140, 150
Francke, Augustus, 54, 56, 65

God
  Foreknowledge, 144
  Love, 51–52, 59, 69, 87, 90, 92, 104, 120, 145, 157, 172–73
  Perfection of character, 98
  Power, 76, 87
  "Righteousness of God," 98, 119
Good works, 8, 11, 12, 13, 15, 16, 18, 21, 23, 25, 27, 28, 44, 45, 51, 67, 71, 75, 84, 90, 95, 101, 104, 115, 131–44, 179–80

198

Goodwin, John, 20, 113, 118–21, 123, 125,
Grace, 12, 24, 25, 35–36, 49, 51, 88–89, 140–41, 142, 154, 159
    Cooperant, 44, 48–49, 50, 87, 89, 90, 109, 136–39, 141–44, 146, 153, 162–63, 167
    Free/sovereign grace, 24, 61, 64, 65, 69, 76, 85, 98, 141, 149, 153, 162, 169, 178
    Justifying grace, 59, 89, 104, 108, 110, 141, 173, 176, 177, 179
    Means of grace, 9, 24, 36, 56, 65, 76, 78, 88–89, 104, 111, 137, 140–41, 142, 156, 179
    Prevenient grace, 28, 89, 104, 108, 110, 153, 154, 155, 162, 169, 179, 140, 142, 143, 154, 176, 177
    "Responsible grace," 137

Hanoverian England, 2–5
Harris, Howell, 26
Heathen, Jews, Muslims, 70, 112, 126, 149, 151–54, 170, 171
Hervey, James, 74, 111, 112, 113–19, 120, 121, 122, 123, 131, 167
Hill, Richard, 27, 111
Hill, Rowland, 27
Holy Communion, 3–4, 30, 32–33, 36, 40, 49, 50, 87–90, 126, 130, 157–59, 177
    Frequent/Constant communion, 33, 50, 157–58
    Sustains justification, 33, 49, 50, 89–90, 158
Holy Living, 9, 11, 18, 37, 39, 40, 44, 51, 87, 90, 95, 99, 101, 124–25, 129, 132–37, 162, 177–78
    Single intention, 37, 41, 42, 57–58, 142
Hooker, Richard, 6, 17, 18, 19, 75
Horneck, Anthony, 31

Huntingdon, Countess of, 26, 131, 134, 135

Imago Dei, 43, 46, 50, 51, 52, 55, 57, 58, 59, 180

Jesus Christ
    Active/passive righteousness, 14, 15, 20, 21, 23, 24, 73, 74–75, 82, 84, 95, 98, 113–25, 146, 162, 176, 180
    Deity, 35, 48, 122
    Federal headship, 31, 34, 170
    Heavenly intercession, 16, 18, 49, 99, 176–77
    Humanity, 24, 43, 48, 98, 115, 122, 124
    Internal/external righteousness, 122
    "Our righteousness," 60, 61, 73–74, 77, 154
    Resurrection/ascension, 18, 35, 48, 49, 50, 70, 71, 77, 163, 177
    Second Adam, 34, 84, 111
    Three offices, 34
    Union with Christ/God, 9, 11, 12, 13, 21, 41, 48, 49, 58, 66, 178
Johnson, John, 50
Justification
    Condition/merit, 8, 11, 12, 15, 27, 70, 84, 86, 90, 99, 118, 133, 137–41, 162, 178
    Degrees, 28, 81, 92–94, 103, 105, 112–13, 125, 130, 146–59, 160, 165, 171–72, 177
    Double, 7–8, 11, 13, 18, 20, 22, 27, 30, 36, 41, 45, 71, 72, 77, 78, 80, 83–84, 93, 100–102, 118, 125, 137, 149, 171–72
    Experience, 71, 160, 164, 165, 177–78

Justification (continued)
- Final, 7, 8, 11, 27, 39, 45, 57, 80, 81, 87, 100–02, 105, 125, 136, 140, 144–46, 158, 171–72, 178, 180
- Forensic, 12, 13, 73
- Full, 83, 84, 87, 93, 103, 146
- Fundamental doctrine, 180
- General, 79, 151–54
- James/Paul, 23, 80, 102–03
- Non-sacramental, 42, 44, 52, 56, 61, 71, 76, 167
- Present/Evangelical, 13, 15, 39, 43–44, 52, 54, 68–72, 81, 84–85, 90, 93, 97–100, 105, 109–10, 113, 119, 136, 140, 144–46, 157, 158, 159–66, 171–74, 177–78
- Relational/real change, 175
- Sacramental, 7, 31–34, 36, 41, 51, 76, 81, 86, 87–90, 107–12, 130, 154–59, 171, 172
- Causes:
  - Formal, 8, 10, 11, 14, 17, 19, 22, 23, 24, 75, 82, 113, 116, 120–21, 123, 125, 176, 180
  - Instrumental, 21, 27, 67, 75, 119, 120
  - Meritorious, 15, 17, 23, 27, 28, 43, 48, 59, 64, 74, 75, 80, 84, 90, 115, 117, 120, 123, 138, 152, 161, 176
  - Originating/Efficient, 77, 80, 142, 172–73
- Conditions:
  - By faith, 9, 11, 12, 14, 17, 28, 34, 44, 55, 63, 67, 70–71, 84, 98, 118, 135, 165, 172, 178, 179
  - By works, 8, 11, 12, 15, 17, 24, 30, 31, 49, 65, 66, 68, 71, 73, 84, 90, 101, 102–03, 115, 119, 135–44, 172, 179–80
  - Faith/works, 8, 12, 17, 27, 45, 68, 75, 102, 103, 167

Justification as…
- Pardon/forgiveness, 11–12, 18, 23, 31, 35, 36, 39, 41, 47, 60, 77, 79, 80, 86, 90, 98, 108, 111, 116, 123, 135, 158, 161, 165, 173–74, 175, 178
- Acceptance, 25, 31, 36, 41, 43, 44, 48, 52, 79, 80, 90, 98, 105, 108, 116, 152, 161, 165, 173–74
- Favor, 35, 64, 79, 89, 100, 103, 104–05, 108, 112, 115, 121, 133, 135, 139, 142, 161, 169, 171, 173, 174, 175
- Title, 35, 38, 47–48, 107, 108, 143, 146, 173, 175, 180

Justification and…
- Freedom from sin, 62, 70, 145, 163
- Holy living, 18, 40, 42, 44, 51, 67, 80, 99, 143, 146, 165
- Methodist identity, 164–66
- New birth, 55, 70, 156–57, 177–78

Thomas à Kempis, 9, 87

Last Judgment, 9, 22, 30, 35, 45, 87, 93, 100–01, 113, 125, 137, 138, 153, 180
Laud, William, Laudism, 6, 18, 22
Law, William, 9, 38, 40–42, 43, 44, 77, 109, 147, 164
Law
- Christ fulfilled the law, 74, 75, 122, 123
- God's law, 14, 15, 26, 66, 68, 70, 73, 75, 82, 99, 102, 116, 117, 119, 120, 122
- "Law of sin and death," 62, 69, 148
- Moral law, 83

Mosaic Law, 31, 66, 68, 70, 83, 86, 170
Luther, Martin, 1, 12–13, 14, 15, 24, 66–67, 68, 73, 80, 119
Lutheran/Lutheranism, 4, 13, 24, 55, 63–72, 71, 73, 85, 164

Monergism/Synergism, 11, 12, 15, 70, 76, 137, 141, 143, 162, 164
Moravian/Moravianism, 5, 24, 45, 53–57, 58, 63–66, 71, 78, 79, 80, 83, 89, 95, 105, 164
Mystics, mysticism, 9, 37

Nelson, Robert, 50, 157
New birth, 12, 24, 40, 41, 44, 56, 67–68, 76, 92, 93, 108, 150, 151, 157, 160, 165, 172, 175, 177–78
New Gospel/New Doctrine, 9, 54, 57, 58, 59, 63, 71, 76, 78, 81, 83, 85, 86, 88, 91, 150, 151, 157, 160, 177

"One thing needful," 42, 43, 46, 52, 53, 57, 68
Ordo Justificationis, 99, 120
Ordo Salutis, 7, 14, 21, 23, 38, 40, 50, 77–78, 105, 147, 168, 172
  Wesley's evangelical *ordo salutis*, 77–78, 105, 110, 112, 144–46, 168, 172, 174
Original Sin, 32, 36, 40, 43, 55, 61, 67, 97, 107, 109, 110, 115, 154, 155
Owen, John, 20, 113

Pearson, John, 35
Pelagianism, 14, 28, 43
Perkins, William, 20
Pietist/Pietism, 23–25, 31, 38, 54–57, 58–61, 63, 95, 97, 164, 179
Protestant scholasticism, 13–14
Puritan/Puritanism, 4, 9, 16, 20–22, 23, 25, 31, 39, 83, 86, 170

Quaker/Quakerism, 4, 5, 24–25, 112
"Real Christian," 92, 93, 113, 125, 149, 159, 160, 165
Regeneration, 13, 14, 16, 24, 30, 42, 55, 70, 107, 108, 109, 124, 150, 155–57, 177
Repentance, 35, 38, 39, 81, 99, 139, 140, 178–79
Responsive Unregenerate, 1, 104, 106, 127, 130, 136, 151–54
Righteousness
  Alien, 12, 34, 73–74
  Declaration, 12, 13, 28, 30, 39, 45, 73, 98, 100, 105, 146, 173, 176, 180
  Forensic, 12, 13, 73
  Imputed, 12, 13, 14, 15, 20, 22, 24, 73–74, 79, 81–82, 84, 86–87, 99, 101, 113, 119, 122–25, 161, 177
  Imparted/implanted, 67, 87, 101, 124–25, 177, 180
  Inherent, infused, 8, 11, 12, 14, 17, 18, 19, 42, 44
  Make, 8, 11, 13, 28, 103, 124, 145, 180
Rutherford, Thomas, 127

Salvation
  Final, 8, 30, 71, 84, 106, 130, 133, 140, 141, 143, 146, 149, 152, 178
  "Full Christian salvation," 104–05, 148
  Present, 12, 44–45, 49, 63–64, 69–71, 79, 81, 83, 87, 91–94, 133, 140, 143, 150, 177–78
  "Proper Christian salvation," 142, 165
Sanctification, 7, 13, 18, 23, 39, 42, 49, 71, 75, 78, 85, 99, 124–25, 136, 142, 164, 165

Subject Index

Sanctification (continued)
   Christian Perfection, 67, 78, 131, 142, 165
Scougal, Henry, 87
Servant/Son motif, 93, 106, 128, 146–51, 153, 160, 171, 174, 180
Simul justus et peccatur, 12
Spangenberg, August, 53
Spener, Philipp, 23–24
Spiritual senses, 178

Taylor, Jeremy, 9, 23, 38–40, 42, 43
Tompson, Richard, 96, 125, 127
Toplady, Augustus, 27, 131
Trinity, 34, 36, 46–52, 59, 77, 83, 85, 87, 101, 120, 141, 146, 162, 163, 164, 168–70
   Divine essence, 101
   Filioque, 47, 51
   Law of appropriation, 46, 169
   Perichoretic coactivity, 46, 51
   Trinitarian roles, 46–52, 77, 101, 141–42, 169, 172–78
Tucker, Josiah, 27

Via Salutis/scripture way of salvation, 7, 28, 140, 142, 143, 146, 147, 159, 160, 162, 164, 165, 168, 172, 173, 179

Wesley, Charles, 88, 92–93, 105, 112, 126, 138, 161
Wesley, John
   Religious life and career:
     1725 spiritual awakening, 37–38, 42
     Aldersgate (1738), 13, 62, 66, 69, 76, 91, 148, 149, 157, 171
     Anglican, Evangelical, Arminian, 167
     Cultural/religious context, 2–9
     Doctrinal theologian, 168, 172

     Doubts his salvation, 52–54, 58, 67, 126–27
     Eclecticism, 167
     Free Grace Controversy, 78, 81
     Imputed Righteousness Controversy, 113–25
     Georgian period, 52–61, 64, 89
     Minutes Controversy, 27, 130–46
     Oxford period, 7, 30, 37–52, 77, 83, 94, 113, 129, 142, 147–48, 168
     Stillness Controversy, 104
   Writings:
     Aldersgate memorandum (1738), 30, 33, 68–69, 73
     Annual Conference Minutes (1744–1747), 79–91, 92, 94, 147
     Annual Conference Minutes (1770), 82, 84, 113, 130–37, 142
     cThe Circumcision of the Heart" (1733), 43–45
     A Collection of Forms of Prayer for Everyday of the Week (1733), 45–52
     Collection of Hymns for the People Called Methodists (1780), 159–64
     Collection of Psalms and Hymns (1737), 59–60
     A Companion for the Altar (1742), 88–90
     The Doctrine of Salvation, Faith, and Good Works (1738), 73, 123
     "The Duty of Constant Communion" (1788), 157–59
     Explanatory Notes Upon the New Testament (1755), 96–106, 147, 159
     An Extract of Richard Baxter's Aphorisms (1745), 81–84

An Earnest Appeal to Men of Reason and Religion (1743), 76, 79
A Farther Appeal to Men of Reason and Religion, Part I (1745), 80–81, 109, 139
Free Grace (1739), 70
Hymns on the Lord's Supper (1745), 88
Hymns and Sacred Poems (1740), 110
"The Important Question," 111
"Justification by Faith" (1746), 84–85
Letter to a Gentleman at Bristol (1758), 118
Letter to James Hervey (1758), 116–18
Letter to Charles Wesley (1747), 92, 104
Letter to Charles Wesley (1766), 126–28
"The Lord Our Righteousness" (1765), 115, 121–25
"On the Discoveries of Faith" (1788), 150–51
On Faith, Hebrews 11:6 (1788), 149–51
"On God's Vineyard" (1788), 164
"On the New Birth" (1759), 108
On Predestination (1773), 144–46
"On Working Out Our Own Salvation" (1785), 141–44
A Preservative against Unsettled Notions of Religion (1758), 106, 114, 117
The Principles of a Methodist (1742), 74
The Righteousness of Faith (1746), 85–86
Salvation by Faith (1738), 69–70, 93
The Scripture Way of Salvation (1765), 139, 154
Serious Thoughts on Godfathers and Godmothers (1752), 106
A Single Intention (1736), 57–58
The Spirit of Bondage and of Adoption (1746), 147
The Sunday Service of the Methodists in North America (1784), 155–57
"Thirteen Discourses on the 'Sermon on the Mount'" (1748, 1750), 86–87
Thoughts on Infant Baptism (1751), 106
Thoughts on the Imputed Righteousness of Christ (1762), 114
The Trouble and Rest of Good Men (1735), 57
Treatise on Baptism (1756), 106–12, 155, 157
A Treatise on Justification, extract of John Goodwin (1764), 114, 118–21
The Wedding Garment (1790), 143, 175
The Witness of the Spirit I (1746), 178
Wesley, Samuel/Susanna, 5, 31–37, 74, 85, 90, 106, 147
Whitefield, George, 26, 113

Zinzendorf, Count, 24, 55

Milton Keynes UK
Ingram Content Group UK Ltd.
UKHW040013250424
441720UK00004B/191